DRUGS AND CRIME

DRUGS AND CRIME
A Complex Relationship
Third edition, revised and expanded

Serge Brochu, Natacha Brunelle and Chantal Plourde

Translated by Julie da Silva

University of Ottawa Press
2018

u Ottawa

The University of Ottawa Press (UOP) is proud to be the oldest of the francophone university presses in Canada and the only bilingual university publisher in North America. Since 1936, UOP has been "enriching intellectual and cultural discourse" by producing peer-reviewed and award-winning books in the humanities and social sciences, in French or in English.

Library and Archives Canada Cataloguing in Publication

Brochu, Serge
[Drogue et criminalité. English]
    Drugs and crime: a complex relationship / Serge Brochu, Natacha Brunelle and Chantal Plourde; translated by Julie da Silva. — Third edition, revised and expanded.

Translation of: Brochu, Serge. Drogue et criminalité.
Includes bibliographical references.
Issued in print and electronic formats.
ISBN 978-0-7766-2632-1 (softcover)
ISBN 978-0-7766-2633-8 (PDF)
ISBN 978-0-7766-2635-2 (Kindle)
ISBN 978-0-7766-2634-5 (EPUB)

    1. Drug abuse and crime. 2. Criminals—Drug use. I. Brunelle, Natacha, 1971-, author II. Plourde, Chantal, 1970-, author III. Title. IV. Title: Drogue et criminalité. English

HV5801 B7613 2018   364.2'4   C2018-900808-3
                                                                 C2018-900809-1

Copy editing: Robbie McCaw
Proofreading: Susan James
Typesetting: Édiscript enr.
Cover design: Édiscript enr.

Originally published as *Drogues et criminalité. Une relation complexe*. Troisième édition revue et augmentée, Presses de l'Université de Montréal, 2016

The University of Ottawa Press gratefully acknowledges the support extended to its publishing list by the Government of Canada, the Canada Council for the Arts, the Ontario Arts Council, and the Federation for the Humanities and Social Sciences through the Awards to Scholarly Publications Program and by the University of Ottawa.

Table of Contents

CHAPTER 6

CHAPTER 7

List of Figures and Tables

Acknowledgments

We wish to thank our research assistants, Isabelle Bastrash, Marie-Ève Bédard-Nadeau, Geneviève Garceau, Vanessa Lapierre, Catherine Patenaude, Alison Pellerin, Alexandra Richard, and Michaël Sam Tion, for their literature search, bibliographic filing, and formatting. We are grateful to Dr. Didier Jutras-Aswad for his meticulous reading of chapter 2 about the effects of drugs and his valuable feedback. Support for this project was provided by grants from the Fonds de recherche du Québec – Société et culture, the Social Sciences and Humanities Research Council of Canada, and the Canadian Institutes of Health Research, which enabled us to conduct a number of studies upon which this book is based. Lastly, we thank the Université du Québec à Trois-Rivières Canada Research Chair in Drug Use Patterns and Related Problems for funding the better part of the work that went into writing this book.

Introduction

The idea that drugs can have negative effects on users and lead people to commit crimes is not new, but is it valid? In this book, we take a practical, scientific approach toward better understanding the relationships between drugs and crime. Our research focuses on how those relationships develop, but before delving into the heart of the matter, we will discuss the factors that enable us to understand the consumption trajectories leading to criminal behaviour, and vice versa. We will conclude on a positive note with a discussion of how to break the drug–crime cycle and the effectiveness of services available to help drug-dependent people involved in the justice system.

Research into drugs and crime is shaped primarily by how these matters are understood and approached, which may be influenced by personal or corporate interests (Szabo 1992). We must remember that scientists function within an economic and socio-political context in which power relations influence the subjects being studied and influences knowledge as a whole. Over half of the scientific literature about drugs and crime is produced in the United States. Our body of knowledge draws heavily on American research, which exerts an undeniable influence on the scientific world. The United States is, however, atypical in its approach to managing people's drug use. Although some states have legalized cannabis, the federal government still exercises strict control over users. The United States imprisons drug users by the thousands, yet is reluctant to enact gun control laws. There can be no doubt that the relationships between drugs and crime are influenced by this social context. Research produced by our neighbours to the south is carried out against a backdrop of repression. Participants in studies on illicit drugs are very often individuals deprived of their liberty (incarcerated, in a treatment program as an alternative to incarceration, etc.). While the results of studies on relationships between drugs and crime are valid for a repressive environment where guns circulate relatively freely, are they valid in other contexts? Science, of course, is never *pure*. Scientists operate in a particular socio-historical context that colours the perception of the subjects and the study's results. In this sense, science is quite simply *human*.

For these reasons, the third edition of this book relies more heavily than previous editions on Canadian studies to paint a picture of our own reality.

Illegal Psychoactive Substances in Canada

Canada's stance on illegal drugs and drug users is incongruous. Moralistic new laws and federal government actions over the past decade have clearly led to greater repression and difficulty accessing substances as well as to potentially dangerous drug use practices. Policies seem to be based on the notion of drugs as diabolical substances that cause social disorder by bewitching weak-minded individuals who seek out hedonistic pleasures. Those who subscribe to this ideological position believe that drug users become marginalized through their own deviance and antisocial behaviour and that it would be pointless to normalize society's relationship with them.

Canadians nevertheless realize that incarceration does not solve drug users' problems and that making appropriate treatment available to those who need it is a better option. Canadians are open to the idea of making treatment available, but many people have a not-in-my-backyard attitude toward services for drug-dependent individuals. Many people believe that heavy users have a disease that requires treatment, perhaps even against their will, and society seems to accept an enforcement regime widely believed to be pro-treatment.

More and more Canadians believe that the use of psychoactive substances is a phase or, at worst, a relatively harmless lifestyle choice. They tend to find the idea of cannabis legalization appealing precisely because they would not have to come into contact with the criminal element. Its status would be more akin to that of regulated drugs in

Canada, such as tobacco and alcohol. It goes without saying that, in 2017, the public's perception of illegal drugs and drug users is quite different from its attitude toward alcohol and alcohol-dependent individuals, which is why we have decided to exclude alcohol from our analyses. We are in no way suggesting that individuals who consume alcohol are not involved in criminal activity; on the contrary, alcohol is the substance most often associated with violent crime. Nevertheless, we have chosen to focus our analyses on illegal substances, which are distinct because repression reinforces user marginalization. This unique relationship is the primary focus of this book.

Drug Use and Criminal Behaviour

This book was written for people who no longer subscribe to pat assertions about psychoactive substances leading to criminal behaviour and who want to dig deeper. The triangular relationship among an individual, a substance, and their context is complex and cannot be boiled down to a pithy phrase, no matter how catchy. In this volume, readers will discover the results of major research projects carried out over the past twenty years that paint an accurate picture of the current situation.

This third edition takes into account the upsurge of research into drugs and crime. It presents robust qualitative studies carried out in recent years that place greater emphasis on the experiences and perceptions of illegal drug users and drug-dependent people.

In chapter 1, we lay out facts and figures to show that drugs and crime are indeed interrelated. We find evidence of very high rates of drug use within the justice-involved population. In chapter 2, we further explore the criminogenic nature of drugs. We examine two situations in particular: the effects of intoxication and the consequences of dependence. Chapter 2 also details documented links between various substances and criminal behaviour. In chapter 3, we delve into the policies and laws governing drugs that are currently illegal in Canada. We review how the existing legal framework came to be and how current policies might be improved upon with respect to drug users. Armed with that knowledge, in chapter 4, we present a review of classic conceptual models that seek to explain the relationships between drugs and crime, and, in chapter 5, we discuss the notion of trajectory and its contribution to our understanding of these dynamic relationships. In chapter 6, we lay out the elements of an "updated" conceptual model that takes into account the latest research about the relationships between drugs and crime. We must be aware that modelling is, by definition, reductionist. It is merely a tool that enables us to better apprehend the facts. The last chapter focuses on treatments available to drug-dependent individuals in the justice system and on factors that can help those who are beginning the rehabilitation process. Our goal is to answer the following basic questions: Who? Why? What? How? Who are the people involved? Why are they involved? What are they involved in? How can we help them?

The relationships between drugs and crime will remain relevant for years to come. This work will have achieved its goal if it succeeds in presenting every facet of those complex relationships.

Chapter 1

Links Between Drugs and Crime in Facts and Figures

Although awareness raising and prevention are appropriate responses to the current state of drug use within the general population and for youth in particular, there is greater cause for concern when it comes to youth and adults involved in the legal system. The proportion of drug users and drug-dependent individuals in adult and youth detention facilities is generally considered to be very large. According to some corrections professionals, up to 80 percent of people in custody have psychoactive substance use problems.

Every year, plenty of studies are published on the prevalence of illegal psychoactive substance use among people involved in the legal system, but it is difficult for conclusions drawn from empirical research to sway unbending opinions about the relationship between drugs and crime. Study results published in scientific journals typically attract far less attention than local media headlines about the latest record-setting drug seizure or a violent crime committed by a drug addict on parole. What conclusions can we draw from the recent scientific findings? Let us begin with a review of prevalence studies involving adolescents in custody and young people with drug dependencies in treatment programs.

Youth

We examine the prevalence of links between drug use and criminal behaviour among youth for two main subpopulations: (1) youth in custody, and (2) youth with serious psychoactive substance use problems accessing addiction treatment centre services. The same individuals may be represented in both subpopulations because, as we will see, a youth who abuses drugs may spend time in custody at some point in his or her trajectory. It is nevertheless important to note that minors who commit offences do not all end up in custody. Jail time is the rarest and most severe penalty and is typically reserved for the extremely violent and for recidivists, those most entrenched in criminal activity (Fortin-Dufour et al. 2015). Then there is the dark figure of crime, crimes that are unknown and lead to neither arrest nor conviction. Nevertheless, authors such as Palamar (2014) show that problems with the police increase in step with frequency of cannabis use. Studies on incarcerated youth therefore do not represent all offenders. On the other hand, young users and those with serious drug use problems are not all in addiction rehabilitation centres. The treatment penetration rate is relatively low for youth with psychoactive substance dependence. For example, although regional variations exist, Quebec's average penetration rate is 22 percent (Tremblay et al. 2014). A number of reasons may account for this: youth deny there is a problem, they lack the motivation to change or accept treatment, front-line services have inadequate screening and detection practices, and so on. Lastly, we must also consider the fact that sample groups in the majority of the studies in this section included only or mostly boys. We must be extremely careful about including the female population in general pronouncements about the results of such studies. On the whole, prevalence findings must be interpreted cautiously because they are mere snapshots of the relationship between drugs and crime.

A brief survey of the studies immediately reveals that the prevalence of psychoactive substance use is much higher among adolescents in custody than among those in the general population (Sedlak and McPherson 2010; Neff and Waite 2007). A 2002–03 American study by the Office of Juvenile Justice and Delinquency Prevention showed that 84 percent of juvenile offenders in custody had used cannabis, compared to 30 percent of their peers in the general population (Sedlak and McPherson 2010).

Similarly, if we compare Quebec studies of young offenders in custody in youth centres (Lambert et al. 2012; Laventure, Pauzé, and Déry 2008) with Institut de la statistique du Québec data on adolescents in the general population (Cazale, Fournier, and Dubé 2009; Laprise et al. 2012), we can estimate that at least four times more of the former (42 percent: Laventure, Pauzé, and Déry 2008) than of the latter (9 percent: Cazale, Fournier, and Dubé 2009) reported having used cannabis at least once a week during the previous year. There is also a significant gap between the two groups with respect to costlier drugs such as cocaine (3 percent of the general population, 11 percent of the youth centre population) (Laprise et al. 2012). We should note that Quebec studies of adolescents in youth centres generally include not only young offenders detained under the *Youth Criminal Justice Act* (YCJA),[1] but also youth in custody under the *Youth Protection Act* (YPA) and the *Act Respecting Health Services and Social Services*, who are in custody in the same youth centres. The proportion of individuals using various psychoactive substances is higher among young offenders under the authority of the YCJA.

A Quebec study of 401 male offenders aged fourteen to eighteen in youth centres showed that more than nine out of ten Montreal youth had used cannabis at least once in their lives. In addition, 69 percent of them reported having used hallucinogens (mescaline, magic mushrooms, LSD), and over half had tried amphetamines (56 percent) and even cocaine (49 percent), the latter a much costlier drug (Brochu et al. 2010).

Similarly, Neff and Waite (2007) conducted a study in the United States using data compiled by the Virginia Department of Justice on incarcerated youth in Virginia from 1998 to 2003 inclusively. Their study results showed that 82 percent of incarcerated youth had consumed cannabis, 16 percent had consumed cocaine, and 16 percent had consumed hallucinogens.

It is important to note that these high rates of illicit drug use among adolescents involved in the legal system may not exist among all youth who commit crimes. Offenders who use drugs are at increased risk of becoming involved with the legal system because drug possession is grounds for arrest and detention (Braithwaite et al. 2003).

With respect to severity of use, incarcerated youth generally have a high rate of psychoactive substance use and dependence (Gretton and Clift 2011; Ahmad and Mazlan 2014). It is difficult to compare data from youth in the general population and from those in custody because of the different measurement tools used. We can nevertheless suggest that, in general, detained youth are much more likely to have significant psychoactive substance use problems (Ahmad and Mazlan 2014; Frappier et al. 2015).

In a Quebec study of 890 young users in addiction treatment centres, Tremblay, Brunelle, and Blanchette-Martin (2007) showed that drug use problems among youth centre inmates sentenced under the YCJA were more severe than among those in custody under the YPA and individuals not in youth centres. The proportion of young people who use cocaine at least once a week is higher among young people under YCJA jurisdiction (12 percent) than among those under YPA jurisdiction (5 percent) and individuals not in youth centres (7 percent). Similarly, in a study of 726 drug-dependent youths in addiction treatment centres, Brunelle and her co-investigators (2014) showed that the most delinquent individuals had the most severe drug use problems. For example, severity scores for alcohol, cannabis, and other drugs are higher in the high-delinquency group than in the low-delinquency group. One of the indicators is frequency of cannabis use, with significantly more of the former group (80 percent) using it at least three times a week compared to the latter (69 percent).

With a number of studies (Chassin et al. 2009; Tripodi, Springer, and Corcoran 2007) showing a directly proportional relationship between drug use problems and levels of delinquency, let us now turn to the link between drugs and crime among youth with psychoactive substance dependence. Myriad studies have shown that delinquency is common among young people being treated for psychoactive substance abuse (D'Amico et al. 2008; Pepler et al. 2010; Reynolds et al. 2011; Van Der Geest, Blokland, and Bijleveld 2009).

A study conducted by Hser and her fellow researchers (2001) showed that 67 percent of young people entering specialized addiction treatment admitted to having committed crimes over the previous year, or they were awaiting trial, on probation, or on parole. Similarly, the U.S. Cannabis Youth Treatment study of 600 young users in treatment who were abusing cannabis showed that 83 percent of them had already committed a crime other than illegal drug possession (Dennis et al. 2004).

A Quebec study showed that nearly a third (29 percent) of youth in addiction treatment in the Quebec City region had been convicted of a crime (Tremblay, Brunelle, and Blanchette-Martin 2007). More recently, Brunelle and her associates (2013) carried out a study involving 199 youth in treatment in Quebec. Their results showed that a high proportion (89 percent) of the participants had committed at least one delinquent act before beginning treatment, and that 43 percent had been arrested by the police. The most common offences were possession and sale of drugs (67 percent), theft (52 percent), and assault (29 percent).

Adults

There are clearly links between drugs and crime among teenagers in custody in youth centres and those in addiction rehabilitation facilities, but do similar patterns exist among adults, including those involved in the justice system? To what extent do adult offenders use drugs?

Justice-involved Individuals

In the United States, the National Institute of Justice introduced the Arrestee Drug Abuse Monitoring[2] (ADAM) program to better gauge illegal drug use among male arrestees in major urban centres (ONDCP 2014). Reimplemented in 2007 as ADAM II, the program initially included ten U.S. cities, but 2012 budget cuts shrank the number of data collection sites to five (Atlanta, Chicago, Denver, New York, and Sacramento). For two fourteen-day periods a year, specially trained staff collected urine specimens from a random sample of individuals who were arrested in the evening or at night and asked them a series of questions. Participation was strictly confidential and voluntary.[3] The purpose was not to collect additional evidence that could lead to conviction but to gauge trends in illegal drug use among arrestees in the major U.S. cities participating in the program. The response rate for the 2013 ADAM II survey was 62 percent for the interviews and 55 percent for the urine tests (ONDCP 2014).

The urine test used in the Office of National Drug Control Policy (ONDCP) survey detected the presence of ten different drugs. The proportion of participants testing positive for at least one of the drugs in 2013 "ranged from 63 percent in Atlanta to 83 percent in Chicago and Sacramento" (ONDCP 2014, xi). In Sacramento, 50 percent of the participants tested positive for multiple drugs. Not surprisingly, cannabis was the most commonly detected drug, ranging from 34 percent in Atlanta to 59 percent in Sacramento. Self-reported cannabis use ranged from 39 percent in Atlanta to 58 percent in Sacramento. Congruence between urine test results and self-reported use is generally very high (84 percent for cannabis and 95 percent for methamphetamine) across all five survey sites (ONDCP 2014). The 2013 ADAM II survey did not investigate the severity of drug use.

Urinalysis may be perceived as more methodologically sound than self-reporting, but test results may be imprecise because the period of time during which different drugs can be detected varies dramatically. For example, cannabis can be detected up to a month after use (for frequent, heavy users), but the window for cocaine and heroin is just forty-eight hours. As a result, the prevalence of cannabis use compared to cocaine and heroin use is often overstated. Moreover, urine tests cannot confirm whether an individual was intoxicated when committing a crime or at the time of arrest, nor can they reveal a serious drug use problem. Regardless, the results show that the vast majority of arrestees had used at least one drug in the days preceding their arrest.

Research on prison and penitentiary inmates reveals a very high prevalence of illegal psychoactive substance use prior to incarceration (Brochu and Plourde 2012; Plourde et al. 2012; Plourde et al. 2013; Zakaria et al. 2010).[4] For example, Fazel, Bains, and Doll (2006) conducted a systematic review of studies on drug use and dependence among inmates. They selected thirteen studies with a total of 7,563 prisoners and found that drug abuse and dependence affected between 10 percent and 48 percent of the men and between 30 percent and 60 percent of the women. Despite there being fewer studies involving women, it is clear that incarcerated women use drugs as much as or more than their male counterparts (Fazel, Bains, and Doll 2006; Johnson 2006; Zakaria et al. 2010). This is especially true for heroin, cocaine, methadone, and psychotropic prescription drugs (Butler et al. 2003; Plourde et al. 2013), which are considered highly addictive.

In a province-wide study set in Quebec prisons, more than half (54 percent) of the inmates surveyed admitted to having used at least one illegal substance during the year prior to their incarceration (Robitaille, Guay, and Savard 2002, 52):

> A significant proportion (48.5%) of individuals who reported using drugs were daily users. Approximately 15% used drugs a few or several times a week. Just 11.3% used drugs only on special occasions. In other words, the vast majority of the subjects used drugs relatively frequently.[5]

A recent study (Plourde et al. 2015) of 292 Quebec inmates with drug use problems using the Assessment and Screening of Assistance Needs – Alcohol/Drug instrument (Tremblay, Rouillard, and Sirois 2004) indicated that 78 percent of participants were in the "red" zone and in need of specialized second-line dependence services. According to the study, 73 percent of the inmates reported regular use of alcohol, 76 percent of cannabis, 63 percent of cocaine, 60 percent of amphetamines, and 15 percent of opiates.

Despite using somewhat different methodology, data from penitentiaries display some similarities. The data showed that half (52 percent) of the inmates used cannabis, a quarter (26 percent) used cocaine, and a tenth (13 percent) used opiates during the twelve months preceding their incarceration (Kunic and Grant 2006).

These statistics stand in stark contrast to the results of major nationwide surveys (Health Canada's Canadian Alcohol and Drug Use Monitoring Surveys 2009, 2010, 2011, 2012), which indicate that, within Quebec's general adult population, approximately one in ten had consumed an illegal psychoactive substance, typically cannabis, in the year preceding the survey (Health Canada 2012). This marked disparity in usage prevalence among offenders and within the general population is even more dramatic in the case of cocaine. A quarter of the inmates surveyed admitted to having consumed cocaine in the twelve months prior to incarceration, whereas the prevalence in the Canadian population is only about 1 percent (Brochu et al. 2001; Health Canada 2012). Though impressive, these results do not establish a causal relationship between drug use and the commission of criminal acts.

Additional data about male offenders' drug use can help us better understand it. According to some of our research team's studies, between a third and half of Canadian offenders are moderately to severely dependent on illegal drugs (Brochu, Guyon, and Desjardins 2001; Pernanen et al. 2002).[6] According to Correctional Service Canada's much less conservative figures, nearly 80 percent of the inmates under its jurisdiction had substance use problems requiring intervention (Weekes et al. 2009). That includes inmates who needed only low-intensity intervention (prevention). When asked if they had a drug use problem before incarceration, a significant proportion of the inmates, both male (56 percent) and female (58 percent), reported that they did (Plourde et al. 2012).

One-fifth of the prison and penitentiary inmates interviewed by Pernanen's team (Pernanen et al. 2002) committed crimes to pay for illegal drugs for personal use. Theft was the crime most frequently committed to acquire drugs. Forty-three percent of penitentiary inmates convicted of theft and 37 percent of those convicted of robbery reported committing their crimes specifically to get drugs. However, when asking offenders to briefly explain why they were arrested, it is important to keep in mind that their answers may very well have more to do with satisfying social acceptability criteria than providing a faithful account of the dynamics involved.[7] Although some degree of circumspection is called for, recidivism statistics offer interesting insights. According to Weekes and his fellow researchers (2009), "offenders with the most serious substance abuse problems are twice as likely to re-offend as others" (recidivism rate = 38 percent versus 19 percent), even though half (54 percent) of federal "offenders on release participated in at least one substance abuse program while incarcerated." Some researchers therefore believe that illegal drug use and dependence are very good predictors of future criminal activity (Benda, Corwyn, and Toombs 2001), particularly for people also suffering from mental illness (Bonta, Blais, and Wilson 2013; O'Keefe and Schnell 2007).

Data for the adult offender population are consistent with data for adolescents in the sense that a significant proportion of them began using illegal psychoactive substances following the onset of criminal activity (Makkai and Payne 2003).

Drugs in Prison

The majority of offenders have a history of heavy drug use prior to serving time, and incarceration certainly does not put a stop to the behaviour. Drugs of all kinds get into prisons and penitentiaries, where they are distributed and consumed.

Drugs are not only easy to get, they are part of prison life (Butler et al. 2013; EMCDDA 2001; Small et al. 2005; Strang et al. 2006). The prison environment is ideally suited to the drug trade because of its population of drug dealers who are, of course, intimately familiar with the ins and outs of the illegal drug distribution network, and the ratio of users to dealers is certainly higher behind bars than on the street: "Substance abuse amongst our offender population creates a high demand that the dealers will undertake significant efforts that ensure a supply" (McVie 2001, 7).[8]

Moreover, day-to-day living conditions in jail are so unpleasant that ex-users have plenty of good reasons to fall back on old habits.

It is natural for inmates to seek freedom and an escape from the miserable prison environment, if only in their minds. Some drugs that produce anaesthetic or euphoric effects serve as an adaptive response for the user (Plourde et al. 2012; Plourde and Brochu 2002; Plourde, Brochu, and Lemire 2001). A 2004 qualitative study of inmates by Seal and his fellow researchers pointed to four main reasons why people use drugs during incarceration: the need to escape their unbearable reality; celebration; addiction; and a more external factor, the many opportunities available. Other external factors associated with psychoactive substance use while incarcerated include gang membership and length of incarceration (Andia et al. 2005).

According to the European Monitoring Centre for Drugs and Drug Addiction (EMCDDA) (2002), "All contacts with the outside world are occasions for smuggling drugs into prison" (p. 48). Inmates use ingenious strategies to turn temporary leave, private visitations, and contact in visiting areas, all of which help inmates maintain social ties, into opportunities to bring drugs into prison.

Ion detectors, sniffer dogs, and manual searches are used routinely, but it is harder to implement mandatory body cavity searches of visitors and of inmates who have been on temporary leave.

When goods are prohibited, their monetary value rises. The cost of street drugs goes up depending on how difficult they are to get in prison.[9] Inmates have very limited access to cash because it is forbidden and confiscated by prison authorities, so users find other ways to pay for illicit drugs. They trade items purchased at the canteen, pay using money deposited in their account by family members or friends, or hand over gifts received from outside (Plourde and Brochu 2002). It seems that a minority of users, unable to cover the cost of their drugs, incur debt that can result in unfortunate consequences (needing correctional authorities' protection [18 percent], smuggling drugs into a penitentiary [15 percent], and inter-prisoner violence [10 percent]; see Plourde and Brochu 2002). A report by McVie (2001) indicates that a quarter of inmates experienced pressure to smuggle drugs into the institution:

> When supply is reduced, sometimes through effective interdiction efforts, prices are increased and offenders and their families and visitors are pressured to pack drugs into our facilities, perpetuating an underground economic cycle characterized by threats, intimidation and, too often, violence. (McVie 2001, 7)

In addition to consuming illicit psychoactive substances, inmates seek temporary escape using a variety of other products, such as glue, aftershave lotion, shoe polish, paint, "pruno" (prison wine) made with fermented fruits and vegetables, and alcohol distilled using various creative processes. Then there are the psychotropic medications prescribed by institutional doctors to treat specific conditions, which inmates sometimes stockpile so they can take higher doses, or sell in the prison black market.

Putting illicit drug users behind bars does not necessarily resolve their drug use problems. In fact, drug use during incarceration is relatively common (Cope 2000; Strang et al. 2006). In Canada, a third of men and 12 percent of women in penitentiaries report having consumed a drug at least once during a three-month period of incarceration (Plourde et al. 2012; Plourde et al. 2014).[10] However, frequency and quantity of drug use decline dramatically during incarceration (Plourde et al. 2012; Strang et al. 2006; Zakaria et al. 2010). When asked why drug use declines, most inmates (81 percent) said they chose to use less while incarcerated. A third (36 percent) of the respondents said it was because drugs are expensive in prison (Plourde and Brochu 2002).

The majority of inmates reported switching to different drugs. Most cocaine users switched to cannabis (Plourde et al. 2012; Plourde and Brochu 2002; Zakaria et al. 2010). It is important to understand that cocaine and other stimulant cocktails heighten the user's awareness of reality and that very few inmates seek this kind of experience, preferring a high that is more compatible with their circumstances. Cannabis produces a feeling of euphoria, helps users relax, and passes time (Cope 2000; Plourde and Brochu 2002). It is nevertheless a somewhat surprising choice considering its pungent smell and given that it can be detected in the user's urine a long time after use. When asked about this, the vast majority of inmates, particularly those who reported having used drugs, said that guards know prisoners use cannabis but tolerate it. In fact, cannabis is considered more acceptable than alcohol and other drugs that can have a negative effect on the prison climate (Plourde and Brochu 2002).[11]

Surprisingly, at first glance, the highest levels of drug use occur in maximum and medium security institutions (Plourde 2001), although illicit drugs are seemingly easier to obtain in minimum security institutions. A partial explanation for this apparent paradox may be that inmates in minimum security institutions have greater contact with the outside world, which makes it easier to bring drugs into the facility. Still, constant contact with the outside world is considered a privilege that inmates fear losing if they are caught using drugs.

Younger inmates, those who have been incarcerated several times, and people with pre-incarceration drug use problems are among the heaviest users during incarceration (Plourde and Brochu 2002).

According to a study by Zakaria and her colleagues (2010), "the proportion of inmates who reported injecting drugs in prison compared to the community declined by about 30% for men (16% vs. 22%) and 50% for women (15% vs. 29%)" (p. 13). More specifically, the proportion of injection cocaine users dropped considerably compared to pre-incarceration rates, but the proportion of opiate users who continued to use while incarcerated remained fairly stable. It is thought that their level of dependence explains this relative stability (Strang et al. 2006). Although injection is not the most frequent route of administration during incarceration, the fact that the distribution of new needles is prohibited makes injection equipment a rare commodity that is often shared, doctored, and reused, with the attendant health risks (Farrell et al. 2010; Small et al. 2005). According to Zakaria and her colleagues (2010), 36 percent of injection drug users reported sharing a needle in the community, while 44 percent of them reported doing so in prison.

The use of psychoactive substances in penal institutions is not exclusive to North America. A report by the EMCDDA indicates that between 8 percent and 60 percent of offenders report having used illegal drugs while incarcerated, while between 10 percent and 36 percent report regular drug use. Most users tend to consume less while incarcerated and to prefer cannabis (EMCDDA 2002). However, heroin use in Europe (close to 50 percent of the inmates or more in some cases) appears to be more popular and of greater concern from a public health perspective than in Canada. Numerous cases of initiation to drug use in prison have also been documented (EMCDDA 2002).

Substance-dependent Individuals

We can consider the drug–crime relationship from another angle by examining criminal activity among substance-dependent adults receiving treatment, but little research exists on the subject, especially in a Canadian context. McIntosh, Bloor, and Robertson (2007) report that 35 percent of the participants (n = 653) in their Scottish study had committed at least one gainful offence during the three months preceding entry into treatment for substance use. In England, the National Treatment Agency for Substance Misuse (2012) reported that the average number of financially motivated offences committed by 1,698 drug users in the month prior to treatment was 10.24. A Swedish study by Fridell and his fellow researchers (2008) involving 1,052 adults in treatment for substance use showed that at least 43 percent of them had been convicted of a violent offence, at least 76 percent of a property offence, and at least 61 percent of a drug-related offence.

In Quebec, Brunelle (1994) demonstrated that no less than 74 percent of the clients in three publicly funded rehabilitation centres had been arrested and convicted at least once for a criminal offence prior to entering treatment. That study inspired two complementary studies that focused on justice-involved individuals in a number of drug rehabilitation centres in Quebec (Brochu et al. 2002; Brochu et al. 2006). A study by Brochu et al. (2002) on the criminality of 149 substance-dependent individuals receiving treatment (thirty in a general treatment program and 119 in a specialized drug treatment court program) showed that 47.4 percent had been arrested for theft and 42.8 percent for assault prior to entering treatment. In a second study that focused specifically on offenders in treatment, Brochu and his fellow researchers (2006) showed that 55.6 percent of the participants (n = 124) were awaiting trial or sentencing and that legal proceedings had been undertaken with respect to 71 percent of them upon entering a rehabilitation centre.

* * *

This chapter focused on the results of prevalence studies, which clearly show that the majority of offenders, be they adolescent or adult, female or male, use illicit drugs. In addition, it appears that a significant proportion of individuals in treatment for substance use problems have committed at least one crime or been involved with the justice system. In light of these results, it would be easy to believe that drug use motivates them to commit crimes. However, these studies reveal little about the nature of the relationship between drugs and crime because they present only associative statistics. We must therefore refrain from jumping to conclusions.

Clearly, justice-involved individuals constitute a subpopulation that deserves the attention of public health authorities with respect to the use of illegal drugs. These people, especially female offenders, use drugs much more than the general population. Incarceration may reduce their consumption, but it does not address their drug use problems. Drug use in correctional settings must be interpreted in light of the inmate's history. Regular users tend to use drugs in prison. However, they adapt their usage patterns to their circumstances, much as they do on the street. Choices and decisions are key to understanding offenders' drug use in general, including in correctional settings.

Before concluding this chapter, we must emphasize that this is only a partial portrayal of the phenomena. By nature, crime statistics take into account only individuals who are caught and convicted. This raises more questions about our understanding of drug–crime dynamics for all offenders. Many offences are never reported or detected.[12] Many lawbreakers against whom complaints are filed are never caught, and those who do get involved in the justice system are typically from underprivileged socio-economic classes. Some arrestees are released for lack of evidence. It is likely that drug-dependent individuals who are not involved with the justice system have a different relationship with illicit drugs than their peers who get caught. As such, it is reasonable to believe that the relationship we have described between illicit drug use and individuals caught by the criminal justice system cannot be generalized to all offenders, and even less so to the majority of people who use or are dependent on drugs.

A thorough understanding of the nature of the relationships between drugs and crime requires a more in-depth examination than the brief statistical overview provided in this chapter. As far back as 1981, Zinberg articulated a seminal observation about drugs: knowledge of the properties of a substance does not fully explain its effects; one must also take into account characteristics of the user and the context. This word of caution is particularly apt when we are trying to tease out the relationships between two events (drug use and crime). In the following chapters, we examine the potential criminogenic properties of drugs, analyze the impact of repression on the relationships between drugs and crime, and strive to better understand the nature and development of those relationships.

Notes

1. Canadian federal law on juvenile delinquency.
2. Previously the Drug Use Forecasting System.
3. The obvious concern is that participation may not be truly voluntary, given that the survey takes place in a police station and involves individuals who have just been arrested. Subjects may well be concerned about the possible repercussions of refusing to collaborate.
4. Prisons are for individuals serving sentences of up to two years less a day; penitentiaries are for inmates serving longer sentences.
5. Translation of "Parmi les personnes qui ont déclaré faire usage de drogues, une pro-portion très importante (48,5 %) en consomme tous les jours. Environ 15 % en prennent quelques fois, voire plusieurs fois par semaine. Seulement 11,3 % des consommateurs en font usage uniquement lors d'occasions spéciales. C'est donc dire que pour la très grande majorité des sujets, l'usage de drogues est, somme toute, plutôt fréquent."
6. Multiple dependence is a common problem because offenders who abuse illegal drugs often consume alcohol to excess (Pernanen et al. 2002; Robitaille et al. 2002).
7. This is the case for alcohol, with men who engage in intimate-partner violence preferring to blame their actions on intoxication rather than a more complex gender/power dynamic (Pernanen 2001).
8. Nearly a quarter of offenders serving time in a penitentiary were convicted of a drug-related offence (Motiuk and Vuong 2006).
9. A gram of cannabis that may cost between $10 and $20 in Montreal can sell for $100 to $200 in a maximum security institution (Plourde and Brochu 2002). However, prices vary greatly from one facility to another and may depend on the user and his network (Cope 2000).
10. In penitentiaries, the use of illegal drugs is more prevalent than that of alcohol (Plourde and Brochu 2002).
11. This observation is consistent with the results of studies by Cope (2000).
12. This may include tax evasion, employee theft, or any number of victimless or consensual crimes, such as buying and selling drugs.

Chapter 2

Drugs: A Detailed Criminogenic Profile

In chapter 1, we presented a general overview of drug use among juvenile and adult offenders. Epidemiological data show that illicit psychoactive substance use is often associated with the commission of crimes among offenders apprehended by the criminal justice system. In this chapter, we examine the main characteristics of the most commonly used substances, intoxication, and dependence, and we detail documented links between criminality and various types of substances. We consider each of these factors in turn to fully understand the role of drugs in the drug–crime relationship.

We have organized this chapter to help the reader understand complicated issues while avoiding the intellectual pitfalls of addressing each theme in a separate chapter. We begin with a discussion of the pharmacological properties of various substances with respect to intoxication, the role intoxication plays in decisions to commit crimes, and, briefly, victimization associated with intoxication. We then look at the criminality of people who have developed drug dependence, a phenomenon that calls for a different analytical approach because a pharmacological lens alone is insufficient here. The complexity and sheer quantity of information about different substances is such that only health experts can find their way through the flood of data, so we concentrate on the essentials for the sake of concision and simplicity because our goal is not to write an in-depth pharmacological treatise.

There is clearly a difference between people who consume too much of a substance and become intoxicated once and those who do it so often and to such excess that they develop tolerance and dependence, or *substance use disorder* (SUD). Two effects of psychoactive substances are often associated with criminality. The first, intoxication, is a short-term effect. The second, SUD, results from a particular drug use pattern. For one thing, it appears that intoxication by one or more drugs can change the user's behaviour, opening the door to certain criminal tendencies, such as violent and aggressive behaviour, that would not emerge under other circumstances. For another, black-market drugs are very expensive, so people with increasing tolerance may turn to criminal activities to cope with a mounting financial burden.

Selected Important Definitions

Intoxication: A condition that follows the administration of a substance and results in disturbances in the level of consciousness, cognition, perception, judgment, affect, or behaviour, or other psychophysiological functions and responses.[1]

Tolerance: A gradual decrease in the effect of a substance when consumed at the same dosage. To achieve the effects originally produced by a particular substance, the user may have to increase the dosage: more is needed to produce the same effect. Tolerance is not dependence.

Withdrawal: Symptoms that occur when individuals stop using psychoactive substances. Repeated drug use disrupts neurotransmission in various brain structures. The brain adapts to the disruption by modifying neuron function. Withdrawal syndrome occurs when substance use is discontinued abruptly because it takes time for neurons to get back to normal. Those who wish to prevent or relieve the symptoms and discomfort associated with withdrawal have two options: re-administer the substance and maintain dependence, or give their body time (days, weeks, even months for certain symptoms) to recover original neural function with or without pharmacological treatment.

Substance Use Disorder (SUD): According to the fifth edition of the *Diagnostic and Statistical Manual of Mental Disorders* (DSM-5), the presence of at least two of the following symptoms within a twelve-month period:

- tolerance
- withdrawal
- substance taken in larger amounts or over a longer period than was intended
- persistent desire or unsuccessful effort to cut down or control use
- a great deal of time spent in activities necessary to obtain, use, or recover from the effects of the substance
- activities given up or reduced because of use
- continued use despite knowledge of problems caused or exacerbated by use
- craving, or a strong desire or urge to use the substance
- recurrent use resulting in a failure to fulfil major role obligations at work, school, or home
- continued use despite having persistent or recurrent social or interpersonal problems caused or exacerbated by the effects of the substance
- recurrent use in situations in which it is physically hazardous

Previously, an individual displaying at least three of the symptoms listed was considered dependent, but the DSM-5 now assesses the severity of the disorder on a continuum according to the number of symptoms an individual displays, from mild (two or three symptoms) to moderate (four or five symptoms) to severe (six or more symptoms).

According to Ben Amar (2007), psychoactive substances affect an individual's mind by changing how the brain functions, thereby altering perceptions, mood, consciousness, behaviour, and physical and psychological functions. Intoxication may be occasional or chronic (almost continuous or frequently repeated), and abuse of particular substances may result in tolerance or psychological or physical dependence.

We will begin with a brief discussion of the main categories of illicit substances and links between intoxication (effects and after-effects) and primarily expressive crime (violence). We will then examine dependence, or SUD, not in terms of different substances but in terms of repercussions on individuals and potential implications for their delinquency trajectories. Here we will focus on acquisitive crime (theft, trafficking).

Intoxication and Criminal Behaviour

Traditional and social media have played a significant role in reinforcing the conventional wisdom that intoxication plays an active role in the commission of crimes. Offenders themselves attribute their actions to intoxication, perhaps because it alleviates their feelings of guilt. Over 80 percent of Canadian federal inmates participating in a study on this subject stated that using illicit drugs on the day of the offence impaired their judgment,[2] and a third said that drugs had made them more combative[3] (Pernanen et al. 2002). Various psychoactive substances seem to have properties that make people more likely to commit crimes. Some people even suggest that drugs have criminogenic properties: users commit crimes that they would not have committed had they not been under the influence of a drug. Although it is clear that consuming a substance that acts on the central nervous system (CNS) can affect cognitive function, mood, and even certain physiological functions, giving rise to reprehensible and sometimes violent conduct, the vast majority of drug use episodes do not result in the commission of crimes. Before we review the properties of the main psychoactive substances that can be linked to criminal behaviour, we must remember that a whole host of factors may influence an individual's intoxication and behaviour. These include the dose ingested and the context of use, which comprises the setting; the user's expectations regarding the effects of the drugs; personality; neurobiological and psychological characteristics (such as impulsive propensity); and past experiences. In other words, it is a dynamic interaction of various features of the drug-set-setting triangle (Valleur and Matysiak 2006).

Let us now examine, one by one, the illicit psychoactive substances most frequently consumed by offenders so that we may better understand the relationship between their individual properties and the perpetration of crimes. Because our theme is drugs, we will not be looking at alcohol in this chapter; nevertheless, we must bear in mind that alcohol is the psychoactive substance most commonly associated with violent delinquency (Makkai and Payne 2003; Pernanen et al. 2002).

Cannabinoids

Although cannabis use is declining in Canada (Health Canada 2011a), it is the most frequently consumed illicit drug here and around the world and has been since prevalence study results were first reported (UNODC 2011). Cannabis (reefer, pot, ganja, weed) is the scientific name for Indian hemp, a plant used to produce marijuana and other derivatives. At different times and for different reasons, experts have classified this substance as a depressant, a psychotropic, and a hallucinogen. It is now typically classified as a psychotropic drug because it modulates the CNS. Tetrahydrocannabinol (THC) is the active ingredient in cannabis that produces the desired psychoactive effects. Cannabis is consumed in several forms, including marijuana (dried leaves and stems mixed with tobacco), hashish (compressed slabs consumed in cigarettes or water pipes), and oil (more concentrated, consumed in pipes). The THC concentration varies enormously from one product to another: marijuana contains between 1 percent and 20 percent, hashish between 2 percent and 30 percent, and hash oil between 10 percent and 20 percent or even up to 70 percent in some cases (Health Canada 2013a). According to the RCMP (2015), THC content in marijuana was between 1 percent and 3 percent 20 years ago; it is now 12 percent on average. A recent meta-analysis by Cascini, Aiello, and Di Tanna (2012) revealed high variability in the increase in THC levels worldwide but a general increase in cannabis potency between 1979 and 2009. "Of course, this is just an indication of the overall increase, but it is clear that this rise in mean THC seems to have been more rapid in the last decade" (Cascini, Aiello, and Di Tanna 2012, 34). Even so, the increase in THC concentration "does not exceed 5% globally" (ibid.)

Cannabis intoxication produces a state of relaxation, a sensation of well-being, and euphoria. It alters the user's perceptions and may cause anxiety and psychosis. Physically, it increases the heart rate, slows reflexes, and stimulates appetite (Ben Amar and Léonard 2002; Centre québécois de lutte aux dépendances 2006).

Evidence suggesting that the properties of cannabis directly induce people to commit crimes is inconsistent. As Ostrowsky (2011) points out, the properties attributed to the substance are many and varied, as are the reported relationships between cannabis use and violence:

> Taken together, the results of some studies suggest that marijuana use and violence are positively associated, some research has found no association, and other studies even reveal that marijuana use can reduce aggressive behavior. These conflicting findings are

not overly surprising, considering that marijuana has been classified at different times by different investigators as a depressant, a
stimulant, a hallucinogen, and a narcotic. (Ostrowsky 2011, 383)

Our own work has shown that some offenders use cannabis to reduce
anxiety or manage stress related to a planned criminal activity or one
that is under way (Brunelle, Brochu, and Cousineau 2005). In such
cases, the psychopharmacological properties of the substance do not
cause the crime, but they do enable the offender to commit it.

Although many consider cannabis to be relatively harmless,
studies increasingly support the idea that cannabis may be a risk factor
for the development of mental illness. In some people who are prone
to psychosis, exposure to cannabis may trigger the illness, which is
sometimes a precursor to violent behaviour (Boles and Miotto 2003;
Fergusson et al. 2006). Studies on the links between cannabis, mental
health disorders, and violence highlight the complex role that cannabis can play in violent behaviour and the importance of thoroughly
analyzing the problem. It is becoming clear that we must pay special
attention to the interaction between the drug and the individual as
well as to the characteristics that make individuals more or less sus-
ceptible to the effects of cannabis if we want to understand how the
substance can be involved in the emergence of violent behaviour. We
must bear in mind that not everyone who develops a mental illness
becomes violent. A minority of cannabis users develop mental health
disorders, and only a few of those become violent.

Synthetic cannabinoids (e.g., Spice) are illegal substances that
look and smell like natural cannabis and produce similar effects.
These illicit substances may be sold in shops and online as "natural"
products, a label that boosts their appeal and conveys a false sense
of security about their effects. According to the National Institute on
Drug Abuse, in 2012, use of Spice among adolescents in the United
States was second only to natural cannabis (NIDA 2012). It is more
potent and addictive than cannabis. Its growing popularity is no surprise considering its "promise of a stronger high than cannabis, easy
access, affordability, [and] perception that the products are legal"
(Spaderna, Addy, and D'Souza 2013, 526). Clinical studies and a very
few empirical and other research undertakings suggest that synthetic
cannabis can cause agitation, anxiety, aggression, mood swings, and
odd behaviour (ibid.). We cannot generalize from these findings
because they are drawn primarily from case studies, which tend to be

extreme situations, and from personal accounts. To date, no study has established a clear connection between this substance and criminality.

One issue in particular is of growing public concern: driving while under the influence of cannabis. Unlike substance-induced paranoia, drug-impaired driving is not a direct consequence of drug use, but it is nevertheless a crime. Research on drug-impaired driving is not nearly as advanced as that on drunk driving. Bergeron et al. (2007) studied the issue of driving under the influence of cannabis and alcohol. They recruited seventy-five male drivers aged seventeen to forty-nine (median age twenty-three; mean age twenty-seven) who had consumed cannabis within the previous twelve months. The volunteers were asked to complete a series of questionnaires about their perceptions, attitudes, and behaviours with respect to various driving situations.

A third of the men in the sample reported driving within an hour of having consumed cannabis (alone or in combination with alcohol) during the previous year. Unlike other participants, these men were regular thrill-seekers and heavy drinkers. They frequently engaged in risky driving, drove faster than the other participants, and were involved in more accidents. Curiously, although they recognized that cannabis can impair driving, most of them failed to perceive their own risk exposure. Moreover, they considered drunk driving to be more dangerous than driving under the influence of cannabis. Another study (Fischer et al. 2006) showed that forty-five Toronto university students who had consumed cannabis before driving at least once in the previous twelve months held similar beliefs. Although most of them recognized the risks associated with driving under the influence of cannabis, they believed they had ways to compensate for some of the drug's effects.

In a 2008 roadside survey of 1,533 randomly selected British Columbia motorists (median age thirty-four) driving between 9:00 p.m. and 3:00 a.m., almost 90 percent of the drivers provided a breath sample and just over three-quarters provided a saliva sample. Survey results showed that 10.4 percent of the drivers tested positive for at least one drug and 8.1 percent for alcohol. Cannabis and cocaine were the two drugs most frequently detected in the sample. The researchers also found that "drivers believed that one was significantly more likely to be stopped after drinking too much than after using drugs" (Beirness and Beasley 2010, 219).

A compendium of studies published by the Department of Justice Canada (2007) revealed conflicting findings about driving under the influence of cannabis. While some studies suggest that the use of cannabis reduces accident risk because of its effects on the CNS and the precautions drivers take so as not to attract police attention, others conclude that it significantly increases risk because of its effects on psychomotor function. Given the paucity of scholarship in this area and the technological limitations on the ability of the police to detect this substance, it is still difficult to arrive at a sophisticated understanding of the precise role of THC or the dose and level of intoxication that affect driving performance. However, the effect of cannabis on the cognitive functions involved in driving appears to be dose-related (Ramaekers et al. 2004). This may partly explain the variable results of studies on the effects of cannabis on driving and accidents. Considering the number of accidents and the human and financial losses attributed to impaired driving, let us hope that more research will be done in this area and that the coming decade will bring advances in impairment detection tools and technology.

A final note on cannabis: recent work has shown that although it is not a significant predictor of criminality due to user intoxication, it is nevertheless strongly associated with drug-specific crime (possession and petty trafficking), especially in countries that adopt a repressive approach to the substance and those who use it (Pedersen and Skardhamar 2010), as we will see in a later chapter.

Stimulants

There are two categories of stimulants: major (cocaine and amphetamines) and minor (caffeine and nicotine). After cannabis, major stimulants are the most commonly consumed illicit drugs in North America. As the name suggests, their primary function is to stimulate the CNS and produce a burst of energy. People under the influence of stimulants experience greater alertness, endurance, and mental acuity. In addition to their stimulating properties, these substances suppress appetite and induce a state of well-being and a feeling of euphoria. We will concentrate on the two major stimulants: cocaine and its derivatives, and amphetamine-type stimulants.

Cocaine

According to the United Nations Office on Drugs and Crime, in its *World Drug Report 2013* (UNODC 2013b), cocaine (coke, crack, base, freebase) is one of the most commonly used substances in the world. Cocaine, a psychostimulant derived from the leaves of the coca plant, comes in two main forms: cocaine hydrochloride and cocaine base. The first is a water-soluble powder that is typically snorted or injected, and the second is a non-water-soluble solid that can be smoked. Freebase and crack are the two most widespread forms of cocaine base.

Short-term effects of cocaine include heightened alertness and energy. It suppresses fatigue and hunger and induces a feeling of confidence. Undesirable effects of cocaine intoxication include agitation, anxiety, insomnia, hallucinations, and delirium. Withdrawal symptoms include irritability, fatigue, hunger, and depression (Government of Canada 2015).

Let us keep in mind that researchers investigating the criminality of cocaine users typically study individuals who are dependent or who misuse the substance, not occasional or recreational users. There is a clear distinction between a psychologically and socially healthy individual who uses cocaine occasionally and an individual who regularly uses crack on the street.

A study by Prisciandaro et al. (2012) revealed "associations between behavioural disinhibition and cocaine use in cocaine-dependent individuals" (p. 1185). An Ontario study of people in treatment for substance dependence (MacDonald et al. 2008) showed that "frequency of cocaine and alcohol use, disrespect for the law, aggressive personality, age, and sex were significantly related to violence" (p. 201). While the research suggests multi-causal explanations, cocaine use (often in combination with alcohol) appears to play a significant role in the perpetration of violence, which supports the hypothesis that the psychopharmacological effects of certain drugs are associated with violence.

Research from over a decade ago, though less careful than recent work, found that certain psychological symptoms associated with using cocaine could contribute to violent behaviour (Boles and Miotto 2003; Friedman, Terras, and Glassman 2003; Moeller et al. 2002). Cocaine use can induce extreme suspicion and intense paranoid delusions that the user may or may not recognize as psychotic experiences (Special Committee on Non-Medical Use of Drugs 2002; Erickson et al. 2000). It is not unusual for users to report trying to find a person they believe is hiding in a closet or watching the sky to spot a police helicopter that they believe is monitoring them. Others have been gripped with suspicion about a neighbour's true identity, believing him or her to be a police informant. Individuals tend to respond to feelings of paranoia in one of two ways: flight or fight. This is where another property of cocaine comes into play: it produces a sense of power that causes some users to engage in situations that have the potential to become very violent rather than retreat from them. Fortunately, some users who are prone to experiencing paranoia deliberately take other psychoactive substances that act as depressants (benzodiazepines or other popular black-market psychotropic substances such as Seroquel or cannabis),[4] to mitigate these undesirable effects. Irritability produced by what cocaine users call a post-high "crash" can also lead to violence (Goldstein 1998).

We must nevertheless be extremely cautious in directly attributing criminal behaviour to the use of a psychoactive substance such as cocaine. Attempts to establish a straightforward, one-way association between cocaine and violence quickly break down when other causal factors and the methodological flaws of the studies are taken into consideration.

Amphetamine-type Stimulants

The most popular of the amphetamine-type stimulants (ATSs) are amphetamines, methamphetamine, and MDMA (ecstasy). According to the UNODC (2013b), "the use of ATS . . . remains widespread globally, and appears to be increasing in most regions" (p. x). Methamphetamine,[5] which "accounted for 71% of global ATS seizures in 2011" (ibid., xi), continues to dominate the market for such substances. In 2015, methamphetamine use was not as widespread in Canada as elsewhere. The threat of a so-called looming meth epidemic made headlines for years, but, fortunately, it never really materialized, at least not to the extent predicted.

ATSs are CNS stimulants. Users experience higher levels of consciousness and dramatically enhanced perception. ATSs were initially prescribed for narcolepsy, depression, obesity, hyperkinesis, and even alcoholism, but are no longer necessarily indicated for these conditions (Goode 1999). People use them recreationally to derive greater pleasure from certain activities and to achieve euphoria; some like the fact that ATSs can help them lose weight, too (Boys, Marsden, and Strang 2001). Many of the effects of ATSs are similar to those of cocaine, described above.

These substances can have adverse effects when hyperresponsiveness to environmental stimuli induces annoyance, impatience, and irritability, particularly during withdrawal (Wright and Klee 2001). Intravenous administration and pathological use of ATSs can lead to hypervigilance, a distorted sense of reality, panic, emotional instability, hyperactivity, poor judgment, reduced impulse control, paranoid thoughts, and even prolonged psychotic episodes that can later lead to out-of-control aggressive behaviour (Boles and Miotto 2003; Miller 1991). According to Makkai and Payne's study of incarcerated male offenders (2003), "regular amphetamine users were more likely to be engaged in violent offending . . . and were significantly more likely to act impulsively with no planning" (p. xvi).

It is important to note that not all users experience violent episodes. In fact, these effects are virtually non-existent among truckers who use the drug to stay awake longer and among individuals for whom it was prescribed to treat obesity (Greenberg 1976). Aggressive behaviour is clearly not ubiquitous among those who use major stimulants. Even so, some people seek out these drugs believing that they will become more aggressive if they use them. The drugs' reputation alone gives people the confidence to carry out planned acts and a way to excuse their actions by blaming an external factor (Makkai and Payne 2003; Wright and Klee 2001).

Because of its connection to a particular subculture, ecstasy (MDMA) merits special consideration to achieve a better understanding of the drug and its effects. According to the UNODC (2013b), its prevalence in 2011 (19 million users, or 0.4 percent of the population) was lower than in 2009. Typically associated with raves, electronic music, and uninhibited sexual behaviour, and classified as both a stimulant and a hallucinogen (Health Canada 2013b), this drug is a powerful CNS modulator. Parrott (2013) reported that MDMA was primarily used recreationally twenty-five years ago and is now used mainly by subgroups of young people (ravers), and that "population surveys have revealed that it is the third most widely used illegal drug, after cannabis and cocaine" (p. 291). Ecstasy has several desirable and popular properties:

> Like some other substances in the amphetamine family, ecstasy has hallucinogenic properties that produce marked changes in sensory perception to which are added certain specific properties. Ecstasy decreases psychic inhibitions, makes it easier to express emotions, creates a sense of empathy with others, and produces a feeling of freedom in interpersonal relations. (Rouillard 2003)

Ecstasy's combined empathogenic[6] and entactogenic[7] properties make users feel "connected" to one another. They want to be close to other people and tend to touch each other and allow themselves to be caressed. According to a recent study, ecstasy makes users feel "relaxed, happy, loving and sexually uninhibited" (Lee et al. 2011, 533). Some of the known undesirable effects, which may intensify if usage shifts from recreational to chronic or from moderate to heavy consumption, include irrational, impulsive, and even obsessive behaviours, impaired cognitive function, intensified negative emotions, and mental hallucinations (Parrott 2013; Rouillard 2003). Lee and her fellow researchers (2011) reported that the "thizzin'" effects of ecstasy (energizing, disinhibiting, numbing, etc.) can result in "violence and aggression as well as fun" (p. 528): "Violence and aggression were also attributed to an overall disinhibiting effect from the drug as well as to feeling 'superhuman'" (p. 534). According to Reid, Elifson, and Sterk (2007), "those with a higher prevalence of lifetime ecstasy use exhibit higher levels of aggressive and violent behavior" (p. 104). Basically, the more people use this substance, the more violence and aggression they exhibit. Reid and her co-investigators found that the effect of ecstasy use on the aggression levels of those with low self-control is not as great as on those with high self-control. In other words, "at high levels of lifetime ecstasy use, those with high self-control actually exhibit more aggression than those with low self-control" (p. 115). Ecstasy's effects are related to self-control: it has little effect on those with low self-control. On a related note, some ravers describe coming down from an ecstasy high as a "descent into hell" with adverse effects including depression, generalized anxiety, agitation, trouble sleeping, and erectile dysfunction (see, for example, Lee et al. 2011). It is easy to imagine how consuming large doses of a powerful stimulant combined with sleep deprivation during long nights of dancing can put people on edge.

Benzodiazepines

Doctors widely prescribe benzodiazepines (CNS depressant drugs: Ativan, Dalmane, Librium, Halcion, Restoril, Rohypnol, Serax, Valium, Xanax) for their anxiolytic and sedative effects. According to data published in 2011 by the U.S. Substance Abuse and Mental Health Services Administration, admissions for benzodiazepine abuse and dependence almost tripled from 1998 to 2008. Of those admitted,

95 percent "reported abuse of another substance in addition to abuse of benzodiazepines: [82 percent] reported primary abuse of another substance with secondary abuse of benzodiazepines, and [13 percent] reported primary abuse of benzodiazepines with secondary abuse of another substance" (p. 1). Generally speaking, doctors recommend this treatment for people with problems such as anxiety, insomnia, and alcohol withdrawal (Konopka et al. 2013; Landry, Gervais, and O'Connor 2008).

Most benzodiazepines are available in pill form and are administered orally, but some are administered intramuscularly, intravenously, or sublingually (Landry, Gervais, and O'Connor 2008). Benzodiazepines administered intramuscularly are fast-acting tranquilizers often used in emergency situations to control agitation, violence, and aggression, particularly in individuals with severe mental health disorders (Gillies et al. 2013; Landry, Gervais, and O'Connor 2008). Adverse effects associated with this class of substances include drowsiness, psychomotor retardation, confusion, hallucinations, impaired attention and judgment, memory loss, and withdrawal symptoms[8] (Ben Amar and Léonard 2002; Landry, Gervais, and O'Connor 2008).

Benzodiazepines frequently turn up on the black market. Some users turn to these drugs for their disinhibiting properties, which can sometimes (though rarely), lead to aggressive or violent behaviour. In that sense, the pharmacological properties of these substances are similar to those of alcohol. Intoxicated individuals may show signs of emotional instability, cognitive and motor disorder, poor judgment, and memory loss. Benzodiazepines are rarely consumed alone. People use them to avert the side effects of cocaine and other stimulants, to partially counteract the effects of opiate withdrawal, or to replace a drug of choice when it is not available (Boles and Miotto 2003). Paradoxical reactions to this drug include anxiety, restlessness, psychomotor agitation, and insomnia.

Once again, other mediating factors complicate our understanding of the relationship between drugs and criminality. These include concomitant alcohol consumption, dose, history of aggression, personality disorders, impulsivity, and anxiety (Jones et al. 2011; Lader 2011; Saïas and Gallarda 2008). In their study of young offenders,[9] Forsyth, Khan, and Mckinlay (2011) examined the link between violence and alcohol and benzodiazepine consumption, and found that diazepam (Valium) was the illegal drug most often identified as a factor related to the respondents' offending behaviour, despite the fact that it is not the most popular illicit substance. The researchers hypothesized that diazepam is more likely to be a factor in violence when used together with alcohol. Diazepam seems to exacerbate many of the negative effects of alcohol, including loss of control. A study by Lundholm and her co-investigators (2013) of a modest sample (*n* = 194) of remand prisoners yielded similar findings: "Influences of alcohol and unusually high doses of benzodiazepines are proximal risk factors for violent crime" (p. 110). In addition, withdrawal from sedative-hypnotic drugs is linked to irritability and anxiety, which may lead to violent behaviour. According to Boles and Miotto (2003), "in severe cases, sedative withdrawal may produce visual and auditory hallucinations" (p. 165).

As we have seen, the link between benzodiazepine use and violence is complex and still only partly understood. On the one hand, benzodiazepines are considered psychotropics and are used to treat aggressiveness and violent behaviours in certain clinical contexts. On the other, this class of substances may be linked to violent behaviour. The risk is modulated by factors such as the user's personality, the context of use, and the dose.

Heroin and Other Opioids

According to Canadian Alcohol and Drug Use Monitoring Survey results for 2011, 0.4 percent of Canadians aged fifteen and older had consumed heroin at least once in their lives. That number, relatively low, is on the decline; in 2004, lifetime prevalence of heroin use was 1 percent. For youth, the rates have been steady at less than 1 percent for several years (Laprise et al. 2012).

As far back as 1925, Lawrence Kolb noted that, "both heroin and morphia in large doses change drunken, fighting psychopaths into sober . . . non-aggressive idlers" (p. 88). The psychopharmacological properties of opiates and opioids (codeine, hydromorphone, heroin, methadone, morphine, oxycodone, and meperidine) do not generally produce violent behaviour. Rather, in many cases, the sedative properties of heroin calm combativeness.

Heroin is a synthetic water-soluble salt, typically heated and injected intravenously. It can also be sniffed, smoked, or inhaled ("chasing the dragon"). Some users combine heroin with cocaine, amphetamines, benzodiazepines, and cannabis. Users typically describe a three-stage experience: the "flash" or "rush" (power, euphoria, wellbeing), relaxation, and the comedown (return to reality, depression).

The most acute phase may be accompanied by miosis, hypothermia, sweating, nausea, and vomiting (Touzeau and Courty 2012).

Methadone, which is available in Canada in pill form or as an oral solution, is a synthetic opioid that acts on the same receptors as heroin. Used for heroin withdrawal or in substitution programs, it is sometimes diverted to the black market for its analgesic properties. This is also the case for hydromorphone (Dilaudid), a molecule used to relieve pain such as post-operative pain; it exists in both oral and injectable forms.

Withdrawal, which usually begins a few hours after the last dose, is characterized by agitation, aggressiveness, irritability, dysphoria, anxiety, muscle pain, cramps, and diarrhea. Regular users fear withdrawal and try to avoid it at any cost. Cravings and an intense desire to get more of the substance to end withdrawal may drive people to commit crimes. Just trying to procure the substance can make people aggressive.

Here again, interpreting the relationship between opioids and criminality involves a complex assortment of interconnected psychopharmacological (including withdrawal symptoms), personal, and contextual variables.

Hallucinogens

The use of hallucinogens among people of all ages remains a relatively rare phenomenon. In 2012, about 1 percent of the Canadian residents surveyed reported using hallucinogens (Health Canada 2013), a rate that has been stable for the past decade. In this section, we will look at two types of hallucinogens: LSD-type (psychedelics) and dissociative anaesthetics.

LSD-type hallucinogens produce major cognitive and behavioural distortions. While the user's experience depends on his or her temperament and mood, these substances generally produce hallucinations and alter perceptions, thoughts, and feelings but do not cause persistent confusion or memory problems (Ben Amar and Léonard 2002). Taking a hallucinogen in an anxiogenic or traumatic setting can lead to a "bad trip" or flashbacks that can last anywhere from a few hours to several years (Pflieger 2005).

Dissociative anaesthetic hallucinogens are drugs with multiple properties and kaleidoscopic effects. PCP in particular is a very powerful hallucinogen that produces general anaesthesia by reducing or eliminating sensation and the perception of pain. Its effects last between four and six hours.

> They are more frequently associated with memory problems, strange or violent behaviour, and toxic psychosis. In addition to behaviour problems, overdosing can cause problems with the breakdown of muscle tissue (rhabdomyolysis) that may result in the accumulation of metabolic waste and lead to renal blockage. Chronic intoxication produces intellectual, psychological, and psychiatric problems.[10] (Léonard and Ben Amar 2000, 148)

It is widely believed that PCP and similar substances (such as ketamine, also known as Special K), seriously impair the user's interpretation of external stimuli and that some people become disoriented after consuming it. However, scientific studies have not found a clear association between PCP use and hostile behaviour (Crane, Easton, and Devine 2013; Hoaken and Stewart 2003). This is partly because it is difficult to differentiate its effects on such behaviours from the direct effects of other substances it is usually used in conjunction with and partly because many other factors, including the user's personality, must also be taken into account (Crane, Easton, and Devine 2013). Once again, users' psychological characteristics (antisocial personality) and psychiatric history may be better predictors of the expression of violent behaviour than PCP use (Hoaken and Stewart 2003). It remains that "violence may be more likely to occur when PCP is present" (Crane, Easton, and Devine 2013, 155).

Drug Interactions

As we saw in our review of the various substances, using more than one drug at once is evidently a widespread practice. It is not uncommon for users to consume a cocktail of several substances, one of which may be alcohol. The terms *polyconsumption* and *polydrug use* apply when drug users voluntarily and deliberately engage in this practice. Polyconsumption may be simultaneous or sequential. Users may practice polyconsumption to enhance the effects of a drug or ward off its adverse effects.

Obviously, products sold on the black market do not have to meet quality control standards or comply with strict manufacturing practices that ensure the product sold is actually what the buyer believes it to be. In many cases, while the substances sold contain some measure of what they are supposed to contain, they are cut with cheaper products that produce similar effects but may have psychoactive properties unlike those the user is seeking.

Intentional or *accidental* consumption of a combination of drugs can have a major impact on the user's reaction to environmental stimuli. Although the simultaneous or sequential (within a certain period of time) use of certain substances simply produces an additive effect, mixing certain other drugs can synergistically produce effects the user would not expect from any of those drugs taken alone. Given that the effects of even a single drug are not always well understood, it goes without saying that the effects of drugs in combination are difficult, if not impossible, to predict with any accuracy. As we probe the relationship between drugs and criminality, this synergistic phenomenon makes establishing "pure," direct associations between a drug and a behaviour much more complicated, if not downright impossible. Since studies take place not in an experimental context but in a "natural" environment, polyconsumption, more often the norm than the exception, must be taken into account when interpreting and drawing conclusions from results (Dafters 2006; Reid, Elifson, and Sterk 2007).

Victimization While Under the Influence of a Psychoactive Substance

In this chapter, we have focused on the properties of drugs that may cause people to engage in unlawful behaviour while intoxicated or in withdrawal, but we feel it is important to draw the reader's attention to another facet of the drug–crime dynamic: victimization of the user. Psychoactive substances may increase the user's risk of becoming a victim of violence. The death rate among drug-dependent people is higher; while this is due in part to disease, overdose, and suicide, it is also due to violent acts such as homicide, assault, and robbery.

Australian researchers Darke, Duflou, and Torok (2009) conducted a study of toxicology and violent death over a ten-year period ($n = 1,723$), comparing analyses of suicide and homicide cases. Their findings were consistent with those of other studies and indicate the relatively frequent presence of psychoactive substances in victims of violent death. However, certain differences were observed between homicide and suicide cases, with the former being more likely to have an illicit substance (cannabis, opioids, psychostimulants) detected. A meta-analysis (Kuhns et al. 2009) of toxicology study findings among homicide victims indicated that, "on average, 6% of homicide victims tested positive for marijuana, 11% tested positive for cocaine, and 5% tested positive for opiates. [In general,] the proportion of homicide victims testing positive for illicit drugs has increased over time" (p. 1122).

Another major study of 1,565 ethnically diverse and socioeconomically disadvantaged U.S. high school students examined the association between dating victimization and psychoactive substance use. The study concluded that, "compared to their nonabused counterparts, youth who experienced dating violence were more likely to smoke cigarettes, drink alcohol, binge drink alcohol, . . . use marijuana, [and] use ecstasy" (p. 701), among other things. However, multivariate analyses showed no association between substances other than alcohol and cigarettes and dating violence, possibly because of underlying variables such as antisocial personality or the co-occurrence of polydrug use (Temple and Freeman 2011).

A number of studies have examined the link between intimate partner violence among adults and psychoactive substance use from the points of view of perpetration and victimization (Smith et al. 2012; Afifi et al. 2012). Although they differ in some respects, these studies all found a relationship among the perpetration of violence, victimization, and specific psychotropic substances.

> The findings from this study, especially when adjusting for the correlation between victimization and perpetration, were largely consistent with what might be expected when considering the psychopharmacological effects of the drugs. Alcohol and cocaine were most strongly associated with intimate partner violence, while cannabis and opioid analgesics were most strongly associated with victimization. (Smith et al 2012, 244)

In recent years, certain illicit substances, known as date-rape drugs, have been specifically associated with sexual victimization. These include two odourless, colourless substances that dissolve easily in alcoholic beverages without altering their taste and are rapidly eliminated in urine: Rohypnol and gamma-hydroxybutyrate (GHB). Rohypnol, or flunitrazepam, is a benzodiazepine hypnotic not approved for medical use in Canada or the United States.[11] Its effects manifest as sedation, muscle relaxation, and sleep. It can produce anterograde amnesia.[12] Rohypnol is sometimes deliberately used with other CNS depressants, such as alcohol, heroin, or marijuana, to enhance their effects (Negrusz and Gaensslen 2003).

GHB was first synthesized in the 1960s. Little effort has been put into commercializing GHB, but it has long been available in health food stores as a food supplement. It is often sold illegally as an aphrodisiac. Some bodybuilders say that GHB helps metabolize fat and build muscle mass. Ravers use it for its euphoria-inducing properties. Only a few cases of sexual assault following the administration of GHB alone and unbeknownst to the victim have been scientifically documented. Victims have no memory of events during and after victimization. According to data from Quebec's Addiction Prevention Centre (2006), 19 percent of Montrealers attending raves had used GHB in their lifetime, which suggests that many people choose to consume it voluntarily. Considering that people use the substance to reduce anxiety and inhibition, it is worth monitoring the evolution of GHB use in relation to criminality closely.

Many people who use drugs do so socially. Substance use can affect how people interact, increasing the risk of arguments, disagreements, quarrels, and violent altercations within groups of users. Intoxication can compromise people's ability to detect situations that could put them at risk of victimization and take adequate measures to protect themselves. It can also lower their defences and weaken their coping skills, thus drawing them into altercations that are likely to end poorly for them. Drug users may also be considered ideal targets for victimization, not only within communities of users, but also by non-users who see them as people who will have a hard time defending themselves, who may find it difficult or embarrassing to report incidents, or who may not seem credible to the police or the courts. It is also worth noting that the illegality of the drug market and barriers to setting up supervised consumption sites force users to consume their drugs in hiding, unprotected, which can place them in uncomfortable situations and expose them to a higher risk of victimization.

To sum up, intoxication makes users vulnerable to victimization because of its deleterious effects on judgment and decision-making and because it exposes individuals to high-risk situations (Temple and Freeman 2011), such as physical confrontations and having unprotected sex, and to places they would not otherwise frequent.

The Role of Intoxication

Certain illicit drugs may have a mediating effect on criminal behaviour, such as violence, our focus in this chapter. Since the general pharmacological characteristics of most of the more common psychoactive substances are quite well known, we can infer the different mechanisms by which certain drugs contribute to the user's behaviour. However, studies have so far failed to provide us with a thorough understanding of the specific role intoxication plays in the perpetration of crime. Research into the nature of the intoxication–crime dynamic appears to have stalled because the factors involved are numerous and extremely complex. Among other things, researchers have to take into account dose, product purity, route of administration, frequency of use, and the individual's natural and acquired tolerance. Moreover, in their quest for intense sensation and quick and easy pleasure, many users consume drug cocktails, most of which include alcohol. This makes it difficult to distinguish the effects of each individual substance in the mix. To further complicate matters, personal and contextual variables must also be taken into account.

Dependence and Criminal Behaviour

We turn now to another repercussion of taking psychoactive substances: the potential for developing dependence and possible links between dependence and criminality. Only a minority of users develop dependence, but it can be devastating. The consequences of addiction include the heavy financial burden of procuring drugs, mounting debt, and engaging in criminal activity to pay off that debt. That certain drugs are illegal makes them very expensive relative to the income of most drug-dependent people. For example, participants in the North American Opiate Medication Initiative (NAOMI), a clinical research project on diacetylmorphine[13] treatment for opioid-dependent people, spent an average of $1,500 a month on drugs (Oviedo-Joekes et al. 2008). However, a number of studies, including our own and some of the major classic studies, show that, before getting involved in criminal activity, people who regularly and frequently use drugs generally employ seven main strategies to manage the cost of their drug use (Faupel 1991; Grapendaal, Leuw, and Nelen 1995; Manzoni et al. 2006). These strategies are not mutually exclusive. On the contrary, engaging in more than one type of income-generating activity is often the only way to get enough money. Let us look at the strategies drug-dependent people employ to support their habit so that we can better understand another facet of the drug–crime dynamic.

How Users Support Their Habit

Some drug-dependent people manage to hold down a *job*, at least for a period of time. Under-the-table or part-time work is common, but many have regular jobs. For a significant number of these people, working provides some structure in their lives, which limits their drug use and involvement in criminal activity.

A drug-dependent individual having trouble making ends meet may try to *reduce overall spending* and will even for ego necessities. Many drug-dependent people *turn to friends and family* for money and other forms of help. Some try to get free meals, live with a succession of family members, friends, and acquaintances, or get drugs in exchange for doing odd jobs for other users. Those whose needs are not met by their social network may turn to panhandling.

Many heavy psychoactive substance users receive *government income support*. The recently employed claim employment insurance benefits. Others collect workers' compensation, and still others are on social assistance.

Some users engage in *activities associated with the drug business*. They may act as steerers who direct potential customers to dealers. They may rent their needle and other paraphernalia to rookies, help less experienced users inject their drugs, or test the quality of a substance for a reseller (Johnson et al. 1985, 63–65). These are just a few of the possibilities available to regular users, who engage in these activities opportunistically. Compensation is commensurate with risk.

Some perceive *prostitution*, or rather, *sex work*,[14] as a feasible way to make money, but it is not the most common income-generating activity for people who misuse illicit drugs (Manzoni, Fischer, and Rehm 2007). For those who do engage in sex work, it is often a supplemental activity that they avoid for as long as possible. Many drug-dependent people who feel they have no other choice find sex work so distressing that they use even more drugs to bolster their courage or numb themselves (Cobbina and Oselin 2011).

A more common drug procurement strategy, particularly among female cocaine (crack) users in North America, is to *exchange sexual favours for drugs* (Logan and Leukefeld 2000; Maxwell and Maxwell

2000; Young, Boyd, and Hubbel 2000). Many women report receiving cocaine as a gift (Marsh 2002) and think it is normal to perform sexual favours in return. The costlier the product, the more personal favours are performed. We wish to make it clear that exchanging sex for drugs is not the same as sex work. The people participating in the exchanges generally do not consider these transactions to be sex work because it is not a job for them and no money changes hands.

For users who have exhausted some or all of these options but still cannot generate enough income to pay for their drugs, crime becomes a viable option. The extent to which people engage in criminal activity (usually lucrative crime), essentially for the purpose of acquiring drugs, varies from one person to the next and is proportionate to how much they are using.

Crime as an Income-generating Activity

Acquisitive crime is just one of many ways to fund dependence on an expensive substance, but it is preferred by a significant proportion of drug-dependent people (Casavant and Collin 2001). In a study of drug-dependent young offenders in addiction rehabilitation centres, Brunelle and her associates (2014) found that 67 percent of those in the high-delinquency group (compared to 38.9 percent of those in the low-delinquency group) said they committed their crimes to get drugs.

Manzoni, Fischer, and Rehm (2007) found that about 40 percent of people who used opioids and other drugs had engaged in illegal income-generating activities in the previous thirty days, but NAOMI researchers found even higher prevalence rates among participants in their study, all of whom were opioid users. In the month preceding assessment, 73.3 percent of the participants were involved in illegal acquisitive activities; the median number of days during which they were involved was fifteen; 94.4 percent had been charged in their lifetime for a crime; 81.7 percent had been convicted; and the median lifetime number of months of incarceration was twelve (Oviedo-Joekes et al. 2008). Other researchers have observed income-generating crime (including trafficking) among amphetamine and cannabis users (Lacharité-Young et al. 2017; Wilkins and Sweetsur 2011).

We know that it is difficult to separate acquisitive offences from the need to satisfy cravings. Individuals may engage in different criminal activities simultaneously or successively; some drug-dependent people develop a main hustle, while others are opportunistic, taking advantage of situations that crop up. It seems that a proportion of drug-dependent people commit more crime at certain points in their drug use trajectory, especially during periods of heavy drug use. The drug–crime relationship becomes firmly established when people progress to heavy, regular drug use, with its attendant financial demands, which can be difficult or impossible for most users to manage via conventional means. However, the pattern of association between drugs and crime is not the same for everyone. Manzoni and his collaborators (2007) observed "substantial differences among the cities regarding both the extent and frequency of illegal activities . . . . Crack use was strongly associated with property crime in Toronto, while cocaine use was strongly related with sex work in Montreal" (p. 342). The authors concluded that local drug culture dynamics are associated with particular crime dynamics. They found that, generally, use of a specific drug is associated with a specific type of crime. For example, frequent use of crack increased the risk of involvement in all three types of crime studied (drug dealing, property crime, and sex work), while heavy heroin use increased the risk of involvement in property crime and sex work, but not drug dealing. Heavy cocaine use was strongly associated with sex work, though heavy use of prescription opioids was not associated with any particular type of crime. This suggests that subculture is another factor in the specific associations between drugs and criminality.

Let us now turn to the criminal activities most common among people who are dependent on costly drugs.

Acquisitive Crime

Acquisitive crime is probably the best-documented type of crime associated with the use of costly drugs. The results of a study by Manzoni and his fellow researchers (2006) clearly showed that "frequency of heroin, cocaine, and crack use, gender, housing status, and past criminal justice involvement were excellent predictors of property crime" (p. 351). This categorical statement must be qualified, however. In 2007, the same researchers published a follow-up study in which they reported that only 16 percent of the participants (regular heroin users) reported having committed a property crime (mostly non-violent theft) in the previous thirty days. This suggests that theft is not necessarily a part of everyday life for drug-dependent people.

Their trajectory is not linear; they cycle into and out of periods of unlawful behaviour. Nevertheless, it is clear that no matter the type of drug consumed, people who are dependent on illicit substances commit more property crime than those who are not (Makkai and Payne 2003). Thus, there is every indication of a positive association between dependence and non-violent theft.

Petty theft is one type of acquisitive crime committed by regular illicit drug users. These offences are relatively simple to carry out and unlikely to be prosecuted. An individual may "borrow" mom's jewellery without telling her, filch some cash from a buddy's kitchen table, or betray the boss's trust by pilfering the till. Some people take the opportunity when visiting acquaintances to rifle through drawers looking for objects of value. These victims are unlikely to report the thief, who likely can resolve matters amicably if caught. Even when the police do get involved, diversion is the most likely outcome (Casavant and Collin 2001; Faupel 1991; Grapendaal, Leuw, and Nelen 1995).

We must keep in mind that money is not the only method of payment in the black market. Small-time drug dealers may accept stolen goods as payment. Some dealers will even tell deeply indebted clients to procure specific items as payment. Big stores are targets of choice because of the vast selection of products they carry and the anonymity factor (Faupel 1991).

Shoplifting generally accounts for a larger proportion of the income of drug-dependent females than of their male counterparts. Although there are advantages to this type of theft, the risk of arrest and prosecution is higher than for stealing from acquaintances, particularly as technology now enables merchants to monitor and stop thieves on the spot. Many shoplifters resort to a well-worn justification to assuage their guilt so they can keep stealing: the stores belong to rich owners (shareholders) who will not notice the missing goods and who will even get their money back from insurance payments or by raising their prices (Grapendaal, Leuw, and Nelen 1995). Common consumer goods, such as clothing, food, and alcohol, are the items most frequently stolen by heavy illicit drug users, but they may also pocket cough syrup containing codeine or other products that can help alleviate withdrawal symptoms. Goods are kept for personal use, offloaded within the thief's network, or fenced for, at most, a third of their retail value.

Breaking and entering is another lucrative offence, but it demands certain skills that not all drug-dependent people possess. The thief must be lucid and clever enough to case the target and figure out the best time to break in without arousing neighbours' suspicions. The thief must have an intimate knowledge of alarm systems and be able to quickly assess which goods will fetch the highest prices on the black market. Stolen goods are either sold by the thief on the street or in bars, passed on to a fence, exchanged with a dealer for drugs, or offloaded to a shopkeeper who may or may not be aware of their provenance. Regular thieves typically prefer to do business with fences so they can get their money quickly and relatively hassle-free, but they get paid just a small fraction of the stolen item's retail value. Proceeds of breaking and entering can enable the thief to buy drugs, but some report using drugs to fortify themselves to commit the crime or to enhance the thrill of the illicit activity (Brochu and Parent 2005; Brunelle et al. 2005).

Although *robbery with violence* is one of the fastest ways to acquire large sums of money, most heavy drug users who commit crimes avoid this type of theft because it involves direct contact between offender and victim (Grapendaal, Leuw, and Nelen 1995). The most common form of robbery with violence committed by heavy users of illicit drugs is mugging, which usually happens in relatively isolated public places. The victim, too, may be involved in illicit activity, such as buying drugs, or may be intoxicated. Drug dealers are also frequently the target of robbery with violence (Faupel 1991). Some drug-dependent individuals come to enjoy the rush of certain types of crime, which they compare to using powerful stimulants (Brochu and Parent 2005). In many cases, these violent acquisitive crimes are a last resort for people desperate to get enough money to satisfy their cravings or avoid withdrawal.

Acquisitive crime may go hand in hand with dependence because it enables people to buy drugs, but we must keep in mind that intoxication and withdrawal can make it more difficult to engage in these activities and increase the risk of arrest.

Trafficking

Drug trafficking comes in all shapes and sizes. Who could have predicted that drugs would one day be sold on the Internet? As surprising as that may seem, Décary-Hétu has shown that cryptomarkets—illicit online drug markets—are having a significant impact on the drug trade (see, for example, Aldridge and Décary-Hétu 2016) and are likely to play a larger role in the coming years. Still, many dealers prefer more traditional approaches: setting up shop in their apartment; offering home delivery and never being out of earshot of their cell phone or pager; and doing business on the street, in bars, or at raves. Some are actively involved in an organized network, and others are involved indirectly (runners, lookouts).

Some users resell a portion of the drugs they have purchased to finance their own habit. These micro-traffickers buy their drugs in larger quantities to lower their cost, then resell small amounts to novice users. According to a study by Small and his fellow researchers (2013), "dealing was perceived to be an effective means to support one's own drug consumption" (p. 482). As a fringe benefit, they always have drugs available, which means they never have to experience withdrawal.

Users may nevertheless hesitate to get involved in micro-trafficking, particularly in the early stages of their criminal career, opting instead for other activities associated with the drug trade, such as transporting varying quantities of drugs from one place to another or temporarily storing drugs in their apartment. Some resell their prescribed methadone.

These users may have no idea that their minor involvement is considered trafficking in the eyes of the law. Their ignorance of laws (such as Canadian laws) that consider the possession of small quantities of drugs to be trafficking, and therefore an offence, puts them at risk of getting caught and saddled with a criminal record. This typically comes as a surprise: "I thought it was okay to have a small amount like that at home," and "I didn't think I was trafficking; I was just selling some of my stash to my friends to pay for my own drugs," are common refrains among justice-involved people in treatment.

While it is not easy to accurately estimate the proportion of individuals who are involved in reselling drugs and use drugs regularly and frequently, we can say with certainty that, sooner or later, a very large number of them are drawn to drug trafficking, if only on a small scale. According to Manzoni, Fischer, and Rehm (2007), "The most prevalent criminal activity among all [study] participants was drug dealing, in which about 27% had been involved in the previous 30 days" (p. 354). A significant proportion of heavy users, particularly of heroin and cocaine, opt for this activity because their drugs are very expensive. It is important to note, however, that gender is a determining factor. The world of drug trafficking is still so macho that women have a hard time carving out a niche for themselves. They do not sell the same drugs as men, and they are often systematically victimized (Brochu and Parent 2005; Felson and Bonkiewicz 2013; Sommers, Baskin, and Fagan 1996).[15] Manzoni, Fisher, and Rehm (2007) also noted that the men in their sample were "twice as likely to have committed a property crime or to have been involved in drug dealing and had a much lesser likelihood of having engaged in sex work than females" (p. 361).

Another factor that motivates people to get involved in the illicit drug trade is the lure of fast money. It does not take long for psychoactive substance users to figure out that this an excellent way to ensure easy, convenient access to drugs without spending a lot of money. Earnings vary dramatically from one study to the next and can be anywhere from $500 to $10,000 per week for what is, in many cases, a part-time activity (Denton and O'Malley 2001; Jacobs and Miller 1998). It all depends on the quantity and quality of the drugs sold, the level of the transaction, and many other factors.

Neophytes are also attracted to this work because they think it is easy and they are unlikely to get caught (Decorte 2000). Some heavy users of illicit psychoactive substances say they worked for a long time and did many deals before they were arrested (Hunt 1990). However, once an individual becomes known to the justice system, the risk of arrest rises dramatically (MacCoun and Reuter 1992).

Arrest is certainly not the drug dealer's only worry. Those selling on consignment may be far more concerned about having their goods or revenue stolen. Other "occupational hazards" include being threatened, injured, or killed (Jacobs, Topalli, and Wright 2000; Pearson and Hobbs 2001). Naturally, under the circumstances, people take steps to protect themselves, such as carrying a gun, but here again, there is significant variation depending on the type of market. Felson and Bonkiewicz (2013) found that "participants in crack-cocaine markets are more likely to possess guns than participants in powdered-cocaine, opiate, and marijuana markets" (p. 319).

Drug trafficking as an occupation is compatible with the lifestyle of regular illicit drug users. Their schedule is conducive to catering to their clients' needs. Sharing and small-scale reselling may help cement social relationships (Kokoreff 2005). They tend to sell drugs in their own neighbourhood and to people they know or friends of friends.

Even though a considerable proportion of people dependent on heroin or cocaine eventually end up involved in small-scale dealing to friends and acquaintances, few of them depend on it as their sole source of income despite the benefits we have described. In most cases, it is something they do intermittently (DeBeck et al. 2007; Denton and O'Malley 2001; Small et al. 2013).

Other Lucrative Criminal Activities

Another relatively common criminal activity among drug-dependent people is *pimping* (Evans, Forsyth, and Gauthier 2002), an activity that profits from the sex work of others and typically goes with other types of crime, such as dealing in drugs and stolen goods.

People sometimes specialize in the *sale of stolen goods*, but it is more commonly practiced as a lucrative side hustle by people with the right kind of network (Denton and O'Malley 2001). The illicit drug distribution scene usually provides plenty of opportunities for the exchange of stolen goods, which are sometimes used to pay for drugs.

A small number of people who use illicit psychoactive substances *commit forgery, cash fraudulent cheques,* or *use stolen credit cards*. Forgery requires specific skills and membership in certain socio-economic groups, which are not available to all heavy drug users (Johnson et al. 1985).

Links Between Dependence and Criminal Activity

The most obvious link between drug dependence and criminality has to do with the economics of buying drugs. Some drugs, such as heroin and certain stimulants, including cocaine, can create dependence in many users. People become unable to function without their drug, and dependence dictates how they live their lives. A user who is dependent on one of these substances must use it several times a day to avoid physiological or psychological withdrawal. Over time, buying drugs becomes terribly expensive. Heavy users support their habit in a variety of ways. One or more paid jobs may be a substantial source of income for those who function in normal society. Others reduce their spending elsewhere, depend on family, friends, and government income support, and engage in activities related to the drug business to support their habit. For some, these income sources eventually dry up or no longer suffice. At that point, income-generating crime begins to look like a good way to support a very expensive habit. Small-scale drug trafficking and thefts of all kinds are among the most common crimes that drug-dependent people commit.

The vast majority of small-scale dealers used psychoactive substances before getting involved in drug trafficking. In fact, the likelihood of being involved in the illicit drug trade escalates in step with the individual's drug use beyond a certain level. Resellers are introduced to the business through contacts, and tend to be relatively young people who work part-time selling their merchandise to a circle of people they know, most of whom live in roughly the same community as them. In most cases, there is little structure involved. This very profitable venture enables them to support their own habit and make ends meet. Small-scale dealing is more of a lifestyle choice than a criminal specialization for most, and they willingly employ other means to earn a living.

Theft is also an important source of income for many drug-dependent people, but it is impossible to identify a single pattern linking the use of psychoactive substances and acquisitive crime. Trajectories differ depending on the circumstances, the individuals, and the drugs involved. A particular individual's lifestyle is certainly an important factor to consider in any attempt to understand the relationship between drugs and criminality. Still, it seems that people who adopt deviant lifestyles are more inclined to employ illicit means to meet their needs. They steal not only to support their habit, but also because it is part of their lifestyle.

One might think that a user from an affluent background with access to money would be less likely to resort to crime to finance a drug habit and that users from different backgrounds and socio-economic classes will engage in different types of crime. Many an office worker has confessed to supporting a drug habit by selling stolen company property. Similarly, it is easy for some medical professionals to divert a portion of their patients' prescriptions for personal use. Studies of this phenomenon are few, however; most research focuses on the criminal activities of low-income heavy users who do not practice well-paid professions. No surprise then that existing scholarship all but excludes occupational crime and high-level fraud.

Involvement in crime varies from one person to the next. It depends on the individual's relationship with drugs (tolerance, dependence, etc.), the cost of drugs, the appeal of certain types of activities, time, place, socio-economic class, contacts, opportunities, and other circumstances.

* * *

The abuse of illicit psychoactive substances is a serious problem. Among users, drugs and crime intersect to a significant extent. Although stemming partly from drug use itself, involvement in criminal activities has more to do with difficulty managing drug use: taking too much at once, using a synergistic combination of drugs, withdrawal symptoms, and dependence.

Research on illicit drugs and crime tells us that any substance that affects the CNS can influence the intoxicated person's behaviour in some way. Since the general psychopharmacological characteristics of most of the more common psychoactive substances are well known, they may serve to explain the unlawful behaviour of some intoxicated individuals. Drug use can diminish an individual's behavioural repertoire to such an extent that alternatives to violence may not be available to him or her. What is more, dependence on certain substances can further limit the options available to an intoxicated person experiencing the early symptoms of withdrawal who will do anything in his or her power to stave it off. These are the ideal conditions for both criminality and victimization.

Still, even though drugs have the potential to induce specific effects that may result in (violent) expressive criminality, scientific observation makes it clear that these properties do not cause all intoxicated or dependent individuals to act the same way. All of the following and more must be taken into account for each individual: the dose ingested, product purity, route of administration, frequency of use, the individual's natural and acquired tolerance, his or her personality and genetic makeup, the setting, acceptance or rejection, and access to the substance or substitutes. Drug use may even make it harder for some people to commit crimes. There is more to intoxication and its consequences than pharmacology. The molecule itself is not solely responsible for the link between drugs and crime; user- and context-specific factors are also part of the equation.

We know that many people who use illicit psychoactive substances regularly and frequently, particularly high-cost substances, are involved in unlawful activity. For some, crime is their primary source of income. Their need for drugs demands an ample income stream that seems best assured by criminal activity. We must nevertheless point out that others resort to crime only on "bad days" (such as when a dealer who has waited too long to get paid starts making threats). Some drug users' criminal careers are brief, abandoned at the first sign of trouble. For others, criminal activity delivers a rush of adrenaline and a supply of cash that they come to depend on. Criminal involvement varies considerably, depending on the individual and his or her context, as well as where they are in their dependence trajectory. A considerable proportion of dependent users' acquisitive crime stems from the need for money arising from dependence on high-cost drugs. However, it may be misleading to think of pharmacodependence as being at the root of that relationship because pharmacological properties alone do not lead to dependence, and dependence alone does not drive criminality.

Cautious interpretation is called for because research in this area is methodologically flawed. First and foremost, it provides information about a subgroup of users, not all users. Participants tend to be recruited from among dependence rehabilitation service clients or the incarcerated population. The first thing to keep in mind is that not all people who use licit or illicit drugs misuse them or become dependent. Some manage their drug use well for long periods of time. Furthermore, not all drug users engage in criminal activity other than buying and possessing drugs, where this is criminalized. Among those who do get more involved in illegal activities, motivation and frequency can vary enormously, depending on the individuals and their socio-economic status. And of course, not everyone who commits a crime gets caught or convicted.

As we have said, the relationship between drugs and crime does not spring solely from the toxicity of a given substance or from dependence. To achieve a better understanding of the dynamics, we must take other factors into consideration. For example, buying, selling, and consuming certain substances may occur within a criminal context or coincide with high-risk illegal activity. Some people who misuse drugs have a compromised behavioural repertoire due to exposure to a combination of risk factors in childhood. In many cases, the delinquent response is implicitly linked to the personal and social context within which intoxication and dependence are just some of the many factors to consider.

In light of this complexity, some researchers have abandoned the idea of a direct causal relationship, focusing instead on personal and psychological factors that can lead to the development of problematic behaviours. We will address that later in this book. For now, we turn our attention to the Canadian political context and what it means for the use of psychoactive substances.

Notes

1. Lexicon of alcohol and drug terms published by the World Health Organization (available at http://www.who.int/substance_abuse/terminology/who_lexicon/en/#).
2. Ninety-two percent said that alcohol affected their judgment.
3. Half of the study participants attributed this effect to alcohol.
4. Alcohol is also very popular among cocaine users.
5. Twice as potent as amphetamine, it is considered a "club drug," a category that includes ecstasy, gamma-hydroxybutyrate (GHB), PCP, and ketamine. These drugs are associated with raves and after-hours clubs.
6. Putting oneself in another person's shoes, empathizing with what that person is feeling.
7. Sensation of floating, happiness, and physical well-being.
8. Nervous system dysfunction upon cutting back consumption (Léonard and Ben Amar 2000).
9. Study participants were aged fifteen to twenty; the average age was 18.5 years. One hundred and seventy-two completed a survey and thirty participated in qualitative interviews.
10. Translation of: "Ils sont plus fréquemment associés à des troubles de la mémoire, à des comportements étranges ou violents et à une psychose toxique. Outre des problèmes de comportement, le surdosage peut causer des troubles du métabolisme musculaire (rhabdomyolyse) susceptibles de provoquer un blocage rénal dû à l'accumulation de déchets métaboliques. L'intoxication chronique entraîne des problèmes intellectuels, psychologiques et psychiatriques."
11. This substance is used legally under medical supervision in over eighty countries around the world.
12. Forgetting events that occurred following consumption.
13. Pharmaceutical grade heroin.
14. The term "prostitution" implies a moral judgment and has criminal connotations. The term "sex work" helps to distinguish between the economic activity and the individual performing it. Sex work is no longer illegal, but Canadian laws have always been written to discourage the sale of sexual services. In its historic December 2013 ruling, the Supreme Court of Canada unanimously struck down three prostitution laws that banned soliciting, brothels, and living off the avails of prostitution. The Court reasoned that these laws were incompatible with the Canadian Charter of Rights and Freedoms because they exposed vulnerable women to violence and murder by preventing them from protecting themselves. The *Protection of Communities and Exploited Persons Act* of 2014 prohibited purchasing and advertising sexual services, receiving material benefit derived from such services, and all activities related to procurement and communication in a public place for the purpose of selling sexual services. The Act protects sex workers because the sale of sexual services remains legal. While the government maintains that the act creates safe working conditions for sex workers, many advocacy groups argue that it recriminalizes sex work and exposes sex workers to violence.
15. Victimization may take the form of assault with the intent to take over a seller's territory, robbery with violence, threats relating to debt repayment, arguments about the quality of the drugs sold, or assault to assert dominance or control within the organization.

Chapter 3

The Legal and Political Landscape

I n this chapter, we describe how psychoactive substance use fits into the Canadian legal and political landscape. We analyze how our relationship with drugs changed to the point that some were criminalized. We try to understand how legislation and policy affect the relationship between drugs and crime. We also discuss recent policy developments that offer realistic alternatives to repression.

The Road to Repression

As surprising as it may seem, there was a time when some of the drugs that are illicit today appeared not in law books but in ledger books. Some drugs went from being an important legal commodity to the target of a "war on drugs," a vicious battle that has claimed many lives around the world. In a matter of years, certain drugs fell dramatically into disrepute. How did such a sudden shift come about?

Globalization of Trade

In the eighteenth and nineteenth centuries, following the Seven Years' War (1756–63), the British controlled opium production in India through the East India Company.[1] For a long time, much of the output was exported to China, which was considered a stable, secure market. By 1729, China was importing 200 chests of opium annually, and by the end of the eighteenth century, over 4,000.[2] In 1838, it imported more than 40,000 chests.

Despite a 1729 Chinese imperial edict prohibiting the sale of opium, China began to produce it in addition to importing it. Production levels were high because it was ten times more profitable than growing rice. In addition to its use as a recreational drug, opium was also used "as an antispasmodic, as an analgesic, as a cough [and] fever . . . suppressant" (Lovell 2011, 34).

> During the time between the first [Chinese] prohibition edict of 1729 and the imperial authorities' stricter enforcement around 1800–10, a distinction was made between opium for smoking and medicinal opium. Producing, trading, and selling the former were prohibited; the latter was a legal substance. (Rapin 2013, 57)[3]

Government-ordered eradication campaigns were doomed to fail because of official corruption. A common strategy was to cut off the head of the plant but spare its roots.

After turning a blind eye to the corruption of many of their officials and the disastrous public health effects of feeble enforcement of the 1729 law for many years, Chinese authorities eventually saw things differently. In 1796, as China's economy was collapsing due to the flow of capital to European countries, it published an imperial edict prohibiting opium importation on pain of death.[4] Yet even this extreme measure failed to put an end to the lucrative business, and it is estimated that there were 2 million opium smokers in China in 1835 ((Lovell 2011). Despite constant problems enforcing the policy and the fact that opium abuse was no longer the province of the lowest classes but was ensnaring young people from good families (Lovell 2011), Chinese authorities ordered all foreign merchants to hand over their opium stocks. The English protested vociferously, but over 1,400 tonnes of their merchandise was thrown into the river at Guangzhou (Canton) (Bell 1991).

In England, some 300 trading companies demanded that their government intervene and force Chinese authorities to compensate them for the destroyed merchandise. A press campaign was launched. News from China told of skirmishes between British ships and Chinese junks (Wikipedia 2017). These actions were interpreted as direct attacks on the British Crown, and the reaction was merciless:

In June 1840, an Indo-British fleet reached the Chinese coast. The attackers' superior firepower brought Canton down quickly. Her majesty's troops sailed up the Yangtze and took control of the movement of goods on the river, thereby depriving the imperial treasury of trade-generated tax revenues. Two years later, the Qing gave in. (*La Tribune* 2013)[5]

In August 1842, intending to secure additional trade advantages for the Crown, "a British squadron sailed up the Yangtze River to Nanking and forced the Daoguang Emperor to capitulate and sign the Treaty of Nanking on August 29, 1842" (Wikipedia 2017).[6]

The treaty opened the Chinese market to British imports. Opium imports reached 12,000 tonnes in 1886. At that point, the British themselves imposed restrictions (De Choiseul-Praslin 1991).[7]

England triumphed in what may have been the first true drug war. Merchants defeated the Chinese empire, and trading nations, such as France and Portugal, applauded the victory (ibid.).

Meanwhile, at the end of the eighteenth century, and in the nineteenth, opiates were regularly prescribed in Western countries to treat certain medical problems (Montigny 2011). In 1789, at the venerable age of eighty-three, Benjamin Franklin wrote to a confidant that he had been using opium to combat "grievous pain" (Benavie 2009, 22).

It was against this political backdrop that the first international conventions on controlling the opium trade—and later, several other psychoactive substances—were signed.

The nineteenth century was a turning point for the history of drugs in many other ways too. The method for extracting morphine and heroin was discovered, hypodermic needles were perfected, the chief alkaloid of coca was isolated, and Vin Mariani and Coca-Cola, which contained relatively small amounts of cocaine, hit the market.

All of these developments, combined with extravagant marketing on the part of pharmaceutical companies and a growing number of opiate prescriptions, led to a surge in the number of users and a gradual change in society's attitude toward drugs and drug users. Nobody in America was particularly concerned about drugs at the beginning of the nineteenth century, but by the turn of the twentieth century, that had changed dramatically. The rapid spread of drug use was antithetical to the aims of certain religious groups[8] and professional associations[9] that backed vigorous anti-drug crusades.

Prohibition

With the late nineteenth and early twentieth centuries came a new outlook on drugs and drug users. There was a growing sense that people who consumed opium derivatives could become pharmacodependent (Benavie 2009). Chinese-American minorities, some of whom used opium regularly, drew the ire of moral entrepreneurs. Anglo-Saxon America, including Canada, made up its mind to do something about this "devilish" substance, as it was described by certain commentators more concerned with sensationalism than with truth (Montigny 2011). Did this mindset find fertile ground in the widespread racism whose target was a minority that was "stealing" jobs from whites? Some are quite certain that it did.

> Around that time, when "Chinese" was synonymous with "opium fiend" and "yellow peril," the United States bowed to union pressure and enacted "exclusion laws" designed to protect American workers. (Béroud 1991, 69)[10]

> However, at the end of the nineteenth century, in Western Canada, puritanical groups were calling for major restrictions on this front. Methodist evangelicals in particular were very vocal in their conviction that atheism and belief systems other than Protestant must not be tolerated because it would lead to the downfall of Anglo-Saxon power. Alcohol, sex, and opium were considered three wellsprings of vice and sin that posed a threat to white Anglo-Saxon Protestant families and their way of life. (Beauchesne 1991, 127)[11]

> The first antiopium laws, beginning with city ordinances in San Francisco in 1875 and Virginia City, Nevada, in 1876, were directed at the smoking of opium, which was associated with Chinese immigrants and deviant whites. Their use of the drug was perceived as symbolic of the immigrants' decadence and as a potential weapon that could be used to undermine American society. In the South, the white majority feared that cocaine use among blacks might cause them to forget their assigned status in the social order. (Nadelmann 1990, 506)

> Beginning in an era of morally tainted racism and colonial trade wars, prohibition-based drug control grew to international proportions at the insistence of the United States. (Sinha 2001, i)

From that point on, the crusade gained momentum; it was only a matter of time until non-medical use of these drugs would be prohibited. The early twentieth century witnessed the creation of new laws prohibiting opium in Canada and the United States. In February 1909, the United States convened a thirteen-member meeting of the International Opium Commission in Shanghai.[12]

> The Commission approved nine resolutions that, while they may look like so much wishful thinking, actually represented phenomenal progress at the time. In the resolutions, the Commission recognized China's right to eradicate the production and abuse of opium (resolution 1). It recommended the immediate closure of opium divans (resolution 7) and the adoption of drastic measures to control the manufacture, sale, and distribution of opium and its derivatives at the national level (resolution 5). It also recognized the duty of all countries to adopt reasonable measures to prevent the shipment of opium to any country which prohibited its entry (resolution 4). (Bell 1991, 4)[13]

These were non-binding resolutions intended to restrict the opium trade. Three years after that, on January 23, 1912, an international convention was ratified in The Hague calling on signatory nations to enact national legislation restricting the production, importation, possession, and use of opiates (UNODC 2013a).

A little over a century later, the current state of global co-operation on drug matters is now laid out in the following three United Nations conventions:

- The Single Convention on Narcotic Drugs, 1961 (amended by the 1972 Protocol), signed by 186 states.
- The Convention on Psychotropic Substances, 1971, signed by 183 states.
- The Convention against Illicit Traffic in Narcotic Drugs and Psychotropic Substances, 1988.

These twentieth-century conventions criminalized the cultivation, manufacturing, trafficking, and distribution of certain drugs except for medical or research purposes. At the instigation of the United States and the United Nations, they endorsed a "war on drugs" strategy.

An array of false impressions combined with major gaps in scientific knowledge about the potentially "criminogenic" effects of certain psychoactive substances misguided many decision-makers and legislators and played a decisive role in the evolution of repressive measures prohibiting the consumption of certain substances in industrialized countries. This brief glimpse into the history of our relationship with drugs helps us better understand the backdrop to the United States' merciless twentieth-century war on drugs and drug users.

The War on Drugs

For the past century, American and Canadian governments have opted for repressive strategies aimed at eliminating the supply of and demand for drugs. Such strategies have consumed the better part of U.S. funding for action on drugs. To eliminate supply, governments have taken two main approaches to crippling supply chains: waging war against drug producers and hunting down importers and distributors. To eliminate demand, governments criminalized users.

Action Against Drug Producers

Except in the case of cannabis and synthetic drugs, producer countries are generally distinct from the most voracious consumer countries. Southeast and Southwest Asia are known for opium poppy production,[14] and Colombia, Peru, and Bolivia for coca cultivation. Without oversimplifying, we can say that, by and large, southern nations produce drugs for northern markets.

In North America, cocaine was clearly the first target of the cross-border battle. According to the United Nations Office on Drugs and Crime, or UNODC, in 2007 and 2008, Americans and Canadians consumed about 470 tonnes of the white powder, which "is generally transported from Colombia to Mexico or Central American countries . . . and then onwards . . . to the United States and Canada" (UNDOC 2017). Although Mexico is not a major producer, it is deeply involved in drug trafficking. Its many well-organized cartels compete to control the transportation of drugs to the American giant, leaving countless "collateral" victims in their wake.

Cracking down on drug producers located outside consumer countries calls for a foreign policy that relies heavily on military action, such as the Mérida Initiative, a $1.6-billion United States–Mexico partnership launched in 2008 to combat organized crime. Its objective is to take down Mexican organized crime groups by capturing their leaders and disrupting their drug-related revenue streams (production, distribution, money laundering). The program also aims to enhance Mexican law enforcement capacity and border controls to stop drugs entering the United States from Mexico. Lastly, the program strives to promote an anti-drug culture among Mexicans (U.S. Embassy, Mexico 2015).

The Mérida Initiative escalated the war on drugs in Mexico, resulting in a monumental death toll[15] and the glorification of a *narco cultura.*

> Alongside the violence emerged new cultural identities that embraced the values espoused by criminal gangs. *Narco cultura* celebrates the drug trafficker lifestyle through popular music and telenovelas. *Narcocorridos* ("sick songs") portray criminals as heroes who have achieved wealth and success in a country where poverty prevails. (Légaré-Tremblay 2014)[16]

In producer countries such as Peru, Bolivia, and Colombia, and others farther afield, such as Afghanistan and Myanmar, drug crops are not only part of the local flora, they also bring in more revenue than any other crop. Drug lords step in where an ineffectual state cannot provide segments of the population with a decent income. Cultivating plants that supply the raw material for drugs is part tradition and part response to economic factors because so few other national products enjoy such stable—and in some cases, growing—demand. Persuading small farmers to cultivate cereal crops, fruit, or coffee instead of coca or poppies is no easy task.

Feeble political and territorial control is largely responsible for the tens of thousands of hectares of illegal crops cultivated in many drug-producing countries. Chouvy (2014) concluded that efforts to reduce supply have failed. Basically, some small farmers deny the legitimacy of such legislation and do not hesitate to engage in activities that they feel are within their rights, particularly in lawless regions where the authorities are impotent or quite simply corrupt (ibid.; Polet 2013a, 2013b).

Action Against Drug Importers and Distributors

Even as it targets producers in foreign countries, the war on drugs is also being fought on the home front, taking aim at importers and distributors in the consumer country. The objective is to seize all drugs being manufactured or cultivated and intercept drugs being smuggled into and distributed around the consumer country.

At the turn of the last century (1908), when opiates were widespread, Canada enacted the *Act to prohibit the importation, manufacture and sale of opium for other than the medicinal purpose*, otherwise known as the *Opium Act*. Unemployment, racism, and the rise of temperance movements converged to create ideal conditions for the enactment of this first Canadian drug law (Brochu and Magrinelli Orsi 2008). In 1911, cocaine and morphine were added under the *Opium and Drug Act*. Codeine, heroin, and cannabis joined the ranks of proscribed substances in Canada in 1923 following a series of articles by Judge Emily Murphy—the first female magistrate in Canada and in the British Empire—that interwove statistics, medical information, and racist and moralistic anecdotes that were later assembled in a book entitled *The Black Candle* (Brochu and Magrinelli Orsi 2008). Canada's current legislation on narcotics, the *Controlled Drugs and Substances Act* (CDSA), was adopted in 1996 (Government of Canada 1996).

In 2012, the Government of Canada adopted Bill C-10, the *Safe Streets and Communities Act*. Among other things, it amended the CDSA by adding minimum prison sentences for the production, importation, exportation, and possession with the intent to export of substances such as cocaine, heroin, and methamphetamine. Minimum sentences were also established for the cultivation of six or more marijuana plants and the production of cannabis oil and resin. It is worth noting that section 720(2) of the *Criminal Code* provides for the provinces to implement a treatment program for drug-dependent individuals under court supervision, which gives judges the option of not imposing the mandatory minimum sentence if the offender successfully completes the treatment program offered.

Under the CDSA, the maximum penalty for importing or trafficking drugs such as opiates, cocaine, PCP, amphetamines, GHB, and large quantities of cannabis is life imprisonment. An individual convicted of dealing drugs for organized crime purposes, of using violence or a weapon, or of a repeat offence is liable to a minimum penalty of one year in prison. The minimum penalty for offences involving minors or for dealing drugs in a prison as defined by the Criminal Code is two years in prison. Trafficking less than 3 kg of cannabis is liable to imprisonment for a maximum term of five years less a day. Trafficking in certain other drugs, such as mescaline, LSD, and magic mushrooms, is liable to ten years in prison.

Harsh penalties may serve as something of a deterrent to the few drug dealers who are aware of them, but the biggest challenge when it comes to catching traffickers is thwarting their schemes to import and distribute drugs, an undertaking further complicated by the sheer size of Canada and the United States combined with the massive quantity of goods of all kinds imported every week. Is it even possible to monitor every potential point of entry closely enough?

Criminal networks are in a constant state of flux. If an entry point is blocked, drug traffickers quickly find another to get their products in (Thoumi 2002). With the dawn of the digital era, some distributors are opting to do business in online marketplaces. An estimated $90 million worth of drugs changed hands on Silk Road, a darknet market or cryptomarket, shut down in 2013 by the FBI (Nancy 2015; The Economist 2014a). Since then, dozens of cryptomarkets that look like legal e-commerce sites but that guarantee the buyer's anonymity have sprung up, enabling resellers and consumers in areas without ready access to traditional dealers to purchase drugs (Aldridge and Décary-Hétu 2016; The Economist 2014b). The recent expansion of cryptomarkets has implications for the people behind them, as well as for legislators. As Aldridge and Décary-Hétu (2016) point out:

> One important question must therefore be asked: given the potential we've discussed here for harm reduction to arise from the online drug trade—for drug dealers, for users and within the markets themselves—should drug cryptomarkets be a high priority for law enforcement? We might consider reframing the problem: instead of deeming cryptomarkets problematic because the criminals operating there are harder for law enforcement to reach, perhaps we should consider the possibility that cryptomarkets reduce the problems associated with this kind of criminality. (p. 28)

According to the most optimistic police estimates, only about 10 percent to 20 percent of drug imports are intercepted, which is a drop in the bucket. Seizures have very little impact on the criminal organizations involved. Even if police agencies managed to completely halt the inbound flow of illicit drugs, clandestine laboratories would step into the breach and quickly bring substitute products to market. It has become relatively easy to synthesize substances with the stimulating effects of cocaine or the natural properties of opiates. These products are already on the market and regularly consumed by users.

Action Against Users

Launched in 2007, the Government of Canada's National Anti-Drug Strategy focused on three main areas: prevention, treatment, and enforcement (Nasr and Phillips 2014).[17] Enforcement is just one of the three pillars of Canada's strategy, but since this chapter is about political and legal aspects of drugs, its repercussions are our primary focus here.

Let us now turn to enforcement provisions that affect users. Under the CDSA, a person found to be in possession of opiates, cocaine, or PCP may be sentenced to up to seven years in prison. For cannabis, the penalty can be up to five years less a day, but if the quantity does not exceed 30 g (or 1 g of resin), it is a summary conviction offence with a maximum penalty of six months in prison or a $1,000 fine. For mescaline, LSD, and magic mushrooms, the maximum penalty is three years' imprisonment.

Although the CDSA is slightly less repressive than the previous law on drugs, at least when it comes to small amounts of cannabis, the number of drug cases reported by the police has been rising steadily for more than two decades in Canada. Erickson and her collaborators (2013) estimate the arrest rate for illicit drugs at 225 per 100,000 residents. Our analysis of Statistics Canada data indicates that police reported close to 57,000 drug-related offences in 1993, and almost twice that many, 109,000, in 2013 (see fig. 3.1) despite a steady decline in the overall crime rate (see fig. 3.2).

While 2 percent of all offences reported by the police in 1993 were drug-related, that proportion grew to 5 percent in 2013 (see fig. 3.3).

This is due primarily to arrests for simple possession of cannabis, which in 2013 accounted for 54 percent (58,965 offences) of all drug-related offences reported by police (see fig. 3.4). Ontario's Centre for Addiction and Mental Health (CAMH) estimates that more than 500,000 Canadians carry a criminal record for simple possession of cannabis (CAMH 2014).

A more in-depth analysis, however, actually reveals a downward trend in the proportion of all prosecuted offences that were drug-related. In 1995, 8 percent of prison sentences were for drug-related offences; in 2012, only 4 percent were. Drug-related offences resulting in probation dropped from 10 percent in 1995 to 4 percent in 2012; those resulting in fines slid from 10 percent in 1995 to 5 percent in 2012 (Statistics Canada 2013a). Simply put, more Canadians were being arrested but fewer were being sentenced.

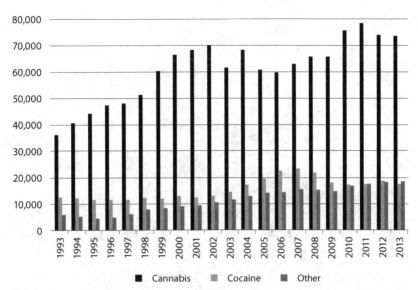

Figure 3.1. Drug-related offences reported by police in Canada from 1993 to 2013 (Statistics Canada 1998, 1999, 2000, 2001, 2002, 2003, 2004, 2005, 2006, 2007, 2008, 2009a, 2010, 2011, 2012a, 2013e, 2014).

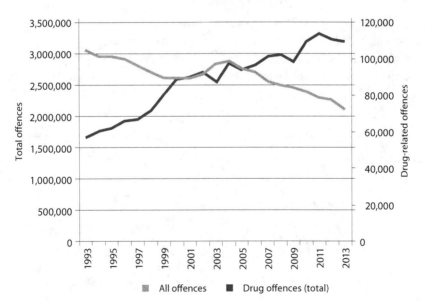

Figure 3.2. Offences reported by police in Canada from 1993 to 2013 and drug-related offences for the same period (Statistics Canada 1998, 1999, 2000, 2001, 2002, 2003, 2004, 2005, 2006, 2007, 2008, 2009a, 2009b, 2010, 2011, 2012, 2013e, 2014).

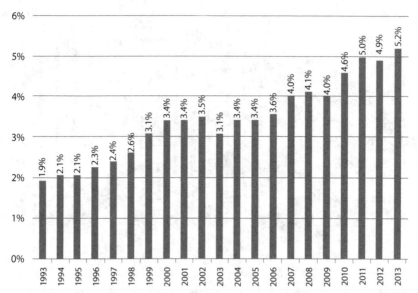

Figure 3.3. Drug-related offences as a proportion of total offences reported by police in Canada from 1993 to 2013 (Statistics Canada 1998, 1999, 2000, 2001, 2002, 2003, 2004, 2005, 2006, 2007, 2008, 2009a, 2009b, 2010, 2011, 2012, 2013e, 2014).

To better understand how existing laws affect drug users—particularly cannabis users, who are arrested in greater numbers than other drug users—we interviewed 165 regular users (who had consumed cannabis more than twice a month for at least five years) in four

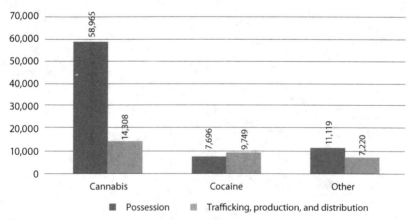

Figure 3.4. Number of police-reported offences related to possession, trafficking, production, and distribution of drugs in Canada in 2013, by substance (Statistics Canada 2014).

Canadian cities: Halifax, Montreal, Toronto, and Vancouver (Brochu et al. 2011). To be eligible for the study, users had to be relatively well integrated socially (regular employment or studies). More than half the participants reported annual household incomes over $35,000, which is much higher than the average income of previous samples made up of drug-dependent people in treatment. The interviews (which lasted between forty and seventy minutes) revealed that these users, who smoked an average of twice a day, were rarely arrested. When we read the existing legislation to them, the respondents were surprised and told us very clearly that neither their own experience nor that of people they knew was consistent with the law. We should point out that very few (10 percent) of the people in our sample used cannabis in public places. The vast majority used it at home (95 percent) or at a friend's place (78 percent).

To gain a deeper understanding of how the law affects cannabis users, we compared the number of self-reported users with the number of arrests for simple cannabis possession for years in which prevalence studies were conducted. Figure 3.5 substantiates the perceptions of the people interviewed by Brochu and his fellow researchers (2011) because the number of people arrested is miniscule (between 1 percent and 2 percent) compared to the number of people who reported using cannabis that same year (see fig. 3.6).

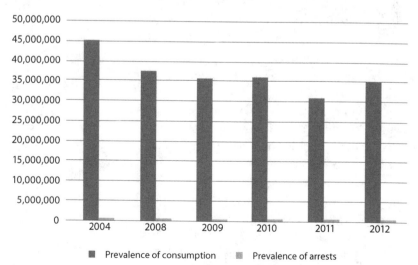

FIGURE 3.5. Prevalence of cannabis consumption and prevalence of arrests for simple cannabis possession from 2004 to 2012 in Canada (Health Canada 2013c; Statistics Canada 2009a, 2010, 2011, 2012, 2013c, 2013d, 2013e, 2014).

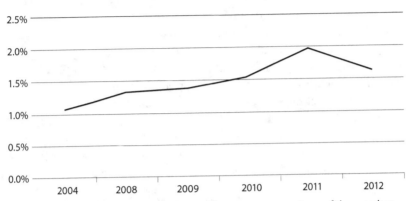

Figure 3.6. Simple cannabis possession offences as a percentage of the number of cannabis users in Canada from 2004 to 2012 (Health Canada 2013c; Statistics Canada 2009a, 2010, 2011, 2012, 2013c, 2013e, 2014).

This suggests that the individuals arrested under the CDSA are either the most visible users (other offences, consumption in public places) or the most marginalized (criminal record, homeless).

The percentage of arrests varies from one Canadian province to another. In 2012, the rate of cannabis-related offences as a percentage of the number of users was 1 percent on Prince Edward Island but more than twice that (3 percent) in Saskatchewan (table 3.1). This federal law appears to be less strictly enforced in some provinces than in others.

The CDSA has not gone unchallenged. In 2000, *R. v. Parker*, which involved a person with epilepsy who wanted legal access to cannabis to ease his suffering, led to the implementation of the Marihuana Medical Access Regulations, replaced in 2013 by the Marihuana for Medical Purposes Regulations (MMPR), which were themselves replaced by the Access to Cannabis for Medical Purposes Regulations in 2016. The regulations set out the conditions for access to and production of dried marijuana for medical purposes. To register with a licensed producer, individuals must follow this procedure: (1) consult with a doctor, (2) obtain a medical document stipulating the daily quantity authorized, and (3) register as a client and order the quantity required from a licensed producer.[18] In other words, under the regulations, Canadians may purchase marijuana for medical purposes if a doctor agrees to sign an official document authorizing them to purchase a specific quantity of the substance from a licensed producer (Nasr and Phillips 2014). At the time of writing, there were thirty-five licensed marijuana growers in Canada, seventeen of them

TABLE 3.1. Number of cannabis-related offences and number of cannabis users (previous twelve months) reported in 2012 in Canada, by province.

Provinces[1]	Number of cannabis-related offences	Number of cannabis users	Offences as a percentage of cannabis users
Newfoundland and Labrador	854	57,953	1.5%
Prince Edward Island	186	15,388	1.2%
Nova Scotia	2,378	114,352	2.1%
New Brunswick	1,300	64,345	2.0%
Quebec	14,825	727,565	2.0%
Ontario	22,123	1,220,492	1.8%
Manitoba	1,935	165,004	1.2%
Saskatchewan	3,449	110,930	3.1%
Alberta	7,412	443,316	1.7%
British Columbia	17,670	626,977	2.8%

1 Prevalence of cannabis users is available for Canadians provinces, not territories.
Sources: Health Canada (2012) and Statistics Canada (2013a, 2013c).

in Ontario. Health Canada regularly updates the number of licensed producers on its website.[19] The 2013 regulations were challenged in Federal Court, which in February 2016 struck down the provisions prohibiting patients from growing their own marijuana at home. Justice Michael Phelan found the MMPR to be unconstitutional, so some 40,000 Canadians with prescriptions for medical marijuana can now grow their own plants at home under the Access to Cannabis for Medical Purposes Regulations.

Europe

A number of European countries have adopted a more tolerant approach to drug users. In the United Kingdom, police can refer offenders to treatment services. Other countries, such as France, Norway, and the Republic of Malta, suspend prosecution while individuals attend courses on the dangers of drugs or motivational interviewing sessions (EMCDDA 2015). Let us take a brief look at the Netherlands and Portugal as examples of countries that have opted for liberalization.

The Netherlands

Contrary to what many tourists think, buying and possessing cannabis is not legal in the Netherlands, but it has been tolerated since 1976. People can purchase cannabis for personal use (less than 5 g) in one of the many coffee shops (businesses with special licences) that are open about what they sell, even though advertising is forbidden. Most of these establishments have a bar serving non-alcoholic beverages and a counter for cannabis sales. There is usually a menu with a variety of cannabis and hashish options. Prices vary from one coffee shop to the next, but one can generally purchase a gram of one's favourite strain for €5. Bongs are generally available upon request. More information about coffee shops is available on the City of Amsterdam's official website. At the time of writing, the website offered the following information:

> Coffee shops are, first and foremost, social spaces. They exist for the sale and consumption of cannabis, but they are also about atmosphere and meeting people, just like cafés and bars. Coffee shops are an integral part of Amsterdam's urban landscape; they contribute to the city's charm and reputation for tolerance. Coffee shops invite patrons to enjoy an alternative ambiance even if they are there just to drink coffee. Alcoholic beverages are generally prohibited, but coffee and tea are available, often alongside a variety of baked goods. People can hang out, have a good time, watch the world go by, read a magazine, and cross paths with a diverse mix of people.[20]

Coffee-shop cannabis sales do not have legal status but are tolerated to a point. A coffee shop can be shut down for selling to minors, if its clients disturb the peace, if it sells more than the maximum amount per transaction, or if so-called hard drugs are found on the premises.

Consumption in public places is subject to relatively strict regulation. Users may not disturb the peace or consume cannabis in the presence of minors. Possession in excess of 5 g is subject to a fine; possession in excess of 30 g is an indictable offence.

It is important to note that the Netherlands' liberal cannabis policy has not been associated with an increase in cannabis use. The Dutch model has, however, separated marijuana sales from sales of other drugs (CAMH 2014; Van Ooyen-Houben 2008). A study comparing the prevalence of cannabis use among high school students in the United States, Canada, and the Netherlands found no difference between the three countries (Simons-Morton et al. 2010). If we were to criticize anything, it would be that, as with decriminalization measures elsewhere, cannabis production is illegal in the Dutch regulatory framework, which leaves the supply part of the equation and its attendant profits in the hands of criminal organizations.

Portugal

Portugal opted for a different model: decriminalization of all drugs (CAMH 2014; Greenwald 2009). Drug use is still prohibited in Portugal, but the possession of small quantities was decriminalized on November 29, 2000 (effective July 1, 2001) (Domosławski 2011). It is important to note that a de facto decriminalization policy had been in place since the 1990s, and fines were the typical penalty for drug possession (Laqueur 2014). The law does not distinguish between so-called hard and soft drugs (Greenwald 2009), and authorizes the possession of amounts sufficient for one person for ten days (e.g., 1 g of heroin, 2 g of cocaine, 5 g of hashish, 25 g of cannabis). Violations of the rules are considered administrative, not criminal, offences. In keeping with a public-health orientation, violations are now adjudicated by "commissions for the dissuasion of drug addiction." Three-member commissions in each region are made up of legal advisors, medical professionals, and social workers. Commission members try to understand the user's family background and economic situation, reasons for drug use, drug use history, and whether there are addiction issues (Domosławski 2011). If addiction is a factor, users are referred to treatment services. If not, in the case of a first offence, the proceedings are suspended for two years once the offender has been informed of the dangers of drug abuse and the consequences of repeat offences. In the case of a repeat offence, the commission may impose fines ranging from €25 euros to €150, as well as non-monetary penalties (community service) (Greenwald 2009; Senate of France 2002). Significantly, from both the offender's and society's perspective, the commission process does not carry the same stigma as a criminal conviction (Domosławski 2011). Acquiring and possessing small quantities of drugs for personal use is tolerated. The law is designed to help drug-dependent people get treatment.

Once the new drug law came into force, far fewer individuals faced criminal charges, which relieved Portuguese courts of a substantial portion of their workload, and there was no increase in the prevalence of problem substance use (CAMH 2014; EMCDDA 2011; Greenwald 2009; Hughes and Stevens 2010; Quintas 2011; Tavares and Portugal 2012). Although substances became more accessible (cheaper), and drug use increased slightly (though no more in Portugal than in Spain and Italy), decriminalization has enabled public health authorities to intervene with heavy users earlier and has enhanced collaboration among addiction service providers (Domosławski 2011; Hughes and Stevens 2007, 2010). Finally, reported recidivism rates are surprisingly low (8 percent) (Domosławski 2011).

One drawback may be that a substantial majority (74 percent) of the individuals appearing before the commissions were arrested for cannabis possession (Domosławski 2011). Certainly cannabis is the most prevalent drug, but are these the people most in need of a conversation with commission members? It is also important to note that, although monetary fines are relatively small and are imposed infrequently, they can have a much greater negative impact on people from underprivileged socio-economic backgrounds (Domosławski 2011). Lastly, it is worth pointing out that consumers still have no choice but to do business with the criminal element because cultivating and selling drugs remains illegal. Nevertheless, Portugal stands out for two reasons. First, it decriminalized *all* drugs, thus eliminating the artificial distinction between soft and hard drugs. Second, and most importantly, Portugal's policy is truly public-health driven.

* * *

Many European countries have changed their cannabis laws since the early 2000s. The European Monitoring Centre for Drugs and Drug Addiction, or EMCDDA, carried out an interesting exercise that involved compiling and comparing the prevalence of psychoactive substance use before countries relaxed their laws or, conversely, began to impose harsher penalties. The EMCDDA's 2011 report concludes that new laws have very little impact on people's drug use. This suggests that enforcing tough laws may not be the best way to curb consumption, since they do almost nothing to deter people from using drugs.

The Americas

Strikingly different approaches prevail in the Americas. Whereas decriminalization is the most common liberalization policy in Europe, the spread of cannabis legalization has been slow in North America, often contrasting sharply with more repressive measures in neighbouring jurisdictions. The following is a brief overview of the situation in a number of countries, including, of course, Canada and the United States.

The United States

At the time of writing, twenty-three states and the District of Columbia have legalized cannabis for medical purposes (INCB 2015). In November 2012, four states and the District of Columbia took their drug liberalization policies a step further. Adults in those jurisdictions are now permitted to consume cannabis recreationally. In those states, cannabis is now treated like alcohol and tobacco despite a federal statute that prohibits the production, trafficking, and even possession of cannabis (INCB 2015). In a number of states, it is now legal to grow a certain number of plants per individual and, in some states, even to sell cannabis. Licensed shops can sell up to 28 g to adults (aged twenty-one or older with ID) for consumption in their own homes. Consumption in public places is prohibited. Washington State's legalization model is slightly different. As of June 2014, people can buy up to 28 g of marijuana from a licensed retailer, but only people who use cannabis for medical purposes can grow their own. In contrast, in the District of Columbia, retail sales are permitted for medical use only; recreational users must grow their own plants (up to three mature plants at a time). Oregon phased in Colorado's model: in 2015, it authorized the cultivation of up to four plants per household; in 2016, it legalized retail sale for recreational use.

Colorado was the first state to legalize cannabis for recreational use in the United States and now serves as a model to several others. Let us look briefly at its legalization model. First of all, the government does not produce cannabis but authorizes the cultivation, processing, and sale of it. When we visited Colorado in February 2016, the City of Denver had issued 557 licences for cultivation, 121 licences for marijuana-infused product manufacturing (chocolates, candies, cookies, juices, etc.), 326 retail sales licences in 215 stores, and 9 licences for private laboratories that analyze the THC content of retail products. According to a March 10, 2014, article in the *Huffington Post*, the state collected $2 million in a single month thanks to cannabis legalization. That kind of revenue could make legalization attractive to governments that are constantly looking for new sources of income. It is our belief, however, that drug policies should not be profit-driven because things could get out of hand. There are ethical considerations involved, and governments must understand that legalization has to go hand in hand with regulation (licensing, inspection, and such) and adequate and effective prevention.

Uruguay

In December 2013, Uruguay passed an act regulating the importation, production, stocking, sale, and distribution of cannabis (INCB 2015). According to Room (2014), the act, which met with strong internal opposition, "permits three forms of cultivation: up to six plants at home; through users' co-operatives . . . and for licensed producers who must sell to the government" (p. 346). The law also allows individuals who add their names to a confidential registry (fingerprints are used as ID) to purchase up to 40 g per month from a licensed club or pharmacy. Uruguay wants to prevent pot tourism, so foreigners cannot sign up for the registry.

These legalization measures came into force too recently for us to assess their impact. Nevertheless, as the International Narcotics Control Board states in its 2015 report, "The Board notes that this legislation is contrary to the provisions of the international drug control conventions, specifically article 4, paragraph (*c*), and article 36 of the 1961 Convention as amended by the 1972 Protocol and article 3, paragraph (1) (*a*), of the 1988 Convention" (p. 62).[21]

Canada

In Canada, a commission and two committees were set up to analyze federal laws and policies and make recommendations to improve them.

The first, the Commission of Inquiry into the Non-Medical Use of Drugs chaired by Judge Le Dain (the Le Dain Commission), visited twenty-seven cities and twenty-three universities from 1969 to 1972. The commissioners heard from 639 witnesses and read 14,600 articles, books, and briefs. Their analysis quickly led them to conclude that cannabis should be treated differently from other illegal drugs, so they prepared a separate report for it affirming that there was no scientific basis for cannabis prohibition, which was costly and ineffective. The commissioners recommended removing the prohibition against cannabis possession (Commission of Inquiry into the Non-Medical Use of Drugs 1972). In its final report (1973), the commission recommended gradually decriminalizing non-medical use of drugs, repealing criminalization of simple possession of cannabis, reducing penalties for other cannabis-related offences, and maintaining other penalties for drug offences. For opiate-dependent people, the commissioners recommended improving access to treatment rather than criminal sanctions. Finally, the commissioners recommended that Canada adopt policies to discourage the non-medical use of drugs and that sanctions fit the crime. Two minority reports were issued, one by Commissioner Bertrand and the other by Commissioner Campbell. The former endorsed a more liberal orientation, advocating for drug legalization; the latter took a more conservative view of the problem and called for a tougher stance on enforcement. The commission's work was a representation of the broader conversation happening in the late 1960s about the relevance of Canada's drug policies, particularly those relating to cannabis. It resulted in a modest bill to relax penalties for simple possession of cannabis, Bill S-19, which was introduced and passed in the Senate in 1974 but did not get past first reading in the House of Commons (Bryan and Crawshaw 1988).

Thirty years later, two important committees were established to study Canada's drug legislation once again: the Senate Special Committee on Illegal Drugs and the House of Commons Special Committee on the Non-Medical Use of Drugs.

The Senate Special Committee on Illegal Drugs (2002) heard from 234 experts and studied the twenty-three reports it received. Among other things, it found that: (1) the vast majority of cannabis users use the drug on an experimental or occasional basis (10 percent become regular users, and 5 percent to 10 percent develop a dependence); (2) cannabis is less harmful than alcohol and tobacco; (3) cannabis does not lead to the use of so-called hard drugs; and (4) cannabis prohibition is a significant drain on the public purse, particularly in terms of law enforcement. The committee concluded its report with a series of recommendations, including the adoption of an integrated drug policy (recommendation 5), the legalization of cannabis for therapeutic and recreational use (recommendation 6), and amnesty for any person convicted of possession of cannabis under current or past legislation (recommendation 7).

A few months later, the House of Commons set up the Special Committee on the Non-Medical Use of Drugs (2002). Committee members heard from 222 witnesses in ten Canadian cities. In its report, the committee expressed concern about the lack of good data on the use and harmful use of substances, which was a barrier to the development of optimal drug policies. The committee nevertheless concluded that "the consequences of a criminal conviction for simple possession of a cannabis product are disproportionate to the potential harms associated with personal use" (p. 129). The report ended with thirty-nine recommendations, including decriminalization of simple possession of cannabis. The committee recommended "that the Minister of Health and the Minister of Justice propose appropriate amendments to the *Controlled Drugs and Substances Act* and/or the *Criminal Code* to provide a wider range of sentencing options, including treatment, for substance-dependent individuals involved with the criminal justice system" (p. 101). Another notable recommendation was that "Correctional Service Canada undertake, as a pilot project, the establishment of two federal correctional facilities reserved for offenders who wish to serve their sentence in a substance-free environment with access to intensive treatment and support" (p. 106).

In the wake of the two reports, a bill to decriminalize the simple possession of cannabis was drawn up. Under Bill C-17 (2004), an individual caught with 15 g or less of cannabis would have been fined $150 ($100 for a person under eighteen). The fine for possession of a gram or less of cannabis resin (hashish) would have been $300 ($200 for a minor). The maximum punishment for possession with aggravating circumstances would have been $400 for an adult and $250 for a person under eighteen. However, because of a leadership change within the party in power, an election, and the arrival of a new, more conservative, governing party, the bill was never passed.

Despite these repeated calls for more lenient policies with respect to drug users, little has been done, and law enforcement costs in Canada now exceed $2 billion per year (Rehm et al. 2006). In 2015, Canada elected a Liberal government that promised to legalize cannabis, so the coming years could bring a number of developments on this score.

Different Concepts and Approaches

The Observatoire français des drogues et des toxicomanies produced a glossary of various legislative alternatives to repression (Obradovic 2011). Here are a few terms and brief definitions:

Legalization: Also known as *regulation*, legalization means making a particular behaviour legal. Under legalization, production, distribution, and possession are permitted, although they may be regulated by the government. This is the scenario in Uruguay.

Depenalization: Relaxing criminal sanctions. Depenalization may be de jure or de facto. In the first case, penal sanctions are removed from the law itself. De facto depenalization means not enforcing the sanctions provided for by law.

Decriminalization: Removing a behaviour from the sphere of criminal law. This is the case in Portugal.

As we can see, different legislative approaches are possible. Some people advocate for cracking down on dealers, and even users, while others prefer a more liberal stance. What factors inform an individual's or a society's position on this issue? Beauchesne (2011) produced an excellent analysis of the relationship between social values and drug-related criminal policies. Canadian laws have clearly been grounded in *legal moralism*: a virtuous state has a duty to impose the moral values of a particular group on the whole community for its own good, even if that means promulgating restrictive laws. Typically, drug users are blamed for their own problems: they get what they deserve. Where moral entrepreneurs' good advice fails to have the desired effect, criminal justice must step in to contain drug users' moral defects.

According to Beauchesne, the majority report of the Le Dain Commission exemplifies a somewhat more liberal position she calls *legal paternalism* because it views drug addicts not as people with moral defects who need to be put back on the straight and narrow but as people who are "sick." Here again, the "father knows best" state embarks on a social mission, forcing sick people to accept treatment or face criminal sanctions.

A third philosophy, which Beauchesne calls *legal liberalism*, is embodied in the Bertrand minority report of the Le Dain Commission and, more recently, the 2002 report of the Senate Special Committee on Illegal Drugs. Legal liberalism is rooted in humanism, social responsibility, and respect. The state is responsible for creating a safe

environment while protecting individual freedoms, so it must provide a safe environment for people to use drugs if that is what they
choose to do.

Normalizing the Relationship With Users

Because psychoactive substances affect the central nervous system,
mood, cognition, perception, and actions, their use must be regulated.
Governments do this for tobacco and alcohol, and they must do it for
cannabis, cocaine, and heroin. The issue is how best to regulate drugs
that are currently illegal. Penal control has held sway for a century
with its attendant deleterious effects (such as huge profits for criminals; no quality control for the drugs people use; development of new,
stronger products; and marginalization of users). Given that the majority of young Quebeckers have consumed at least one illicit drug, if only
experimentally, that the most commonly used illicit substance is cannabis, and that the majority of cannabis users will never become dependent on it, society should normalize its relations with drug users. In
our view, normalization is the best way to prevent dependence.

As summarized by Parker (2005), "the concept of normalization
was first utilized in respect of creating 'normal' living conditions for
people with learning difficulties" (p. 205). As applied to our field of
study, normalization refers to how deviant individuals—drug users,
in this case—can be "included in many features of everyday life"
(ibid.).

A harm reduction philosophy is an essential first step toward
normalization. Harm reduction represents a major paradigm shift
because it means redirecting resources away from persecuting users
and toward providing a harm-free context of use (Gillet and Brochu
2006; Quirion 2001; Rozier and Vanasse 2000). As the name implies,
harm reduction strategies focus on the consequences of use rather
than the drug use itself (Fischer 2005). As such, the main objective
of intervention is not abstinence or reduced consumption, though
neither of those outcomes is ruled out if that is what the user wants.
Abstinence is therefore not a prerequisite for action or a short- or
medium-term objective. The fundamental values of this approach are
humanism and pragmatism (Brisson 1997), so its supporters advocate
for measures that combat the harmful effects of drug use. Humanism
favours actions that respect individuals and their choices and reach
out to people where they are. Pragmatism means taking effective

action to tackle the most urgent and harmful consequences of drug use. Harm reduction may involve making clean paraphernalia available to users (at needle and syringe exchange sites or through mobile sterile injection equipment distribution), opening safe consumption sites (with supervised injection services), or offering substitute drugs (e.g., methadone, buprenorphine, and L-alpha-acetylmethadol) or even medically prescribed heroin (as in the NAOMI project in Montreal and Vancouver). In many cases, such strategies have a major public health impact (Magrinelli Orsi and Brochu 2009b) and do not produce undesirable effects such as an increase in drug use or crime (Lasnier et al. 2010).

According to some studies (Brochu et al 2011; Cheung and Cheung 2006; Duff et al. 2012; Parker, Williams, and Aldridge 2002), there are signs that normalization is slowly taking place: high usage rates reported during major prevalence studies, substantial recreational use characterized by decision-making based on cost-benefit analyses, availability of drugs, and tolerance and accommodation on the part of non-users.

Nevertheless, Canadian policies in 2015 retain their prohibitionist slant, still seeking to control drug use through punitive, stigmatizing measures. This approach to managing a non-issue is not only ineffective as a deterrent, but also unsuited to the needs of the vast majority of users who are capable of managing their consumption (Erickson 2005). Existing North American drug policies generally attempt to address the most serious cases at the expense of the majority of users who engage in moderate recreational consumption (Erickson 2005; Parker 2005).

Certainly, the sale and use of drugs calls for some regulation with respect to the products themselves (quality, potency), context of use (points of sale, business hours), and who can buy them (age, primarily), but should anyone get a criminal record just for using drugs? Is jail really the best way to treat an addict? This is not how we treat people who use tobacco and alcohol, two substances whose socioeconomic and public health repercussions far outweigh those of illicit drugs (Rehm et al. 2007).

* * *

For a century, psychoactive substances were a thriving business. The twentieth century ushered in a new era of control over these products and their users. The conversation about illicit drugs tends to focus on one substance: cannabis. It is, after all, the most widely used and controlled substance globally, as illustrated by Canadian arrest statistics. The fact is that most cannabis users limit themselves to occasional use and do not develop a dependence on it or any other substance. As a result, numerous reports have called for more lenient policies on certain drugs and on cannabis in particular.

Still, many countries, including Canada, continue to view illicit drug users as depraved or dissolute and treat them as offenders in the eyes of the law. Society may impose criminal sanctions to punish addicts and make them realize the harm they are doing to themselves, or, if it believes that the greater good (e.g., lowering costs, minimizing the spread of disease) is better served by treating addicts, it may offer (with varying degrees of coercion) services addicts need. Its approach is motivated more by economics than by humanism. This is clear from an analysis of the reasoning over the past twenty years that has led to funding for programs for drug-dependent people in Canada.

Like it or not, drug users are part of society and have the same rights as everyone else. They are human beings too. While circumstance, opportunity, and limitations may have led them down a different path, should we further marginalize them as a result? No. Rather, we must seek to understand their needs and their abilities and to walk alongside them. That is one of the goals Portugal's drug policy achieves.

As we have seen in Portugal and some American states recently, measures that take a more liberal approach to drug users appeal to people, many of whom have experimented with cannabis in what turned out to be just another harmless life experience. This indicates that normalization of drug use is gradually taking hold.

In the nineteenth century, drugs were widely and sometimes aggressively marketed. In the twentieth century, efforts to control drugs via criminalization marginalized countless users. Let us hope that the twenty-first century will witness the normalization of society's relationship with people who use substances that are, for the time being, illicit.

While simple possession of a drug for personal use may be a crime under existing laws, some users engage in other crimes. In the chapters that follow, we will examine why.

Notes

1. An association of English merchants, originally trading in spices and later importing Chinese tea, which held a monopoly on trade with Southeast Asia.
2. One chest equalled 64 kg.
3. Translation of "Durant la période qui sépare le premier édit de prohibition de 1729 du durcissement de la politique répressive des autorités impériales au tournant des années 1800-1810, une distinction était établie entre l'opium à fumer et l'opium médicinal. Alors que la fabrication, le commerce et la vente de l'un étaient interdits, l'autre était une substance légale."
4. Prohibition was first enacted in 1729 but opium imports continued (Wikipedia 2017).
5. Translation of "En juin 1840, une flotte britanno-indienne arrive au large des côtes chinoises. Les attaquants disposent d'une immense supériorité en armement et Canton tombe rapidement. Les troupes de Sa Majesté remontent le Yang-Tsé, prennent le contrôle du trafic sur le fleuve et privent ainsi le budget impérial des taxes que ce commerce lui procurait. Au bout de deux ans, les Qing plient."
6. Translation of "une escadre britannique remonte le Yangzi Jiang jusqu'à Nankin, obligeant le gouvernement de l'empereur Daoguang à capituler et à signer le traité de Nankin le 29 août 1842."
7. The drug trade had grown so large that people in England began to speak out against it. A Quaker-inspired lobbying group called the Anglo-Oriental Society for the Suppression of the Opium Trade was created.
8. Quakers in Great Britain and American missionaries returning from the Far East (Nadelmann 1990, 503).
9. Associations of doctors and pharmacists (ibid., 505).
10. Translation of "À cette époque, où le Chinois était synonyme d'« immonde opiomane » et de « péril jaune », les États-Unis votèrent, sous la pression des syndicats, les « exclusion laws », des lois visant à protéger les travailleurs américains."
11. Translation of "À la fin du XIXe siècle, toutefois, dans l'Ouest canadien, des groupes moraux puritains réclament des restrictions majeures dans ces domaines. Des évangélistes méthodistes, surtout, clament bien haut que les valeurs autres que protestantes, ou encore l'athéisme, ne doivent pas être tolérés, car cela amènera la destruction de la puissance anglo-saxonne. L'alcool, le sexe et l'opium sont, à cet égard, considérés comme les trois sources majeures de vice et de péché qui menacent la famille et le mode de vie anglo-saxon protestant…et blanc."
12. Germany, Austria-Hungary, China, United States of America, France, Italy, Persia [now Iran], Japan, Netherlands, Portugal, United Kingdom, Russia, and Siam [now Thailand] (UNODC 1959).
13. Translation of "La Commission vota neuf résolutions, qui peuvent sembler n'être que des vœux pieux, mais qui constituaient à l'époque un progrès phénoménal. Dans ces textes, la Commission reconnaissait le droit de la Chine de supprimer totalement l'abus et la production d'opium (résolution no 1). Elle recommandait la fermeture immédiate des fumeries (résolution no 7) et l'adoption de mesures draconiennes pour contrôler la production, la vente et la distribution de l'opium et de ses dérivés à l'échelon national (résolution no 5). Elle reconnaissait aussi la nécessité de prendre des mesures raisonnables pour empêcher l'expédition d'opium dans les pays qui en avaient interdit l'importation (résolution no 4)."
14. Used to manufacture heroin.
15. It is estimated that more than 60,000 people have been killed since the start of the war (translation of "On estime à plus de 60 000 le nombre de morts depuis le

début de cette guerre" [Légaré-Tremblay 2014]).

16. Translation of "Cette violence s'accompagne d'une création de nouvelles iden-
     tités culturelles largement imprégnées des valeurs véhiculées par les réseaux
     criminels. La« narco-culture » glorifie le mode de vie des narcotrafiquants à trav-
     ers des manifestations artistiques populaires, comme la musique et les telenove-
     las. Dans les narco-corridos (« chansons malades »), les criminels sont considérés
     comme des héros, des nouveaux riches qui triomphent dans un pays où domine
     la pauvreté."

17. Harm reduction was one of the four pillars of the National Drug Strategy, first
     released in 1987.

18. See http://www.hc-sc.gc.ca/dhp-mps/marihuana/access-acceder-eng.php.

19. See http://www.hc-sc.gc.ca/dhp-mps/marihuana/info/list-eng.php.

20. Translation of "Les coffee shops sont avant tout des lieux de convivialité ; leur
     fonction première est certes la vente et la consommation de cannabis, mais ils
     sont également des lieux d'atmosphère et de rencontre, tout comme les cafés
     ou les bars. Ces lieux font partie intégrante du paysage urbain d'Amsterdam,
     et confèrent à la ville son ambiance de tolérance et son charme. Les coffee shops
     offrent la possibilité de profiter d'une ambiance alternative, même si l'on n'y
     consomme qu'un simple café. Les boissons alcoolisées sont généralement pro-
     hibées, et l'on y boit des sélections de thé et café accompagnés bien souvent de
     gâteaux et tartes divers. On peut y passer un bon moment, admirer la vue sur la
     rue, lire un magazine, rencontrer une population cosmopolite." Accessed May
     20, 2017, http://www.amsterdam.info/fr/coffeeshops/.

21. The 1961/1972 Convention is here: https://treaties.un.org/doc/Publication/UNTS/
     Volume%20976/volume-976-I-14152-English.pdf.   The   1988   Convention   is
     here (p. 127): https://www.unodc.org/documents/commissions/CND/Int_Drug_
     Control_Conventions/Ebook/The_International_Drug_Control_Conventions_E.
     pdf.

Chapter 4

Proximal and Distal Models:
A Static Conceptualization

S tudies show that, in Canada, fully half of all young offenders and inmates identify some connection between their criminality and their use of psychoactive substances (Brochu et al. 2010; Dufour 2004; Pernanen et al. 2002). In the latter half of the twentieth century, such statistics prompted researchers to develop a number of conceptual models in an attempt to fathom those connections. Two main schools of thought about these connections emerge from a review of the scientific literature on the subject. The first concentrates on proximal elements that may explain why drug users and dealers engage in criminal activity. The second concentrates on distal elements that may explain substance misuse and delinquency.

Proximal Elements

Proximal elements include the state of intoxication (*psychopharmacological model*), dependence on a substance (*economic-compulsive model*), and involvement in the illegal drug distribution system (*systemic model*). These three elements were later combined into a single *tripartite model* (Goldstein 1985). Below, we present the three classical proximal models, together with Goldstein's tripartite model. A lesser-known proximal model approaches the issue from a different angle. We call it the *inverse proximal model* because it goes against the grain in its assertion that drug use is a logical outcome of involvement in a deviant lifestyle.

Goldstein's Tripartite Model

Goldstein's tripartite model (1985), the most classical and fully developed of the proximal conceptualizations, incorporates all three ways in which drugs contribute to criminality: (1) the psychopharmacological aspect or intoxication, (2) the economic-compulsive aspect or dependence, and (3) the systemic aspect, which has to do with the illegal distribution of drugs (see fig. 4.1). The integration of these three facets of the causal relationship between drugs and crime into a tripartite explanation is based on numerous empirical studies conducted in North America and Europe in the second half of the twentieth century.

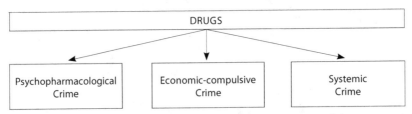

FIGURE 4.1. A proximal conceptualization: Goldstein's tripartite model.

The Psychopharmacological Model

As we saw in previous chapters, the prevalence of drug use within the offender population tends to be high. While the lifetime prevalence of drug use for the Canadian population is around 40 percent (Health Canada 2012), it is nearly double that among offenders (Brochu et al. 2010; Pernanen et al. 2002). We also discussed how some drugs act on parts of the central nervous system, altering the emotional state, cognitive processes, and behaviours of intoxicated individuals. As such, some types of criminality can be attributed at least in part to the psychoactive properties of various drugs (most often illicit stimulants, according to Sutherland et al. [2015]). This is what the psychopharmacological model attempts to describe.

The psychopharmacological model focuses on intoxication and violence: What is the role of intoxication in aggressive behaviour? This model is based on many observations of the presence of psychoactive substances in arrestees (Brochu 2006; ONDCP 2014; Rainone et al. 2006; SAMSHA 2006; United States Department of Justice 1998).

This model holds that a combination of psychological and pharmacological factors may cause a person to behave "abnormally" while intoxicated and give free rein to impulses that would otherwise be held in check. In the psychopharmacological hypothesis, intoxication is a determining contributory factor in the commission of offences that the perpetrators would not have committed had they been sober.

A variant of this model is that intoxication can serve an underlying instrumental purpose. In a study by Havnes (2015), a number of participants reported taking high doses of benzodiazepines prior to committing crimes to help themselves transgress their moral codes, lower their inhibitions, and become unfeeling, and even hostile, toward their victims. Experience with a variety of drugs and information gleaned from various sources enables people to use narcotics deliberately for specific purposes. In addition, cultural norms and situational ecology play an important role in how an individual responds to psychoactive substance intoxication. For example, people with antisocial tendencies may choose to consume a substance that cultural norms and their own expectations lead them to believe will liberate their underlying aggressive tendencies (ibid.). Others may use drugs to facilitate integration into their new environment: to calm jittery nerves or give themselves the audacity to commit a planned crime. Still others, influenced by the symbolic value and cultural meaning of certain substances, may use intoxication as a convenient scapegoat for their socially unacceptable actions, thus alleviating the emotional unease associated with their crimes (ibid.). This pretext is commonly used by people who commit family violence.

In the first version of the psychopharmacological model, intoxication leads to crimes that would not have taken place in the absence of drugs (see fig. 4.2). In the second version, drugs are a tool (much like a weapon or a disguise) or a pretext to achieve very specific ends.

In 2012 in Canada, 75 percent of persons accused of homicide had consumed alcohol, one or more illicit drugs, or some other intoxicant before doing the deed. In addition, 62 percent of the victims had consumed an intoxicant (Statistics Canada 2013b). While we cannot establish a causal link between the perpetrator's or the victim's intoxicated state and the homicide, it is clear that psychoactive substances are often present in homicide cases.

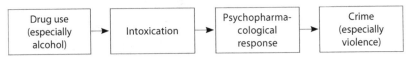

Figure 4.2. The psychopharmacological model.

A study of all crimes committed by Canadian federal inmates serving sentences between 2002 and 2009 showed that 41 percent of the offenders reported being under the influence of drugs the day they committed the crime they were serving time for (Ternes and Johnson 2011). Typically, federal penitentiary inmates have committed serious or repeated and often violent offences.

Lambert and his collaborators (2012) reported that 66 percent of the youth centre clients in their sample had committed at least one offence while intoxicated. For violent offences in particular, 67 percent of the young offenders in a study by Brochu et al. (2010) admitted

The Psychopharmacological Model: Marc-Antoine[1]

Marc-Antoine, thirty, is an all-around good guy. He's athletic, energetic, thoughtful, hard-working, and outgoing. A little while ago, though, his partner of ten years left him, and he was devastated. They had met at sixteen, started dating at eighteen, and moved in together when they started university at twenty. She left him because she fell in love with Charles, a colleague of hers. Ever since, for the past four weeks, Marc-Antoine has been hiding out at home. He barely sleeps, hardly eats, and, for the past few days, has been using whatever drugs he can get his hands on (cannabis, alcohol, anxiolytics, sleep aids). His friend, Louis, thinks he needs a change of scenery and wants him to go out to the bars, so he offers him some speed. Louis is so enthusiastic that Marc-Antoine agrees to take the little white pills before leaving the apartment and heading to the bar. When they arrive, there's a long lineup, and Marc-Antoine gets annoyed. He's very agitated and fidgety, he's talking loudly and bumping into people, and he's making clumsy attempts to flirt with a woman who's there with her friend. The friend gets annoyed by Marc-Antoine's behaviour and calmly but in no uncertain terms tells him to leave the woman alone. That's when Marc-Antoine snaps, insults the couple, shoves the man, and tries to start a fight. The doormen try to intervene, but before they can stop him, Marc-Antoine punches the other man in the face. Bystanders call the police. The couple have every intention of pressing assault charges against Marc-Antoine.

being under the influence of one or more drugs when they committed their most violent act ever. Four in ten young offenders blamed intoxication for the most violent act they had ever committed or been a victim of.

In another study (Parent and Brochu 2002), regular cocaine users told us that their drug use could help neutralize hesitations to commit a crime or violent act; in essence, it served as a buffer between their values and their actions. Users may experience detachment from their values while intoxicated and grow "increasingly distant from their moral center" with repeated drug use (Copes, Hochstetler, and Sandberg 2015, 37). In addition, intoxication "contributes to decision-making errors" by making fewer options available and preventing users from recognizing the consequences of their actions (ibid.). Certain drugs give the timid the nerve to go through with a crime and make criminal activity more pleasurable for the bold (Brunelle 2001; Dufour 2004; Parent and Brochu 2002). As Copes, Hochstetler, and Sandberg (2015) point out, intoxication, particularly repeated intoxication, "offers a fundamental transformation of character that may be more or less stable for a period and that is needed by many to engage in violence" (p. 38). Note that this phenomenon is not observed in the majority of illicit drug users. Most cannabis users never exhibit violent conduct while under the influence.

The Economic-Compulsive Model

One of the primary links between drugs and crime arises from the financial burden of buying illegal substances. A user who becomes dependent on a drug must use it several times a day to avoid physiological and psychological withdrawal. Over time, using these substances becomes extremely onerous. For one of our studies, we asked young offenders in Montreal and Toronto how much they spent on psychoactive substances in a given month. The Montrealers said they spent, on average, $886.81, and the Torontonians $1,107.71 (Brochu et al. 2010). The criminal activity of some users who can no longer control their drug use can be explained, at least in part, by their need for money to buy the drugs they are addicted to.

The economic-compulsive model describes a causal relationship between the use of costly substances that can lead to intense physiological or psychological dependence and involvement in lucrative crime (see fig. 4.3). Unlike the psychopharmacological model, the

The Economic-Compulsive Model: Joël

Joël, sixteen, lives with his mother in Montreal. He hangs out with kids his age and has lots of fun doing things with them, such as playing football. Until recently, Joël was the quarterback for his private high school's elite football team. His mother provides adequate parental supervision, but is not well-off and has to work two jobs (day and evening) to make ends meet and pay for her son's private school. For the past year, Joël and his friends have been using cannabis and cocaine with some older female friends. Joël now feels the need to use drugs every day; without them, he doesn't feel as good. He is taking higher doses than he used to. His coach found drugs in his locker, and he missed several practices, so now he is on the verge of being expelled. His girlfriend dumped him because she didn't like his drug use. Yesterday evening, Joël and his friends robbed a convenience store and roughed up the cashier. That was not their first crime. They started with petty theft a few months ago (taking $20 from mom's wallet, stealing small things from school, and so on) to pay for drugs. Then they began stealing more often, and their crimes got more serious. Yesterday, they scored $150.

economic-compulsive model does not attribute criminality to unregulated impulsivity resulting from intoxication. The hypothesis here is that dependence on a drug and the high cost of that drug motivates individuals to commit crimes.

Empirically, this model predicts a unidirectional relationship between costly illicit drugs and lucrative crime. In fact, nearly one in five Canadian inmates report having committed their most serious crime for the purpose of obtaining a drug (Pernanen et al. 2002; see also Havnes 2015), as do one in ten offenders under the age of eighteen (Brochu et al. 2010). An Australian study (Payne and Gaffney 2012) concluded that heroin and other opiates, along with cocaine

Figure 4.3. The economic-compulsive model.

and other stimulants, were most likely to be involved when people committed crimes because they needed money to buy drugs.

The fact is, drug-dependent people need to get enough money to support their drug needs. However, as we have seen, studies clearly show that criminal activity is not always the only source of income (Brochu and Parent 2005; Grapendaal et al. 1995). Rather, individuals under financial pressure diversify their income streams, choosing from various options that include illegal activity. We have therefore adapted the economic-compulsive model diagram to better reflect reality (see fig. 4.4).

Another problem with the economic-compulsive model is that it is based on disease theories of addiction that view addicts' social behaviours as determined by their addicted state (Grapendaal et al. 1995). In this interpretation, the social actor's illegal act is psycho-socially meaningless; it is merely symptomatic of an overpowering or even hereditary disease. It suggests that criminality is an unavoidable consequence of addiction to costly habit-forming drugs. This ignores, discredits, or denies the personal significance of the act and dismisses the dependent individual's socio-economic background. In contrast, none of the drug-dependent inmates interviewed by Pernanen and his co-researchers (2002) reported committing their crime for this specific purpose. Drug addicts have options and make choices about which income-generating activities to pursue. In their study of Dutch drug addicts, Grapendaal, Leuw, and Nelen (1995) found that acquisitive crime was the main source of income for a minority (22 percent) of the respondents. It is important to note that

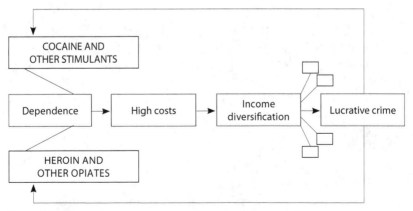

Figure 4.4. The contemporary economic-compulsive model.

many drug-dependent people match their drug use to their available income.

Grapendaal, Leuw, and Nelen (1995) also note that many drug users themselves buy into this economic-compulsive model. The researchers suggest that this reductionist view of reality actually serves the interests of all the social actors involved in the problem. Heavy users disavow moral responsibility for delinquent acts: "It's not my fault. I'm addicted. I'm sick." Therapists use this model to avoid confronting drug users about their unlawful behaviour. Law enforcement agencies use it to justify asking for bigger budgets and to avoid taking responsibility for their failure to curb crime. The model gives everyone permission to shift the blame for their inaction onto the murky properties of drugs.

The economic-compulsive model, which regards drug addiction as a tyrannical disease, does not take into account periods of reduced drug use or even abstinence that correspond to reduced availability of the drug (Brochu and Parent 2005; Faupel 1991; Grapendaal, Leuw, and Nelen 1995). Such periods are significant but difficult to reconcile with classical disease theory. Moreover, the model overlooks people who manage their drug use well (Alexander 1994; Zinberg 1984), who are not among the clientele of treatment centres and tend not to be behind bars. Researchers usually overlook them because they are discreet and hard to find. We believe that it would be misguided to base our understanding of the phenomenon on the most easily observed elements.

Teenagers begin to feel the financial pressure of regular drug use much sooner than adults. Tremblay, Brunelle, and Blanchette-Martin (2007) found that two-thirds of the young offenders in their sample reported committing lucrative crime to support their drug use. Brunelle, Brochu, and Cousineau (2000, 2005) showed that, because of limited access to legal income streams, adolescents venture into lucrative crime—particularly small-scale drug dealing—to pay for their drugs earlier in their trajectory than adults. This has been observed even among frequent users of relatively inexpensive substances such as cannabis. As with adults, their involvement in lucrative crime may increase in step with their drug use. Young people and adults alike who are dependent on costlier, highly addictive drugs are likely to commit more lucrative crimes.

Illegal drug users' economic-compulsive criminality is therefore a function of: (1) their income relative to the cost of their drugs, (2) frequency of use and involvement in a drug-using lifestyle, and

(3) history of involvement in crime (Hunt 1991). Consequently, the economic-compulsive model applies only to people with limited means to support their psychoactive substance use and who are heavily dependent on costly drugs. In addition, it is valid only for a specific phase of their dependence trajectory (Grapendaal, Leuw, and Nelen 1995).

The fact remains that many regular users of high-priced illicit substances get involved in dealing drugs in some capacity to make ends meet. The majority of young offenders in Montreal (69 percent) and Toronto (84 percent) report having been involved in drug trafficking at some point in their lives (Brochu et al. 2010). This means they have been exposed to a parallel universe in which systemic criminality often features very prominently.

The Systemic Model

As we saw in chapter 3, the United Nations Office on Drugs and Crime's Single Convention on Narcotic Drugs (1961, amended in 1972) and Convention against Illicit Traffic in Narcotic Drugs and Psychotropic Substances (1988) were designed to limit, through criminalization, the cultivation, production, trafficking, distribution, possession, and consumption of certain substances. Taking their lead from the United States, many countries have used these conventions as the basis for a "war on drugs." Alongside this repressive approach, a distribution system for illegal drugs has taken shape (Roberts and Chen 2013), with its own laws, obligations, and normative codes. Unwritten internal rules, pseudo-contractual obligations, and implicit standards constitute an operational framework for a community functioning outside the law. Breaking the rules can provoke arguments and confrontations that are never reported to the authorities. Members of this society are well aware that breaking the rules is asking for trouble in the form of threats and violence against themselves and the people they care about (Brochu and Parent 2005; Jacques and Wright 2008).

Goldstein, the father of this concept, observed that violence associated with the illicit drug distribution system generally occurs in connection with *rip-offs*, *debt collection*, and *territorial disputes* (1985). These crimes are not related to the intrinsic properties of drugs (such as intoxication and dependence). They are directly related to the repressive environment, which relegates distribution of the products to a black market not subject to the governance and protection of public health and safety authorities (Roberts and Chen 2013). These crimes are "systemic" in that they arise in direct connection with an operating system.

Johnson, Golub, and Fagan (1995) show that this is a world operating outside the bounds of public authority;[2] its culture and the people involved are not well known. Drugs change hands away from prying eyes, generating the kind of massive unreported profits that can make people greedy and deceitful. *Rip-offs* (higher prices, short-weighting, lower quality, etc.) are commonplace in the illicit drug market because perpetrators can make more money and are unlikely to be reported. Jacques, Allen, and Wright (2014) identified certain types of

The Systemic Model: Charlotte

Charlotte, thirty-two, has a nursing degree. She had a job in the field for a few months, but she could not handle the lifestyle that went along with the profession. She lives alone in a small apartment in Quebec City. She and her family are close, and she visits her parents in Rimouski often. Without a legitimate job, she has been making ends meet with occasional work as an escort and by selling small quantities of drugs to her friends. Charlotte has been using cannabis occasionally since she was sixteen, and she's done cocaine a few times in the past year. Through her escort work, she met Marc, whose "businessman" image is a front for his involvement in organized crime, and has been seeing him regularly. She says he thinks she is trustworthy, which is why he gave her a large quantity of cocaine to hide and sell. That's how Charlotte got more involved in dealing and expanded her client base. A potential buyer paged her a few minutes ago to set up a deal. She is supposed to go meet him in a discreet location at some distance from her place because this is a new contact who was referred by a friend and she feels safer not having him come to her house. A few seconds after they meet, the man grabs Charlotte by the neck and tells her, "You have no business selling dope on my turf, and if you and your boyfriend keep it up, you won't live long." She hadn't realized that she was selling in territory claimed by another criminal organization willing to do whatever it takes to protect its interests.

buyers who are more likely to fall prey to these tactics: "persons who are strangers, first-time or irregular customers; do not have sufficient money on hand to make a purchase; are uninformed about going market rates; are deemed unlikely to retaliate; . . . or are addicted to drugs" (p. 251). These ruses can spark arguments between sellers and buyers (Jacques and Wright 2008). According to a Quebec study (Dufour 2004), 42 percent of young offenders in youth centres have found themselves in a violent revenge situation following a drug transaction.

A dealer may front a buyer drugs on a promise of payment later (after a small-scale dealer's shift or on payday, for example). In many cases, the price of the product will be proportional to the risk of not getting paid at the appointed time. Some dealers may be fairly tolerant, but when their patience runs out, they become more forceful, employing threats, intimidation, ultimatums, and violence to get their money (Brochu and Parent 2005). Fortunately, threats usually serve to resolve the situation quickly (Zaitch 2005). In our study (Brochu et al. 2010) of young offenders and their participation in drug trafficking, violence related to *debt collection* accounted for 27 percent of the systemic incidents in which young Montrealers were involved, second only to turf wars (41 percent).

Many of those involved in this highly lucrative illicit business are motivated to grow their client base and eliminate the competition, which leads to *territorial disputes* between rival dealers. Newspapers regularly report on violent incidents related to drug trafficking. In the late 1980s, conflict between major cocaine and crack distributors in the southern United States frequently made headlines. While the systemic violence associated with certain drug markets in the United States gets a lot of media attention (Zaitch 2005), similar levels of brutality have been observed among small-scale dealers and in other countries, including Canada. Canadian police services estimated that, from 1992 to 2002, 11 percent (684) of all homicides were drug-related, including those motivated by settling of accounts (Desjardins and Hotton 2004). The substance most commonly involved was cocaine (60 percent). Fortunately, the most common type of violence does not end in homicide. In Quebec, 43 percent of young offenders in youth centres reported being involved in a violent incident while selling drugs on someone else's turf (Dufour 2004).

Here too, the systemic model illustrated in figure 4.5 has some flaws, four of which seem especially significant to us. The first is the unidirectional nature of the causal relationship, which suggests that

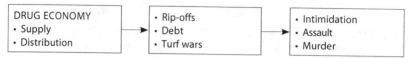

Figure 4.5. The systemic model.

the illicit drug supply and distribution system encourages criminal activity. However, studies indicate that individuals drawn to violence may be strongly attracted to the methods employed in this milieu, where their skills and physical strength can be exchanged for significant monetary rewards (Brochu et al. 1997; Ellickson, Saner, and McGuigan 1997). To protect their reputation vis-à-vis their colleagues and their hold over a given territory, the people at the top of these illegal organizations have every reason to surround themselves with short-fused enforcers prepared to rain down terror whenever it serves the organization's interests (Brochu et al. 1997; Brochu and Parent 2005). In this chicken-and-egg situation, there is no telling which comes first. Does a delinquent lifestyle lead to involvement in drug distribution, or, conversely, does involvement in the drug scene lead to criminal activity? It is also unclear what role the drug scene plays in violence in certain neighbourhoods. After all, neighbourhood deterioration, endemic unemployment, the erosion of traditional values, and delinquency were happening long before drug dealers showed up. Perhaps these areas were fertile ground for the emergence of brutality. Under such conditions, can drug trafficking be blamed for causing the violence we are now observing in these neighbourhoods? Although a significant proportion of the violence we are seeing seems directly related to the illegal drug trade, the trade is often just an excuse for violence (see Copes et al. [2014] and Ousey and Lee [2007]).

The second flaw has to do with whether this model, developed in the United States, accurately describes the situation outside North America. It is important to note that violence associated with the drug distribution system is far more prevalent in large American cities than in major European centres, which suggests that the sociopolitical environment (including repressive drug laws and access to firearms) is involved in some way (Zaitch 2005). Some studies suggest that the level of systemic violence may be related to intensity of repression. Two American economists carried out interesting analyses worth mentioning here. The first, Resignato (2000), correlated drug-related arrest data and illicit substance use statistics for twenty-three major U.S. cities with violent crime in those cities. His results indicated that violent crime may be more strongly related to drug enforcement activities than to people's drug use. A second study, this one by Miron (2001), examined how gun control, drug prohibition enforcement activities (such as seizures), and violent crime (such as homicide) intersect. Unlike the first study, which was limited to the United States, this one compared statistics from sixty-six countries. Here again, the findings suggest that illicit drug prohibition explains the different homicide rates reported by different countries, which in turn explain gun ownership rates (which are correlated but not causally related to violence).

The third flaw is related to the second and has to do with the validity of this model. Aside from journalistic accounts, very few studies have set out to verify it empirically. Perhaps researchers lack enthusiasm for this approach because few victims seek help from the police. It is not really in a drug dealer's best interest to report being robbed of drugs and money, after all. Any dealer reporting such a theft is likely to misrepresent certain pieces of information. He or she might report the amount of money stolen but take care not to say where it came from. This makes it very difficult to accurately identify systemic crime and distinguish it from crime in general. It is also important to note that drug dealers do not commit only violent crime and that drug dealing is not the only type of lucrative crime they commit. Some also commit theft, for example (Kokoreff 2005). A study by Lacharité-Young et al. (2017) of 1,447 students at six Quebec high schools revealed that, among psychoactive substance users, having sold drugs is a predictor of membership in a group of young people that committed personal violence offences in the previous year. The problem is figuring out whether a violent act committed by a person who sells and uses drugs has more to do with the psychopharmacological effects of the substances consumed or the effects the user expects to experience if he or she is intoxicated when committing the act.

The fourth flaw we identified has to do with the fact that this model applies to only a minority of transactions. Studies of buyers and sellers clearly indicate that their transactions are often based on mutual trust or friendship (Belackova and Vaccaro 2013; Moeller and Sandberg 2015). The vast majority (89 percent) of transactions involving marijuana, the most widely consumed drug, take place between friends and relatives. Moreover, in 58 percent of cases, it is shared or given for free (Caulkins and Pacula 2006). Early drug experiences typically happen with friends. Experimental or occasional consumption involves sharing substances. Regular buying is an extension of behaviour learned in previous stages. In the illegal drug scene, trust and friendship provide priceless protection and are much more valuable than threats and violence, at least for small, everyday transactions between people who know each other. Anyone who does not follow the rules, who does not share or pay on time, is likely to be avoided or shunned (Jacques and Wright 2008). This explains why violence and threats are not part of most illicit drug users' day-to-day experience. Systemic violence appears to be an optional dispute resolution technique in the illicit drug trade, not a mandatory one. It is just one of the available informal social control tactics. Of course, there are fewer alternatives in the drug trade than there are for legal transactions, but they do exist: tolerance (doing nothing), avoidance (of the deviant individual), negotiation, mediation (with a third party), and non-physical retaliation (theft, fraud, vandalism). Sellers can also employ preventive measures to avoid problems. They can be selective about their clients, specialize in a particular product (cannabis users, for example, are a less deviant clientele), or do business in safe places (Fleetwood 2014); others work with a partner (one handles the business side and the other is a lookout), place the drugs in a designated location (such as a locker) for pick-up once payment has been received, or even use conventional situational prevention technology (surveillance cameras, alarms) (Jacques and Reynald 2011; Piza and Sytsma 2015). All of these strategies can affect profit margins (Jacques and Reynald 2011), but from the dealers' perspective, they can prevent a lot of problems.

Non–Mutually Exclusive Types of Crime

One might think that crimes committed while intoxicated to procure drugs or in connection with an illicit distribution system are mutually exclusive, but this would be a grave misinterpretation of Goldstein's tripartite model. There is significant overlap among the types of crimes described above. A fairly significant proportion of individuals who commit a crime to procure drugs for personal use do so while under the influence of a substance (Havnes 2015; Pernanen et al. 2002), and in some cases, the offence is related to the drug trade (Brochu et al. 2010). This may give the impression that the proportion of crimes attributable to drugs is larger than it really is (see fig. 4.6).

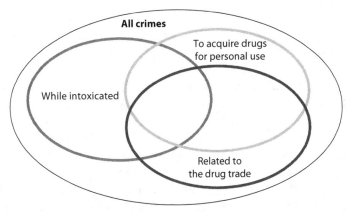

FIGURE 4.6. Goldstein: Three non–mutually exclusive types of drug–crime relationships.

The Inverse Proximal Model

Goldstein's tripartite model hypothesizes a causal relationship between criminality and intoxication, the need for money, and/or the violent nature of the drug economy. In contrast, some theorize that involvement in delinquent behaviour promotes illicit psychoactive substance use.

A number of studies (Doherty, Green, and Ensminger 2008; Fothergill and Ensminger 2006; Monahan et al. 2014; Odgers et al. 2008; Pardini, White, and Stouthamer-Loeber 2007) have shown that, in young people who engage in both delinquency and drug use, the former precedes the latter. Within this population, it is clear that consumption of drugs such as cocaine and heroin appears long after an individual's first property crimes (e.g., break and enter) (Parent and Brochu 2002; Seddon 2000). Even if drug use initiation occurs at an early age (with marijuana consumption), problematic behaviours will already have surfaced in a young adolescent's trajectory long before regular drug use begins and sometimes even prior to initial experiences with certain illicit psychoactive substances.

It is worth examining this simple chronological sequence of the onset of drug use and delinquency in light of findings from the broader field of criminology. Criminological studies such as those by Lanctôt, Bernard, and Le Blanc (2002) and Menard, Mihalic, and Huizinga (2001) generally show that initiation to deviance occurs gradually, beginning with minor crimes and proceeding to increasingly serious crimes. Individuals begin with disobedience, then move on to deceit, and eventually physical violence. Rebellion typically precedes property crime. The more socially acceptable the behaviour, the earlier it is likely to begin. Individuals typically use cannabis, which is considered more socially acceptable, before they use drugs seen as more socially taboo or subject to stricter enforcement.

If we observe the order in which drug use and crime phases appear, we must keep in mind that the most deviant behaviours will "naturally" appear after those considered more socially "acceptable." Accordingly, recent studies place greater emphasis on a more nuanced understanding of why delinquency and drug use emerge than on which came first. For example, a study of 1,076 U.S. college students revealed that early conduct problems, including delinquency, are a major risk factor for very early onset of marijuana use (Falls et al. 2011). Many researchers have noted that juvenile delinquency is a positive predictor of other conduct problems, such as psychoactive substance use (Menard, Mihalic, and Huizinga 2001; Poikolainen 2002; Windle and Mason 2004). Mason, Hitchings, and Spoth (2007) studied a sample of 429 American youths and found that onset of delinquency at eleven or twelve was positively associated with alcohol use at age sixteen and problem substance use at eighteen, with alcohol use at sixteen mediating an indirect relationship between delinquency and problem substance use.

A study of violent offences and substance use among Mexican American and European American adolescents found bidirectional associations between the two behaviours (Brady et al. 2008). Those who perpetrated violence early were more likely to exhibit problem substance use later on, and those who used drugs early were more likely to report violence involvement later on. Xue, Zimmerman, and Cunningham (2009) examined a sample of 649 African American youths and found that "early violent behavior predicted later alcohol use, and early alcohol use predicted later violent behaviour" (p. 2041). Early onset of either behaviour was a positive predictor of the appearance of the other a few years later.

We can see the inverse proximal model at work in the findings of Quebec studies that observed how some individuals celebrate criminal achievements by consuming drugs (Brochu and Parent 2005), while others report that income from criminal activity at a young age can contribute to initiation to drug use (Brunelle, Brochu, and Cousineau 2005).

The Inverse Proximal Model: Tristan

Tristan, fifteen, lives in a well-to-do Montreal neighbourhood with his two parents, both professionals. His friends don't know it, but for the past few months, he has been stealing from local businesses. He pawns the stolen goods and uses the money to buy pizza and energy drinks for his school friends at lunch. Now that he is popular, he gets invited to lots of parties, which he is really happy about. Recently, a friend introduced him to a cousin who invited him to a house party. That evening, Tristan met some teenagers who were bragging about their criminal activity. Laughing, they shared some tips for stealing. At one point, one of them offered Tristan a special discount on a gram of cocaine: just $80. It was a lot of money, but Tristan could afford it and would be able to "share" the white powder with his new friends.

Other factors related to the world of crime play a role too. In addition to the proceeds of crime, the deviant lifestyle puts people in contact with illicit drug distributors and legitimizes drug use through models, norms, protocols, rules, and so on (Brochu and Parent 2005; Grapendaal, Leuw, and Nelen 1995).

As evidence for the validity of the inverse proximal model (see fig. 4.7), researchers usually cite studies showing that delinquent conduct precedes illicit drug use or that users continue to commit crimes even during periods of abstinence. Prior delinquency and residual criminality are evidence that delinquency springs from a constellation of factors other than drug use or dependence. In a way, this model led to the development of the biopsychosocial model, which draws on the notion of problem behaviour syndrome.

All things considered, proximal models fail to convey an accurate understanding of the complex drug–crime relationship. We believe this is because their supporters do not view individuals as social actors capable of logical reasoning and as products of their environment. Other researchers, however, have abandoned this linear cognitive schema in favour of a more comprehensive perspective. They focus on the distal elements (biological, psychological, and social) in the lives of people contending with dependence and delinquency.

FIGURE **4.7.** The inverse proximal model.

Distal Elements

According to this model, biopsychosocial factors present during a person's development, usually during childhood and adolescence, affect the likelihood of that person engaging in deviant behaviour a few years later. Because they are not direct causal factors, they are known as risk factors, and they can be offset by protective factors.

Many studies show that both criminality and psychoactive substance abuse are very unevenly distributed across the population. This structural marginality is associated with general deviance syndrome (Corwyn and Benda 2002; Donovan, Jessor, and Costa 1999; Le Blanc 2010). According to this model, delinquency, drug use, and certain other deviant or marginal behaviours (such as early and often unprotected sexual experiences and dangerous driving) are linked to the presence of risk factors in a person's past that "predispose" him or her to adopt a lifestyle in which intoxication, impaired driving, and crime are part of everyday life. The appearance of one such behaviour could pave the way for further abnormal behaviours or trigger their expression, but this does not necessarily indicate a direct causal relationship (Brochu 1994; Grapendaal et al. 1995). However, as the name suggests, protective factors are thought to play an important role in the development of what researchers and other workers in the field call "resilience."

In essence, studies that look at the role of biopsychosocial factors in the emergence of deviant conduct clearly demonstrate how difficult it can be to establish exclusive linear causal links between psychoactive substances and crime because the relationship is also influenced by distal links and an imbalance between risk factors and protective factors (see fig. 4.8).

Some studies, most of them quantitative and a fair number of them longitudinal, have attempted to identify the risk and protective factors associated with deviant conduct. These factors tend to fall into four categories: biological (gender, heredity, hormonal and

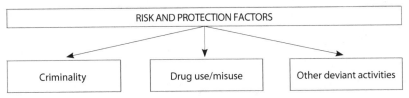

FIGURE 4.8. Distal model: biopsychosocial factors.

neurophysiological elements); psychological (personality disorders, hedonism, failure to adapt to school, work, and social life); contextual (association with deviant peers, poor family environment, mistreatment and abuse, estrangement from social institutions); and social (poverty, endemic unemployment, unfit housing, difficult living conditions) (Bennett, Holloway, and Farrington 2008; Born and Boët 2005; Brown and Larson 2009; Buu et al. 2009; Castellanos-Ryan, O'Leary-Barrett, and Conrod 2013; Fallu et al. 2011; Farrington, Loeber, and Ttofi 2012; Jadidi and Nakhaee 2014; Hartwell et al. 2012; Haug et al. 2014; Henry, Knight, and Thornberry 2012; Krank et al. 2011; Pedersen and Skardhamar 2010; Monahan et al. 2014; Oesterle et al. 2012; Steinberg and Monahan 2007; Stone et al. 2012; Wanner et al. 2009).

The Distal Model: Pier-Alexandre

Pier-Alexandre, fourteen, has been using cannabis occasionally for about six months. He has been an anxious person since early childhood. He suffers from trichotillomania, a psychological disorder that causes people to pull out their own hair. Pier-Alexandre pulls out his eyebrows and lashes so often that he has hardly any left, and other kids make fun of him for this. He also suffers from severe attention-deficit/hyperactivity disorder (ADHD), as does his mother, who was not diagnosed until adulthood. His severe anxiety combined with his ADHD makes it difficult for his psychiatrist to calibrate his medication. He has a lot of trouble at school and often cuts class to hang out with friends who think he's cool and protect him. Sometimes they shoplift and pawn the stolen goods, then use the money to buy pot and smoke it together. Pier-Alexandre and his friends feel that it helps them relax and makes them laugh.

Early onset of deviant behaviour is a major risk factor for the development of a variety of problems (Le Blanc 2010).

Protective factors are much more than the absence of risk factors; some are their opposites. For example, associating with deviant peers is a risk factor for problem drug use and delinquency, but interacting with prosocial peers is a protective factor against deviant behaviour (Dufour 2014). Adequate parental monitoring is a protective factor, while poor parental monitoring is a risk factor (Casanueva et al. 2014). Other protective factors, such as religious faith, have no corresponding risk factor (Kliewer and Murelle 2007). Some protective factors, such as school connectedness, may be present from childhood (Wang et al. 2005); others, such as having and raising a child, may appear later in an individual's trajectory (Casanueva et al. 2014). By focusing on risk and protective factors, this explanatory model provides a much more dynamic interpretation of the drug–crime relationship than do the causal models based on proximal factors discussed above.

The distal model, which incorporates a range of biopsychosocial elements, is an appropriate framework for uncovering factors related to the onset of illicit drug use and delinquency among adolescents. However, it offers little insight into the development and nature of the drug–crime relationship for people whose trajectory includes both behaviours.

* * *

Three observations stand out from our analysis in this chapter. First, humans are drawn to simple linear causal explanations and tend to attribute actions to factors that precede them, are easy to observe, and attract attention. If that factor happens to be deviant or illegal, why look any deeper? It seems perfectly natural to point to illegal drug use as the cause of criminality, hence the popularity of proximal models. Nevertheless, illicit drug use is a "determining factor in the development of criminal behaviour for only a small minority" of users (Grapendaal, Leuw, and Nelen 1995, 190[3]).

Second, a distal conceptualization of the nature of the drug–crime relationship makes it clear that the relationship is much more complex than previously thought. It involves an intricate interplay of risk and protective factors. Proximal models alone cannot account for the full measure of that complexity.

Third, we must keep in mind that the conceptual models of the drug–crime relationship that we have just presented, though crucial to our understanding of the phenomenon, are nevertheless incomplete because they are too static and do not take into consideration the experience of the social actors involved. Studies have shown that drug–crime relationships are not fixed and can be expected to change to varying degrees over time (Brochu and Parent 2005; Brunelle, Cousineau, and Brochu 2005). A range of possible interactions can influence a user's life course and the specific nature of the drug–crime relationship at various stages. In the next chapter, we will detail the drug use and crime trajectories of people who become dependent on drugs.

Notes

1. The sketches in this book are compilations of elements drawn from interviews with drug-dependent individuals.
2. See also Friedman, Terras, and Glassman (2003); Brochu and Parent (2005).
3. According to their Dutch study, only 20 percent of the addicts interviewed "began to commit criminal offenses *after* the use of heroin became an important element in their lives."

Chapter 5

Trajectories: A Dynamic Conceptualization

When the topic of illicit drugs comes up in conversation, the ensuing vigorous debate exposes ignorance of the facts. Though not widely known to the public, studies from the past decade have nevertheless radically updated our knowledge of the field of illicit drugs. Psychoactive substance use has become much more widespread among adolescents and young adults and is no longer a marginal activity reserved for a relatively small number of initiates. Although approximately a third of Canadians aged fifteen to twenty-four report having consumed cannabis (Health Canada 2013c), most consumers use it on an occasional or experimental basis.

Contrary to the gateway drug theory, a comparative analysis of recent prevalence studies (Health Canada 2005, 2008, 2009, 2010, 2011a, 2013c) clearly shows that illicit drug use does not necessarily lead to addiction and that cannabis use does not necessarily lead to cocaine or heroin use. Even though some politicians still like to trot out the gateway drug theory, scientists have long since discarded this kind of explanation. The fact is that a minority of users become dependent on a substance and make drugs the centre of their world. According to the 2012 Canadian Community Health Survey, less than 2 percent of the Canadian population presented problems related to illicit substance use in the previous twelve months (Statistics Canada 2012b).

The continuum from experimentation to dependence includes many stages. As we have seen in previous chapters, the way we perceive illicit drugs and drug use has changed significantly in recent years. Society has become more tolerant. New drugs have gained popularity and quickly become associated with partying (Duff 2005). Some authors have examined the normalization of certain substances (Brochu et al. 2011; Hathaway, Erickson, and Lucas 2007; Parker 2005; Parker, Aldridge, and Measham 1998), revealing the existence of a new category of users: frequent recreational users whose drug use is strictly for pleasure as part of their leisure activities and does not lead to deviant behaviour. Some become regular users of one or more drugs. For example, they may smoke a joint every day but never become dependent (Brochu et al. 2011). In essence, there are four main types of use: experimental or occasional, frequent, regular, and addictive. There is good evidence to suggest a unique drug–crime relationship associated with each type of use.

The Evolving Drug–Crime Relationship

The nature of the drug–crime relationship depends on the substance used (its pharmacological effects, its chemistry, whether it is addictive, its cost, etc.), the characteristics of the person using the substance (his or her resources, values, prior delinquency), and the context of use (influences, opportunities, etc.), but, in general, the trajectory described here reflects the experience of the many people who have participated in our studies over the past two decades.

Some young people who struggle with difficult life circumstances and have trouble with family or school seek out different experiences together. They may be drawn into a fringe culture in which alcohol and cannabis use, intoxication, petty crime, early and unprotected sexual experiences, and risky driving are common and admired. Without even realizing it, many of these young people may embark on a path toward regular and deviant use of costly drugs that are subject to stricter enforcement, and possibly even toward dependence (Brochu and Parent 2005; Brunelle, Cousineau, and Brochu 2002b). Drug use does not necessarily commit the user to a deviant trajectory, but repeated use, the consequences of use, and the significance of drug use to a given individual may do so. Being marginalized may hasten the process (Dérivois 2004).

Taking their cue from Becker (1963), researchers such as Grapendaal, Leuw, and Nelen (1995), Hser et al. (1997), and Duprez and Kokoreff (2000) interpreted the drug user's pathway as a career.

Borrowed from the sociology of professions (Rubington 1967), this notion recognizes elements of belonging, progression, and retirement. In other words, a drug use career is portrayed as a longitudinal sequence marked by a typical series of episodes linked to behavioural changes (Kokoreff and Faugeron 2002; Simpson 2003).

Others prefer to use the term *trajectory* rather than *career* (Brochu, Da Agra, and Cousineau 2002; Brochu and Parent 2005; Brunelle 2001; Le Blanc 2010; Poirier 2011). *Trajectory* incorporates notions of time, development, and transition into our analysis of the drug–crime relationship. It also restores the full meaning of the word "relationship" because it interprets the variables involved from a dynamic interaction perspective. The trajectory approach looks at relationships between systems that evolve over time. Studies that adopt this approach validate work by Castel (1992): "Establishing the drug addict's biographical line involves retracing his or her path specifically as it relates to drugs as well as analyzing how other elements of his or her social baggage crystallize along that line" (p. 14).[1]

Whether one prefers the word *career* or *trajectory*, both encompass the notion of transformation and even evolution. These concepts of change and mutation will serve as our backdrop. In this chapter, the notion of trajectory will help us understand that, contrary to the assertions of classical conceptual models of drug–crime relationships, the links that develop between drug users and criminal activity are dynamic, not static.

A number of longitudinal quantitative studies have been conducted in recent decades to learn more about the paths of drug users and offenders. For example, a clear distinction has been observed between the vast majority of adolescents who present limited antisocial behaviour at a specific life stage and those who engage in life-course-persistent deviant behaviour (Moffitt 1993; Moffitt et al. 2002). Other studies, such as those by Brook et al. (2014), Passarotti et al. (2015), and Pardini et al. (2015), identify different trajectories related to the intensity of cannabis use in adolescence.

Generally speaking, the studies identify four groups of adolescents: (1) a majority who use cannabis experimentally or occasionally, or abstain from use completely; (2) those who use cannabis regularly during adolescence but who gradually stop using it by their mid-twenties; (3) a small group of those who use it regularly from mid-adolescence and continue to use it in adulthood; and (4) those who begin using cannabis during late adolescence and continue using it as young adults (Pardini et al. 2015). These studies also show that delinquency varies from group to group but that intensity of use is generally related to delinquent and even violent activity. There also appears to be an overall stable relationship between substance use and delinquency (Jennings et al. 2016). In Canada, Le Blanc (2010) produced an excellent portrayal of deviant conduct trajectories based on descriptions of the onset, escalation, and desistance processes. These quantitative studies paint an interesting picture that we will refer to periodically. However, they fall short when it comes to explaining the ups and downs that mark the trajectories of the individuals involved, accurately depicting the stages and the often temporary departures from those trajectories, and reflecting the complexity of the phenomenon. To gain a better, more comprehensive understanding of these elements, our team turned to qualitative studies that consider the expertise of the primary social actors involved and their own understanding of their journey.

This chapter draws heavily on qualitative studies of drug users by our research team (Recherche et intervention sur les substances psychoactives – Québec, or RISQ). Brunelle and her fellow researchers (Brunelle 2001; Brunelle, Brochu, and Cousineau 2005) focused on adolescents' deviant trajectories, Brochu and Parent (2005) concentrated on better understanding the trajectories of regular cocaine users, Marsh (2002) and Bertrand and Nadeau (2006) delved into the trajectories of female users, and Couvrette (2014) explored the influence of motherhood on the drug use and crime trajectories of drug-dependent mothers in the justice system. Lastly, Brunelle et al. (2014) studied elements that influence the addiction trajectories of drug-dependent adults.

Deviant Trajectories

First and foremost, we must emphasize that a trajectory is not a linear, unidirectional path. Both quantity and frequency of use, as well as type of drug used, are highly variable over time. Periods of continual consumption may alternate with periods of abstinence. Heavy drug use and criminal activity may be short-lived or may be one of the most constant features of a lifestyle (Brochu and Parent 2005; Cloutier 2014). Le Blanc stated that "the development of deviant conduct begins with a trigger that leads to a progression sustained by contemporaneous interactions among deviant behaviours" (2010, 421).[2] A trajectory is an evolving, ever-changing phenomenon.

Consumption trajectories that lead to dependence can generally be separated into five phases of varying length, during which the drug–crime dynamic evolves. For our purposes here, we will call these phases *experimentation and occasional use, frequent use, regular use, addiction,* and *reduction/cessation/interruption.* An individual's trajectory may or may not follow this sequence, and, of course, a reduction/cessation/interruption phase may occur at any point in the trajectory.

Experimentation and Occasional Use

Generally speaking, illicit drug users begin their trajectory with experimental or occasional cannabis use. They are motivated by pleasure and the appeal of sharing new experiences with friends (Brunelle, Brochu, and Cousineau 2005; Poirier 2011). This is far removed from the worn-out stereotype of a bad crowd of kids pressuring a straight-A teenager to try drugs for the first time. The social context of hanging out with friends is particularly important at this stage because illicit drug use depends on contact with other users. The same is true for many other deviant behaviours, such as delinquency. These early experiences tend to be voluntary, however (Brochu and Parent 2005). Peer pressure is not as significant a factor in illicit drug use as choice of peers in the first place.

With more experienced companions showing them the ropes, some individuals experiment with a variety of psychoactive substances but are usually not heavily involved in drug use. People who use sporadically and don't spend much money on drugs are not under pressure to commit crimes. Intensity of drug use is determined not by income but by events, circumstances, and casual offers from friends (Brochu and Parent 2005; Brunelle, Brochu, and Cousineau 2005). A recent study of 129 adults with substance use disorder showed that peer groups and parties functioned as incentives to use drugs, especially (but not exclusively) at the beginning of their trajectory (Brunelle et al. 2014).

There is no direct relationship between drugs and crime at this stage (see fig. 5.1). However, for young offenders and adolescents on a deviant trajectory, drug use and crime sometimes satisfy the same need to develop their identity and a sense of belonging (Brochu and Parent 2005; Brunelle, Brochu, and Cousineau 2005). Young people already involved in illegal activity may spend some of their proceeds of crime on drugs as well as on a variety of other things (Brunelle, Brochu, and Cousineau 2000). With respect to this first phase of the trajectory, we must avoid establishing a spurious causal relationship between these delinquent behaviours and illicit drug use.

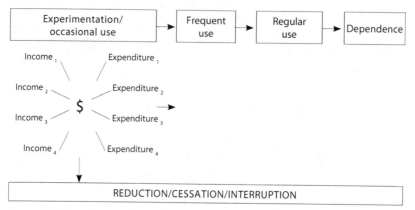

FIGURE 5.1. Experimentation and occasional use.

Frequent Use

For the majority of adolescent drug users, frequent use is one of many other fun activities that precedes or accompanies their quest for strong sensations (Brunelle, Cousineau, and Brochu 2002b). The appeal of a new source of pleasure and the allure of the forbidden play important roles in the genesis of a trajectory that people pursue because they want to recapture those initial pleasurable sensations and experience more of the novel sensations that they come to expect from episodes of drug use. This leads to more frequent drug use (Brunelle, Cousineau, and Brochu 2002b). During this phase, the focus is on pleasure and fun (Brunelle, Cousineau, and Brochu 2005).

In the experimentation phase, some young people choose to use drugs to gain entry into a group. In this second phase, they exhibit a desire to be liked and accepted by the group members (Brunelle, Cousineau, and Brochu 2005). Some young people with low self-esteem, particularly those who feel abandoned or neglected by their parents, find drug use environments appealing because they can bond with friends to make up for lack of attachment to family. Bonding with deviant peers reinforces delinquent behaviour and drug use (ibid.), although one does not necessarily lead to the other.

For some youths already involved in unlawful behaviour, drug use can make committing minor crimes, such as shoplifting, more fun

(Brunelle, Cousineau, and Brochu 2002a). For others, associating with deviant peers and engaging in delinquent behaviour with them can supply the money and contacts required for more frequent drug use.

By the time they reach this phase of their trajectory, many young people are consuming drugs other than cannabis. Having tried a variety of drugs, some users begin to favour one substance (or a class of substances), but others are not so exclusive and will use anything they can get their hands on to get high.

During the frequent use phase, individuals tend to use small quantities of drugs (Brochu and Parent 2005; Decorte 2000; Marsh 2002) and can easily afford the expense just as they would the cost of any other leisure activity. Since they are not dependent, available leisure time and access to drugs are the principal factors that limit their drug use (Brochu and Parent 2005).

Many of these users attend school regularly or have paying jobs. This structure (regular hours of work or study, performance expectations, social relationships, etc.) keeps their drug use in check. Some individuals, however, use drugs, particularly stimulants, to enhance their performance at especially demanding times. Drugs enable them to work longer hours, at least for a while (Brochu and Parent 2005). This specific consumption pattern is self-reinforcing and may lead to regular use for many people (see fig. 5.2).

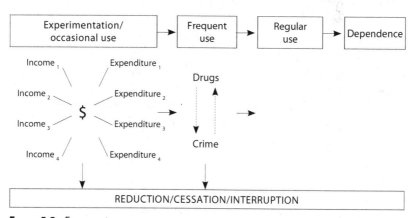

FIGURE 5.2. Frequent use.

Regular Use

Drugs are usually easy to get—even easier for regular users. Regular customers also have access to higher-quality products at lower prices

(Decorte 2000; Marsh 2002). The desirable effects of drugs combined with easier access favour escalating drug use. However, even under such ideal conditions, drug use trajectories are not linear; they vary depending on individuals, contexts, and stages (Brochu and Parent 2005; Decorte 2000; Monahan et al. 2014).

In the vast majority of cases, consumption intensity in this phase is subject to available income (Decorte 2000; Marsh 2002), but some users begin to go into debt. Initially, periods of indebtedness are brief, lasting only until payday or welfare cheque day. As users become known in the community and prove that they can settle their debts within a reasonable time, it becomes easier for them to get their drugs on credit (Brochu and Parent 2005).

Users who have trouble managing their debts may see crime as a convenient solution to the problem. Because certain drugs are sold on the black market, buyers are more likely to meet substantial and pressing financial obligations using proceeds of crime. People in the drug scene do not usually get upset about drug users committing crimes to pay back debt. On the contrary, the scene connects users to an extended network of opportunities to settle their debts faster. As they spend money on drugs, and as their lifestyle exposes them to more chance encounters, some regular users begin to participate in questionable or even outright criminal activities that enable them to use drugs regularly without draining their funds or interfering with their lifestyle (ibid.). Users may spend just a portion of their proceeds on drugs and the rest on other costly consumer goods.

Not being subject to the same constraints as regular employment, criminal activity enables people to become more intensely involved in a lifestyle structured around drug use. For some, fast, easy money can heighten their desire to use more drugs. This sets up a mutually reinforcing behaviour dynamic. The drug scene offers opportunities to make money. Users typically spend that money on increased drug use. The more they consume, the more they feel the need to diversify their criminal activity to generate more income, and so on (ibid.).

Those who are not dependent are free to choose the money-making activities that suit them best. People who stick to legal activities must cut other expenses, while those who engage in lucrative crime can access a much more lavish lifestyle. During this phase of the drug use trajectory, regular users tend not to commit crimes that compromise their core values just to get money. Those who do turn to unlawful activity typically elect to sell drugs to friends and a small network of acquaintances or commit workplace theft and fraud (ibid.).

Drug sales and distribution is the most common category of criminal activity at this stage. It provides easy access to large quantities of higher-quality substances at lower prices, which may at some point result in an unintended consequence: rapidly escalating drug use may become difficult or impossible to manage. Many small-scale drug dealers fall into this trap and never really benefit from the tremendous money-making potential of the drug trade (ibid.).

Some regular drug users discover that their workplace provides opportunities to commit fraud, embezzlement, and other lucrative illegal acts in support of their lifestyle. These people would not likely commit these crimes if not for their drug use (ibid.). When people use costly illegal drugs regularly, their own consumption demands nudge them toward crime.

Often, with the onset of regular consumption, the drug–crime dynamic gradually shifts. This is the point at which many users commit their first crimes, and those already involved in illegal pursuits begin to diversify their activities. At this stage, we can observe mutual reinforcement between certain types of crime and drug use (see fig. 5.3): psychoactive substance use may lead to involvement in delinquent activities, such as drug dealing, which can enable users to cover the cost of regular drug use (ibid.). In this scenario, money is the intermediary between the other two behaviours.

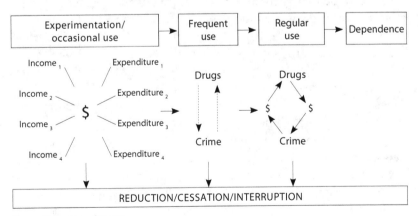

Figure 5.3. Regular use.

It is not uncommon for drug-use trajectories to develop over a decade without ever crossing the threshold of dependence (Decorte 2002). While some users lose control for periods of time, they are generally capable of regulating their consumption (Decorte 2000, 2002). The fact is that controlled drug use is not only possible, it is the norm (Harrison 1994).

Regular drug use may nevertheless lead to addiction for some users. The most deviant users, those who employ the most extreme routes of administration (such as intravenous) and those who use a mix of drugs (opiates, in particular) are at higher risk of succumbing to addiction despite the dysfunction it causes in the vast majority of situations (Brain, Parker, and Bottomley 1998; Brochu and Parent 2005).

Addiction

Certain factors can make it very difficult or virtually impossible for some individuals to control their consumption. These include regular drug use, the effects users experience, their reasons for use, and easy access to drugs via dealing.

Users who become addicted certainly do not do so deliberately. Drug use is associated with active pleasure-seeking and an unrestrained quest for happiness and, as such, choice and free will are part of the equation right from the beginning. However, deliberately and determinedly embarking on an addictive trajectory is rare. Brunelle, Cousineau, and Brochu (2002b) conducted a study to better understand the causes and processes involved in the development of addictive trajectories among young users. They found that, while users' initial experiences with psychoactive substances are motivated by pleasure and curiosity, they eventually begin using drugs to forget their problems and distance themselves from a past or a present that they perceive or experience as deeply painful. Early on, they use drugs for social reasons; later problem use is due to personal reasons (Titus, Godley, and White 2006). Their state of dissatisfaction or discontent may have been present since childhood or it may have materialized more recently following a traumatic event. It may also result from the consequences of regular drug use, and some young people may escalate drug use to escape reality (which may include problems with parents or at school) (Brunelle, Brochu, and Cousineau 2005).

Once individuals are at the addiction stage, their lives revolve around drugs. Dependence certainly has a major economic impact

(Brochu and Parent 2005; Brunelle, Brochu, and Cousineau 2005; Marsh 2002). It is usually difficult for people who are unwilling or unable to stop using drugs to avoid criminal activity, and they typically engage in lucrative crime to support their addiction. Even so, crime is not the only money-making activity available to dependent users. Users who have somehow managed to hold down a job try to work extra hours if they can. They cut their other expenses as much as possible and employ every ounce of their ingenuity and audacity in the pursuit of money and the goods they need to survive (Brochu and Parent 2005; Marsh 2002).

Nevertheless, most dependent users quickly realize that fulfilling their employment obligations is incompatible with satisfying the demands of their addiction. Happily, some choose the former over the latter, but that choice is not available to everyone. Above-board alternatives dry up. Friends stop lending them money because they never pay it back, and they wear out their welcome with relatives. Soon enough, legal avenues alone can no longer meet the demands of compulsive consumption, and illegal activities may seem like the only option (see fig. 5.4) (Brochu and Parent 2005; Cloutier 2014).

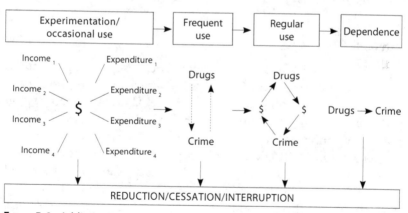

Figure 5.4. Addiction.

Individuals who get involved in lucrative crime at this stage often begin with petty crimes against family members and friends. They may progress along their delinquent trajectory by committing more serious, riskier crimes to get more money to support their drug use (Brochu and Parent 2005; Marsh 2002). Individuals already involved in crime ramp up and diversify their illegal activities.

Although drug users frequently commit their crimes while intox-icated, their actions are often in conflict with their core values and may elicit strong feelings of guilt in those who did not do such things prior to becoming dependent. They then have two options: cease the activity or live with the guilt. Many drug-dependent people try to escape these feelings by consuming even more drugs, and thus begins a vicious cycle in which only addiction prevails (Brochu and Parent 2005).

For both regular and dependent users, the drug–crime dynamic changes depending on where they are in their trajectory. We must nevertheless keep in mind that not all trajectories lead to problem drug use. In fact, the vast majority of drug users never progress beyond experimental or occasional cannabis use.

Factors That Influence the Progression and Maintenance of Deviant Trajectories

Four factors seem to have a significant influence on the progression of drug use trajectories: the properties and effects of substances, income, stigmatizing environments, and traumatic events (Brochu and Parent 2005; Brunelle, Cousineau, and Brochu 2002a).

The Substance Itself

The substance or substances individuals choose may contribute to maintaining their position on a deviant trajectory or progressing along it (Brochu and Parent 2005; Brunelle, Cousineau, and Brochu 2002a; Marsh 2004). Certain drugs and routes of administration that lead to tolerance and strong psychological or physical dependence set the stage for intensification or at least perpetuation of drug use. For a thorough understanding of substances as factors in progression and maintenance, we must take into account the *quantity* used, the *route of administration* (how it is taken), and *frequency of use*. For instance, cocaine is a less influential factor for a person who snorts it once a month than for someone who injects it every day.

Our studies indicate that escalation of use and adoption of a deviant lifestyle depend primarily on: (1) tolerance and (2) drawbacks related to the substance or the route of administration (Brochu and Parent 2005).

Eventually, people who have used a substance regularly or intensively no longer experience the effects they did initially. They must take more to feel those effects again to an appreciable degree. In general, progression is a subtle process as users increase their dose gradually, often while they are no longer in full possession of their faculties because they are intoxicated (ibid.).

Changing the route of administration, perhaps because of problems with the previous method, is another indication of progression along a deviant trajectory (ibid.). A user may switch from snorting cocaine to injecting it to avoid getting a bloody nose. Heroin users may swap sniffing for injecting because it is cheaper and more intense.

Once dependence to a more addictive substance such as heroin or cocaine has set in, fear of withdrawal symptoms (such as nausea) may explain, to some extent, why individuals continue to use it (Brunelle et al. 2014).

Income

As we have seen, once users can no longer support their drug use with legal revenue, they generally turn to illegal sources of income. Drug dealing is often a preferred income-generating crime, partly because it is so lucrative, and partly because it is considered less serious than other crimes such as theft, and much less serious than robbery, which involves contact with the victim. Drug dealing provides greater access to drugs and the income to increase consumption. Young people, who have limited legal means to support their drug use, turn to lucrative crime, particularly small-scale dealing to friends, more readily than adults (Brunelle and Bertrand 2010). We may observe a more rapid progression along the delinquency trajectory among young people with the least legal income (no job or allowance), especially if they consume costlier and more addictive drugs.

Environment

One's environment is not a constant. Changes in a person's social circle may or may not follow a linear progression, and several spheres of influence may coexist. The first sphere of influence, the family, is often a risk factor and continues to influence the individual's development even after independence. The drug scene is another sphere of influence; it includes users, dealers, back alleys, shooting galleries,[3] crack houses, and everything else that goes along with such activities and places. Then there is the world of crime, which includes thieves and fences, sleazy bars, and strip clubs (Cusson 2005).

The effects of certain constants in a person's environment are predictable. The social segregation (limited access to well-paid jobs, endemic unemployment, unfit housing, etc.) prevalent in some areas is conducive to the adoption and progression of a deviant lifestyle (Cusson 2005). Delinquency is a much more attractive option when available jobs offer poor working conditions and pay. Segregation isolates individuals in virtually inescapable marginal conditions and inflicts a deep social wound destined to leave a distressing scar that prevents complete social healing. Segregation drags people down into a subculture and tethers them to a deviant trajectory. People get involved in the world of drugs or with certain criminal groups to fill the void or forget their troubles. For these people, this is an ideal way to cope with, escape, or forget reality (Bouhnik 1996; Brunelle, Brochu, and Cousineau 1998, 2005).

Traumatic Events

For others, the deviant trajectory is related to traumatic events that become turning points in their lives. Such events usually involve loss: a break-up, being fired, the death of a loved one, or an abusive situation that violates the individual's physical or psychological integrity (Brochu and Parent 2005; Brunelle et al. 2014, 2002b). In many cases, such events radically alter the structure of an individual's life and sever important social ties. People may turn to drugs to escape intense feelings that are hard to cope with, while those who are already using need look no further than drugs for help getting through periods of extreme distress. These defining events play varying roles in the adoption of deviant conduct, depending on their nature, when they occur, and the meaning individuals ascribe to them (Brunelle, Cousineau, and Brochu 2002b). That is why not all victimization experiences are considered traumatic by the social actor, at least not to the point of causing them to embark on a deviant trajectory (Brunelle, Brochu, and Cousineau 2005).

Progression along a drug use trajectory may be enabled by certain properties of drugs and routes of administration but is more often a product of the interaction between a stigmatizing environment and a traumatic event (Brochu and Parent 2005; Brunelle, Cousineau, and Brochu 2002b). People try to escape the painful emotions linked to these factors by using more drugs. Over time, an accumulation of day-to-day problems with relationships and at work can also trigger intensification of drug use in the absence of a specific traumatic event (Brunelle et al. 2014).

Reduction, Cessation, and Interruption

The majority of studies examining the links between drugs and crime have focused more on the development of deviant conduct than on disruption of such behaviours. Deviant trajectories tend to twist and turn and may be punctuated by periods when drug use and delinquency are reduced or in abeyance (Brunelle, Cousineau, and Brochu 2005; Brunelle et al. 2014). For the most part, the people we met in the course of our studies on deviant trajectories experienced periods of decreasing involvement. In contrast to factors that fuel deviant conduct, other elements motivate people to distance themselves from the lifestyle to greater or lesser degrees. They may cease their activities entirely or scale back their involvement (Brochu and Parent 2005).

Elements that may drive progression or maintenance in some individuals can cause others to interrupt their activities. For example, one person may react to the death of a friend by going on a bender, but the same event may be the wake-up call another needs to quit using. Similarly, some individuals who move to another community or serve time in prison maintain their behaviour, others quit, and still others progress to using harder drugs. It is important to note, however, that in many cases, a combination of pressures, not just one, leads to a break with the deviant lifestyle.

Peer Pressure

Many respondents reported that they distanced themselves from their deviant lifestyles following suggestions or ultimatums from friends and love interests who steered clear of those lifestyles (Brunelle, Cousineau, and Brochu 2002a; Brunelle et al. 2014). Such pressure can be even more effective if it is applied to an individual who is expecting a child or has recently become a parent (Brochu and Parent 2005), a state that creates a feeling of family and social belonging, at least for a time, and can help an individual cut back on deviant activity (Brunelle, Cousineau, and Brochu 2002a).

Internal Pressure

People who get involved in deviant activities may become aware of their consequences. As they gradually move farther away from their moral bounds, they may suddenly become painfully aware of having betrayed their personal values, of having crossed a line. This crisis of conscience can serve as the catalyst for exiting a deviant lifestyle (Brunelle, Cousineau, and Brochu 2002a; Mercier and Alarie 2002). Participants in our studies said that they sometimes cut back or quit using because they wanted to improve their economic, social, and family situation and their physical and psychological health (Brunelle et al. 2014). They may feel that they have too much to lose, or at least nothing to gain, by maintaining or increasing their drug use.

Organizational Pressure

Organizational structures may exert pressure in favour of quitting a deviant lifestyle. For people who are employed, one of those structures is the job itself. The requirements of paid employment include showing up for work and meeting performance expectations. A life of debauchery and all-night partying is not compatible with regular attendance and productivity at work. In short, committing to a regular job provides some degree of structure to one's day-to-day activities. Failure to fulfil that commitment soon results in organizational consequences. This type of pressure is very effective at halting progression along a deviant trajectory for those who value their professional activities and the associated lifestyle (Brochu and Parent 2005). Many people give in to this kind of pressure because they feel they have too much to lose (status, money, etc.) by flouting the rules.

Deviant Environment Pressures

The world of crime is exciting and scary, and those who break its unwritten rules can expect threats and violence rather than forgiveness. Worry, intimidation, risk, and danger related to deviant subcultures, the world of crime, and the illegal drug distribution system can be excellent reasons to break with the lifestyle (Brochu and Parent 2005; Brunelle and Bertrand 2010).

There is another dimension to these pressures. Individuals may simply mature out or, once they have been immersed in a hedonistic lifestyle for too long, realize that it is not actually compatible with their goals. The fact is, delinquent environments can wear a person down (Brochu and Parent 2005).

Women's Distinctive Trajectory

There is evidence that women's drug–crime trajectory is distinct from that of men. Marsh's study (2002) made an important contribution by shedding light on some characteristics of the trajectories that female cocaine users regularly adopt and the main ways in which they differ from those of men. Women's trajectories seem to include four drug use stages: initiation, gradual intensification, rapid escalation, and enslavement.

According to Marsh (2002), initiation is the first stage in women's cocaine use trajectory, and it is analogous to men's experimental or occasional use. When women have their first experiences with cocaine, it never occurs to them that the drug might one day play a dominant role in their lives. These early experiences happen by chance when cocaine happens to be available at parties. Little cash outlay is involved because women usually get drugs from a friend or boyfriend, no strings attached.

Gradual intensification is characterized by regular but not frequent use of small amounts of cocaine. Through gradual changes in a woman's lifestyle, cocaine becomes increasingly present in her recreational activities. Her new peer group not only accepts more and more frequent consumption but is impressed by and encourages it. There is no downside, yet. By this point, of course, the substance is no longer free, but she is not yet spending more on drugs than she can afford. Eventually, she starts to resent being so dependent on the peer group (Marsh 2002).

The next stage is rapid escalation, characterized by almost daily and frequently excessive consumption. Remaining social structures (e.g., family ties, employment) cannot compete with this pattern of drug use and, neglected, disintegrate one by one. At this stage, a female drug user must begin to contend with limited access to legal income and the prospect of resorting to crime. She may begin dealing drugs, committing fraud, or shoplifting. These criminal activities supply ample positive reinforcement: independence, a kind of freedom, and access to a luxurious lifestyle (Couvrette 2014; Marsh 2002).

The final stage in the trajectory is characterized by enslavement to the drug and the need to use increasing amounts of cocaine to feel the desired effects, which becomes very costly. Women who can no longer do without cocaine have no choice but to escalate their criminal activities. As Marsh (2002) points out, this is the beginning of a dual dependence on both drugs and crime. These women cannot do without either cocaine or their illegal income.

A comparative analysis of the trajectories of men and women reveals two distinct factors that affect female users specifically (Bertrand and Nadeau 2006; Couvrette 2014; Marsh 2002). First, intimate relationships play an important role for the better part of these women. In many cases, women get their first taste of cocaine from an intimate partner who encourages them to use more. However, what began as a passionate relationship often turns out to be pathological, and women find themselves trapped. Second, motherhood often serves as a crucial regulating factor in their trajectory. Women who are heavily dependent on drugs may modify their consumption patterns by using less frequently or in smaller quantities. This socially reviled behaviour naturally pricks at the conscience of mothers who are struggling to reconcile their dependence and their maternal responsibilities, often in a single-parent setting. To capture the complex emotional and social factors at work, Couvrette (2014) called them "good deviant mothers." They love their children passionately, are concerned with their well-being, and want above all to avoid being separated from them, but they are also in thrall to a drug, and do not always see treatment as an option.

* * *

Scientific research sheds only partial light on the role of drugs in the development of a person's criminality. Too often, studies draw on samples made up primarily, if not exclusively, of dependent individuals. While they represent a minority of drug users, they are nevertheless more heavily involved in criminal activity, usually of the lucrative variety.

In this chapter, we looked at the consumption pathways of deviant regular users and addicts, but drug users fall into other categories too. For example, there are people who use drugs regularly but whose drug use is not part of a deviant trajectory and whose participation in society is quite normal (school or work, family and social relationships, etc.) (Brochu et al. 2011). They typically use drugs for pleasure as a recreational activity, and although they account for the bulk of drug users, they have been the subject of little study. As Simpson (2003) suggests, drug use can be categorized based on five factors: regularity of use, amount consumed, type of drug chosen, route of administration, and attitudes regarding the place of drug use in the user's life.

In examining the trajectories of dependent and deviant regular users, we focused on the sustained use of drugs by people whose lives include relatively little structure and organization (mainly in terms of school attendance or maintaining stable employment), so we must take care not to generalize based on the drug–crime relationships described in this chapter.

The term *trajectory* refers to the longitudinal sequence of drug use. The typical trajectory we presented comprises five phases: experimentation and occasional use, frequent use, regular use, addiction, and reduction/cessation/interruption. It is important to note that one phase does not inevitably lead to the next, but entry into any given phase opens some doors and closes others.

Psychoactive substance use entrenches existing delinquent involvement and propels those who were hitherto minimally or not at all involved toward crime. Close and enduring links exist among compulsive use of highly illegal drugs, crimes committed by people whose income is low compared to the cost of drugs and who offend to support their habit, and lack of social structure (e.g., drop-outs, the jobless, those lacking adequate family ties). Criminality does not necessarily emerge at the beginning of the trajectory. Rather, it insinuates itself gradually, harmlessly at first (such as returning a favour), then as an increasingly lucrative pursuit, and finally as an indispensable source of income to support drug use. Once drugs have become central to an individual's life, they become more difficult to procure by legal means alone.

Brunelle's studies show that initiation into an addictive trajectory is a kind of involuntary self-selection phenomenon. In such cases, drug use is polysemic, loaded with meaning and symbols from the user's past. People who embark on this trajectory, usually without realizing it, typically exhibit a deep and abiding discontent that they are trying to escape.

As people progress along the path of addiction, drug use plays an increasingly important role in their lives. The more they misuse drugs, the more they organize their lives around drug use (the drug scene, drugs themselves, and their effects). Eventually, drugs become the be-all and end-all of their lives: the cycle of getting money to buy drugs, procuring drugs, and consuming drugs repeats itself over and over again (Cormier 1993). For quite a few drug-dependent people, lucrative crime is frequently the only way they can get enough money to buy drugs.

Once initiated, addictive trajectories tend to twist and turn. Unpredictable availability can dictate drug use. Abstinence may give way to relapse. Users may be arrested. Nevertheless, it is possible to observe changes in the relationship between drugs and crime over time. Drugs, which may start out as a fun way for young offenders to celebrate criminal success, may draw regular users into illegal activities associated with the illicit drug market (crime brings in enough money to pay for drugs, and drugs enable users to broaden their criminal repertoire) and dependent users toward lucrative crime driven by the need for drugs and fear of withdrawal.

As addictive and criminal trajectories evolve, these two deviant behaviours become entangled to the point that they can no longer be viewed as separate. Drug dependence manifests surreptitiously, first as a habit—a costly one, to be sure, but one that does not outstrip the user's legal income—and then, for some, it gradually morphs to the point that it demands a constant supply of cash well in excess of their legal income. Having crossed line after line, the user adopts not only deviant behaviour but also a deviant identity as a distinct lifestyle steadily takes shape. This condition is not irreversible, however, and most drug use trajectories include periods of hiatus that may be associated with a lull in delinquent activities. The point is, drug use and delinquency trajectories tend to be convoluted.

The notion of *trajectory* helps us understand that, contrary to the assertions of classical conceptual models of relationships between drugs and crime, the connections that develop between drug users and criminal activity are more dynamic than static. They also carry meaning. What does drug use mean to an individual? What does delinquency mean to him or her?

Notes

1. Translation of "Construire la ligne biographique du toxicomane, ce serait bien sûr retracer son parcours de drogué dans ce qu'il implique de spécifiquement lié à la drogue ; mais ça serait aussi analyser la manière dont se cristallisent autour de cette ligne d'autres éléments de l'équipement social d'un individu."
2. Translation of "la conduite déviante se construit d'abord avec un effet de lancement qui se transforme ensuite en continuité et celle-ci est soutenue par les interactions contemporaines entre les conduites déviantes."
3. Locations where drug users can rent or borrow needles and syringes and inject drugs.

Chapter 6

Deviant Lifestyles: An Integrated Conceptualization

I n this chapter, we will integrate the findings we have presented so far as we break down the relationship between drugs and crime.[1] Our goal is to enable the reader to grasp its full complexity and better understand the ins and outs. We will make use of the conceptual models introduced in chapter 4 and the notions of trajectory we analyzed in chapter 5.

A number of authors, chief among them Goldstein (1987), adopted an essentially deterministic perspective to show how drug use can lead to crime. In their view, be it because of the psychopharmacological effects, the need for money to support an addiction, or violence associated with the illegal distribution system, psychoactive substances are the prime mover for a significant number of crimes. Analysis of these causal models reveals that they are typically developed as either/or propositions. The inverse proximal model is a good illustration of that because it pins the origin of problem drug use on delinquency. In chapter 5, we made it clear that the drug–crime dynamic can also evolve over time.

The concepts of *career* and *trajectory* add another dimension to that static analysis (Brunelle 2001; Faupel 1991; Kokoreff 2005). These concepts are useful because they provide a good description of how people who become regular drug users learn and develop patterns of behaviour and because they take changes in the drug–crime dynamic into account (Brunelle, Cousineau, and Brochu 2005).

We can agree that problem drug use is a complex behaviour in constant flux involving the interplay of myriad past and present, public and private, objective and subjective factors (Bellot 2005; Brochu et al. 2014). Our conceptualization of the drug–crime relationship must therefore go beyond notions of intoxication, dependence, and illicit markets to incorporate personal, subjective experiences. The conceptual models we analyzed in chapter 4 probably represented the outcome of time-limited, one-dimensional observations—snapshots—of this phenomenon. Furthermore, although the trajectory concept discussed in chapter 5 seems well-suited to describing drug use as an ever-evolving process, it glosses over how individuals subjectively experience events and interpret facts (Brochu and Parent 2005).

The deviant lifestyle concept is a construct that offers insight into the subjective reality of a social actor constantly interacting with his or her environment. It identifies a propensity for non-conformist, marginal, illegal, and antisocial behaviours, among others. This attitude and the resulting behaviours eventually shape the identity of the person who adopts them (Brochu and Brunelle 1997). This chapter is based primarily on the notion of *deviant lifestyle*.

The Integrative Model

Qualitative, ethnological, and phenomenological studies, which involve more contact with the actors involved, point to the importance of idiosyncrasy and the evolution of the drug–crime dynamic. Knowledge accumulated over the past thirty years, including what our own research group, RISQ,[2] has discovered, has supplied enough pieces to put together an integrative model explaining drug–crime relationships. Our model takes into account risk factors, deviant lifestyle, and progression factors. The following core schematic representation situates these elements relative to one another. The integrative model presented here amalgamates two complementary models, one by Brochu, first published in 1995, and the other by Brunelle, Brochu, and Cousineau, first published in 2005 and refined in 2010 by Brunelle and Bertrand. Merging the two yields a new integrative model. Now that we have identified its principal elements, we can better define and articulate them.

Although the schematic representation of this model (see fig. 6.1) may suggest a linear conceptualization, this is in no way the case. While some conditions are prerequisites for the adoption of particular behaviours, they never fully explain those behaviours. Humans, even when intoxicated or dependent on a drug, have a will of their own and ascribe phenomenological meaning to their behaviour and their path through life. These meanings can continually influence an individual's trajectory.

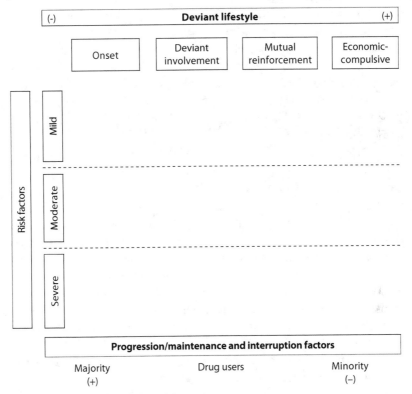

FIGURE 6.1. Core integrative model.

Risk Factors

As we saw in chapter 4, a number of risk factors promote the emergence of a lifestyle that deviates from the norms upheld by the dominant social classes. For example, early drug use and delinquency are much-documented risk factors. Basically, there are situations, contexts, and environments that increase a person's risk of adopting a deviant lifestyle, and the same variables influence the likelihood of a person exhibiting a range of delinquent behaviours or consuming illicit psychoactive substances.

However, our findings put us at odds with traditional research on risk factors that assigns an actuarial value to these risk factors for predicting deviant behaviour. Predicting whether such behaviours will occur based on combinations of risk factors is error-prone (Brochu and Parent 2005; Brunelle, Brochu, and Cousineau 2005). Of greater importance here are the subjective significance and synergies among these factors from the perspective of the social actor, as well as the presence of protective factors, all of which augment or diminish the relative weight of risk factors. From our point of view, individuals must be considered social actors who organize their lives according to who they are, what they experience, what they feel, and what they understand. Risk factors play a greater or lesser role depending on the meaning a social actor attributes to them and the interpretations associated with them.

To assess the intensity of the risk factors present, we must consider not only these subjective elements themselves, but also what happens when they interact synergistically. For example, with respect to socialization institutions, parent–child relationships and school attendance can be good or poor, but cutting class or dropping out can have much more negative repercussions for a student with a dysfunctional or non-existent parent–child relationship. Furthermore, risk factors can have a greater or lesser impact depending on the individual's maturity (self-control, empathy, and attachment), social capital (resources), and the presence of protective factors (family and school environment, certain recreational activities, certain moral values, etc.).

The social actor's subjectivity, risk-factor synergies, and the presence of protective factors interact to determine the degree to which risk factors influence a person's life. The likelihood of embarking on a deviant trajectory varies according to risk factor intensity. For illustrative purposes, our integrative schema depicts three levels of risk intensity: mild, moderate, and severe.

Deviant Lifestyles

It is clear from longitudinal research and large national studies focusing on adolescents that experimental drug use rarely leads to criminality, so its root causes must be found elsewhere. Nevertheless, drugs do mingle quite readily with other deviant behaviours. Is there some explanation for this other than linear proximate cause models? The distal model presented in chapter 4 covered a broad range of socially deviant conduct, including delinquency and illicit drug use by some adolescents. We will now expand on that model by adding degrees of permeation and stages of progression.

The deviant lifestyle concept is based on phenomenological postulates about how individuals and their inherent subjectivity are central to understanding their behaviour. This is a particularly interesting concept because it enables us to integrate new knowledge about risk factors while observing these elements through a different lens. Here, the user's behaviours are seen as linked to the personal meaning they bear rather than resulting from external determinism. There may be more to a drug user's delinquent act than the mere instrumental acquisition of drugs. As we saw in earlier chapters, not all illicit drug users become dependent, delinquency is not the only way for people who misuse illicit psychoactive substances to get by, and not all drug-dependent people are involved in crime to the same extent. People commit crimes not only for economic-compulsive reasons, but also to fulfil marginal aspirations tied to the sociocultural context.

The deviant lifestyle concept offers insight into how individuals exposed to particular risk factors construct their identity and why they adopt certain deviant behaviours. These factors include failure (e.g., school or work) and rejection (e.g., family or ethnic group), a person's resulting self-esteem and beliefs, and meaning ascribed to experiences and deviant behaviour (Brochu and Brunelle 1997; Kaplan 1995). This is how a lifestyle that can be considered deviant comes together for some people (Becker 1963; Brochu and Brunelle 1997; Brochu, Bergeron et al. 2002; da Agra 2002).

At times, this concept has been associated with moralizing, Manichaean, or pathologizing conceptualizations. To avoid attaching a pejorative sense to the concept, and to avoid confusion, we want to clarify exactly what we mean by "deviant lifestyle" here (Brochu and Brunelle 1997; Brochu et al. 2002; da Agra 2005). As we see it, going off the beaten path can open the door to healthy creativity and progress. However, unconventional pathways may sometimes include deviant acts that are harmful to the individual, to those around him or her, or to social institutions. Harmful use of psychoactive substances and delinquent acts are generally associated with deviance. While there is no social consensus around this idea, to many researchers (Brochu and Brunelle 1997; Brochu et al. 2002; da Agra 1986; Grapendaal, Leuw, and Nelen 1995), the word "deviance" is a relatively neutral term meaning the violation of a norm stemming from a social construct. That is how we view the notion of deviant lifestyle in this chapter.

Degrees of Permeation

As with risk factors, deviant lifestyle is not a simple dichotomy—present or absent—but a spectrum of intensity. To varying degrees of intensity, deviant lifestyles may include illicit psychoactive substance use, criminal activity, or in many cases both.

People with weak deviant tendencies (exposed to risk factors that are fewer in number, lower in intensity, or viewed as less significant by the individual) can easily hold down a job while cultivating a rebellious side that they express when it does not conflict too much with their work or social life. They may adhere to many prosocial values that prevent them from adopting a fully deviant lifestyle and try to reconcile their marginal tendencies with the values endorsed by dominant social classes. Their illicit drug use may go on for a relatively long period of time without coming into conflict with their other activities. In fact, it may go hand in hand with some of those activities and can even be used to enhance their performance at work (Peele 1989). This type of drug use is an indulgence that does not put a strain on their budget.

In comparison, the notion of work means something completely different to people with strong deviant tendencies. They have a hard time bending to the yoke of a nine-to-five office job and may opt for unlawful alternatives rather than a more conventional trajectory. Illicit drugs are likely to have a greater presence in their social context. More intense deviant involvement can promote more frequent and more serious consumption and delinquency.

For our schematic illustration purposes, we begin by associating each level of risk with income from deviant activities of varying severity: mild (legal income), moderate (petty theft), severe (more blatant delinquency). As we will see in the next section, these risk levels are also indicators of the length of a drug–crime trajectory.

Stages of Progression

Deviant lifestyles are not fixed in time or bound to a single invariable trajectory. Subtle or substantial evolution can occur due to personal factors (Dérivois 2004) and the influence of external variables (which we will analyze in the section on progression and interruption factors).

All individuals are constantly evolving and adapting in response to internal realities (emotions and beliefs) and external pressures. Our evolution is not sudden and complete; we each follow our own life course, and our lifestyle is affected by our evolution. This is what da Agra (1999) calls a *processual explanation*. As we probe the links between drugs and crime, we must consider the individual's evolutionary process within the context of their life.

At each stage, many possible interactions can influence the direction of the individual's trajectory. Young users typically begin their progression by consuming legal psychoactive substances used by the adults around them (generally tobacco and alcohol, which adolescents cannot legally buy). Some then go on to use illicit substances that society tolerates somewhat (marijuana), while others begin to consume products that are more strictly forbidden (amphetamines, cocaine, crack, heroin, etc.). Type of use also follows a progression. As we saw in the previous chapter, the drug use pathway begins with occasional or experimental use, from which some progress to regular use and a very few become dependent. This progression inevitably alters the drug–crime relationship, which can differ markedly depending on the stage in an individual's trajectory. Our model identifies four stages during which links between drugs and crime appear, evolve, and may crystallize. The stages are onset, deviant involvement, mutual reinforcement, and economic-compulsive.

Onset (see fig. 6.2) is marked by occasional, generally light drug use. Consumption is a function of contact with other users and available funds, and is motivated by pleasure and curiosity. During this first stage of the deviant lifestyle, adolescents and young adults use drugs haphazardly as opportunities arise. People who engage in a mildly deviant lifestyle are likely to pay for their drugs with money from work or other legal sources of funds, but those who adopt a more deviant lifestyle may commit petty theft or more serious crimes to pay for their drugs. In such cases, criminality creates favourable conditions for drug use: crime supplies income, and friends supply contacts and social support for drug use (see the inverse proximal model in chapter 4). Regardless of the degree of deviant lifestyle permeation, available funds constitute both an incentive to use drugs and a rigid, limiting factor. Drugs are a discretionary expense subject to the ebb and flow of income and opportunity.

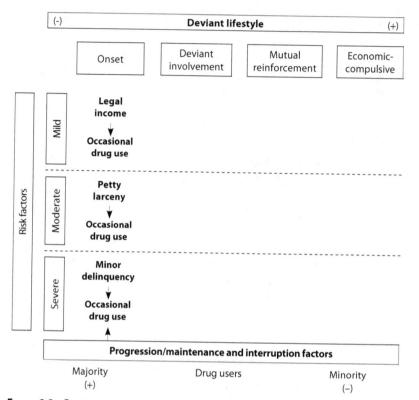

FIGURE 6.2. Onset stage.

For many people, this stage serves as an introduction to a different, unconventional lifestyle, changes how they feel about prohibited activities, and provides access to a peer group that enables them to pursue their nascent deviant tendencies.

Deviant involvement (see fig. 6.3) is marked by more frequent drug use that, though typically not problem use, can be abusive or risky. Initial positive experiences with drugs motivate users to keep using. Users do not experience the negative effects and consequences of drug use while using occasionally. Humans, being what they are, seek to re-experience known pleasure. However, at the deviant involvement stage, individuals may intensify their drug use because they want to belong to a peer group. The inverse proximal model also applies to young people. Their contact with other deviant individuals and their illegal income enables them to consume more drugs. Drug use can also play a utilitarian role because users feel it gives them the nerve to commit certain crimes, and they may be intoxicated during delinquent acts. Drug use, in this case, may facilitate crime. It is difficult to discern whether perpetration can be attributed to the user's expectations about the effects of a substance or to the substance's actual psychopharmacological effects. Regardless, the intention to commit the crime precedes drug use, so the drug is in no way responsible for the unlawful activity. Illegal behaviour is a little more frequent and diversified here than in the previous stage. It may be expressed as minor theft, such as shoplifting, theft of less than $20, and fraud.

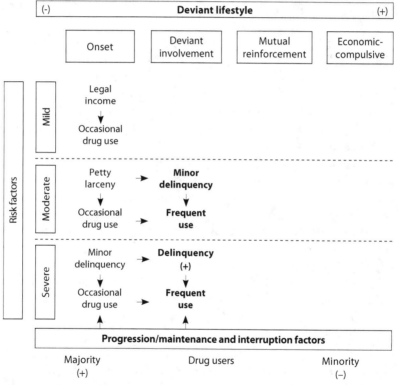

FIGURE 6.3. Deviant involvement stage.

If individuals subsequently begin to consume costly illegal drugs regularly, their delinquent behaviour is likely to become more frequent and varied and to include gradual involvement in drug dealing, first as one-off favours for friends, then in a more organized and regular fashion. As we saw earlier, this type of activity seems virtually unavoidable as a means of supporting sustained use of costly illicit

psychoactive substances, particularly for individuals from disadvantaged social classes. This has less to do with the demands of addiction
than with the user's seeing an opportunity to minimize spending on
drugs and enjoy easier access to the substances they want. Involvement
in the drug trade can also lead to systemic criminality. Easy access
to drugs can in turn have the adverse effect of increasing drug use
significantly (Brochu and Parent 2005).

At the *mutual reinforcement* stage (see fig. 6.4), consumption is still
governed primarily by available income, and it is plausible that some
individuals would never have become involved in drug dealing had
they never consumed illicit drugs. We therefore show a two-way link
between sources of income and regular drug use: drugs become both
the cause and the consequence of delinquency. The drug–crime relationship is one of circular causality, not linear causality, and mutual
reinforcement prolongs both drug use and delinquency trajectories.
More so than at previous stages, crimes are often committed while the
individual is intoxicated. Meanwhile, one's degree of involvement in
crime that is not related to the drug trade is a function of earlier deviant lifestyle permeation.

Generally, the deeper that permeation, the more frequent, varied, and serious (theft of $500 or more) the delinquency. Users may
engage in activities related to sex work (although sex work itself is no
longer illegal in Canada), which can lead to an increase in consumption because they have more disposable income and because drugs
numb the emotional impact of sex work, if only temporarily. At this
stage, users may be motivated by a desire to forget or escape the consequences of delinquency or even drug use itself, as well as feelings
about a traumatic event.

We will return to this consideration below. This general description of the mutual reinforcement stage paints a picture of individuals
who adopt a moderately or highly deviant lifestyle; other users have
probably not progressed beyond occasional drug use. Eventually, the
fact that drugs are always available and that users and their peers
admire drug culture can thrust some individuals into dependence.

Ultimately, drugs claim their due from individuals who become
dependent. Addicts report that the demands are implacable and financially onerous. At this point, delinquency supports drug use, and the
individual has reached the *economic-compulsive stage* (see fig. 6.5). It is
here that the economic-compulsive model truly applies. Initial forays
into lucrative crime escalate as the user spends more and more money

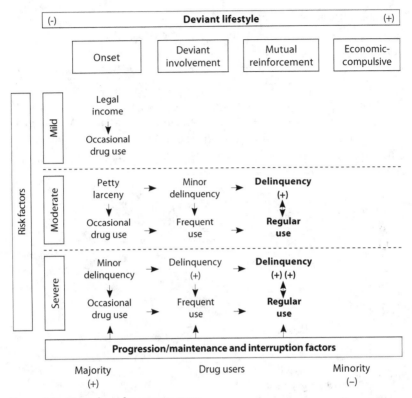

FIGURE 6.4. Mutual reinforcement stage.

on drugs and lacks the legal income to keep up; this is the catalyzing effect of dependence on a costly product. Delinquency also becomes more serious at this stage and may include robbery, which users see as a quick way to get money to buy drugs, especially when they are experiencing withdrawal or are under pressure to repay large debts. Also at this stage, drug use may be motivated primarily by a desire to forget, as users try to escape the negative aspects of their reality. It is only at this stage that a person's drug use can be considered the cause of their delinquency. However, insofar as using psychoactive substances is a conscious and deliberate process, criminal activities appear to increase in frequency and severity primarily among individuals who have chosen a delinquent lifestyle; others put an end to their drug use once the criminal component gets too serious.

The level of deviant involvement prior to initiation of drug use is a major factor in the development of delinquency. Progression toward dependence seems much more likely for individuals who have been exposed to many major risk factors and who have already adopted a highly deviant lifestyle. We must not forget, however, that only a minority of users reach the economic-compulsive stage. It is also worth noting that, since such individuals are frequently intoxicated, they very often commit their lucrative or violent crimes while under the influence of a substance. The psychopharmacological effects of drugs and even the user's expectations about those effects probably play an even more important role at the economic-compulsive stage.

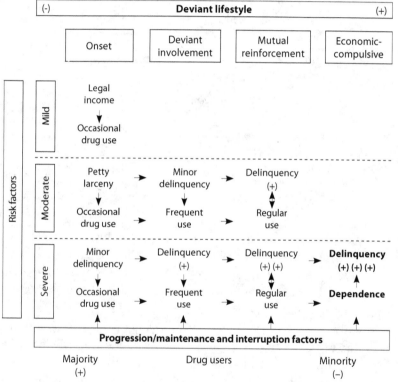

Figure 6.5. Economic-compulsive stage.

By focusing on the stages of progression, we may have given the reader the impression that deviant progression is just a matter of time. Like Dérivois (2004), we must emphasize that progression toward a deviant trajectory occurs when an individual repeats an act and attaches a symbolic value to that act (symbolization). Isolated drug use episodes typically result in few deleterious effects in the long term; repetition, however, can put the user on a drug use trajectory. Even so, repetition alone does not explain the most deviant trajectories. For more insight, we must look to the complexity of psychological processes and users' symbolization of the acts they repeat until they become central to his or her identity.

In essence, the concept of *lifestyle* refers here to the step-by-step construction of a deviant identity that makes it possible for people to cast off certain values and gradually adopt new behaviours. Without really realizing it, the social actor plays an active role in constructing this identity. We see the notion of lifestyle as a construct that integrates the actor's personal dispositions and his or her propensity for adopting behaviours and ways of life that are adaptive, marginal, or deviant to varying degrees, thus validating his or her existence and defining his or her identity. Drugs are certainly part of this lifestyle, but they are not the only part of it. It is created, constructed, and reinforced by the actor–context interaction. Let us now examine in detail the progression/maintenance and interruption factors of the deviant lifestyle.

Although exposure to risk factors, generally in childhood and adolescence, plays a role in deviance permeation, our studies (Brunelle, Cousineau, and Brochu 2002a; Brochu and Parent 2005) suggest that more contemporary factors in the social actor's life have a greater influence over his or her deviant trajectory. These are the progression/maintenance and interruption factors that we discussed in chapter 5.

Certain factors in people's lives create the right conditions for progressing along or maintaining a deviant trajectory; others are linked to a reduction, cessation, or interruption of the behaviours we are examining, an interruption in the trajectory. As we have seen, the most important progression and maintenance factors are the properties and effects of the substances consumed, the individual's income, a stigmatizing environment, and traumatic events.

It is certainly not easy to abandon a way of life that was established gradually over a long period. It is much easier to abandon this path during the earliest stages of deviant progression or after a frustrating trajectory. It is also easier if the individual has maintained a certain degree of social integration. This is probably why various pressures the individual experiences function as interruption factors. In a way, they hinder the progression or maintenance of the deviant lifestyle. For some people, these interruption factors trigger complete cessation; for others, they slow down progression or bring about a temporary cessation.

* * *

It is clear that the drug–crime relationship can vary depending on risk factors, deviance intensity, progression and maintenance stages, and progression and interruption factors. This chapter was organized around the notion of deviant lifestyle, a construct that considers a range of personal and social factors informed by exposure to risk factors, and that is associated with a tendency to adopt conduct and ways of life on the adaptive, marginal, or deviant spectrum. One's lifestyle is established gradually through repeated actions and the meaning attributed to those actions, which eventually shape the individual's identity. This concept takes into account the complex phenomenon of deviance take-up and the numerous interactions among individual, contextual, and temporal circumstances that drive psychoactive substance users toward various types of criminal involvement (Brochu and Brunelle 1997; Brochu and Parent 2005).

As shown in figure 6.5, in a matter of months or years, some individuals can progress from occasional drug use motivated and sustained by the success of delinquent activities (crime → money → drugs) to economic-compulsive crime (drugs → need for money → crime) dictated by drug dependence, while others will limit themselves to recreational drug use that does not exceed their available resources (money → drugs). The two begin with different lifestyles, which change in response to circumstances related to drug use. Many a cocaine user's deviant lifestyle is about cultivating defiance, power, and appearances. However, those who become dependent on cocaine adopt a lifestyle more heavily influenced by multiple attempts to get the money they need to buy cocaine and by time spent recovering from the effects of using drugs.

Initially, the lifestyle is shaped by certain behaviours, repetition of the most symbolic acts, and meaning attributed to those acts. Subsequently, the lifestyle itself dictates priority behaviours and, in a way, becomes the prime mover of activities that arrange themselves into a coherent whole.

In a sense, the integrative model we presented in this chapter represents a conceptual break with the positivist paradigm underpinning the assimilationist and reductionist theories that emerged over the past thirty years. Our model is based on a phenomenological paradigm that fully humanizes the individual and takes into account his or her interaction with a web of systems over time.

The models we have developed to gain insight into the nature of drug–crime relationships make one thing abundantly clear: these relationships are much more complex than we thought, and they evolve. In chapter 7, we look at how services can help addicts in the criminal justice system distance themselves from dependence and delinquency.

Notes

1.   Many sources cited in previous chapters will not be cited again here.
2.   Recherche et intervention sur les substances psychoactives – Québec.

Chapter 7

Treating Addicts in the Criminal Justice System

In this chapter, we focus on the abundance of scientific documentation about treating drug-dependent adults in the criminal justice system and the issues involved. We will also look at key findings from studies on drug-dependent youth. Drawing on our review of the literature, we will highlight the ingredients for successful treatment, and we will conclude with a critical assessment of treatment available to addicts in the criminal justice system.

Access to Treatment

Since the 1940s, tensions between the punitive approach and offender rehabilitation have shaped correctional systems. Publication of compelling data on the outcomes of these two approaches fuelled fierce paradigm wars (Gendreau and Ross 1987; Martinson 1974). Over the past twenty years or so, however, scientific studies have established the credibility of treatment by showing that repressive penal measures have a negligible impact on recidivism and that measures to rehabilitate and reintegrate offenders have a positive impact (Bonta and Andrews 2003).

Predictably, soon after repressive U.S. drug policies were introduced, courts were bogged down and prisons overcrowded. Not long after, things took an unexpected and alarming turn: recidivism among ex-convicts was very high. The authorities needed a better way to deal with the many addicts for whom repression did not produce the desired effect.

As part of the effort to find that better way, many research projects showed that the presence of problematic drug use is a risk factor for criminal recidivism that can be offset by appropriate intervention (Andrews and Bonta 2006; Belenko 2006; Chandler, Fletcher, and Volkow 2009; Degenhardt and Hall 2012; Dowden and Brown 2002; Strang et al. 2012). This finding is valid for offenders who commit their crimes while intoxicated or to pay for drugs and those for whom the drug–crime dynamic is rooted in common underlying factors.

Services available to offenders with dependence issues are usually aimed at reducing criminal recidivism by enabling them to get their drug use under control. Although we are sensitive to the ethical issues surrounding correctional interventions, we agree with Chandler, Fletcher, and Volkow (2009) that not giving an offender the chance to treat a drug use problem is a missed opportunity to improve the offender's life as well as public health and safety.

We begin with a brief review of how the thinking on treatment in a correctional setting has evolved, and then dedicate the rest of the chapter to drug rehabilitation interventions for offenders who use illicit drugs. We will examine the impact of these programs on reducing crime as well as their limitations and other issues, particularly ethical issues.

Punishment or Rehabilitation?

In the 1950s, North American prisons gradually took to the idea of rehabilitation. With humanist schools of thought dominating psychology, the corrections sector became more receptive to the benefits of clinical psychology, but it was not until the 1970s that the field of clinical criminology research emerged. It was the golden age of clinical criminology and offender rehabilitation. Professionals were playing a prominent role in North American prisons and penitentiaries and were determined to rehabilitate offenders using therapeutic tools borrowed from contemporary clinical psychology.

Then, in 1974, hitherto obscure American sociologist Robert Martinson published an explosive article titled "What Works? Questions and Answers About Prison Reform," in a journal called *Public Interest*.

"Nothing Works"

In the article, Martinson (1974) examined the outcomes of measures to help offenders. His conclusion, entitled "Does nothing work?," made waves. In it, he posed a crushing question: "Do all of these studies lead us irrevocably to the conclusion that nothing works, that we haven't the faintest clue about how to rehabilitate offenders and reduce recidivism?" (p. 48). It was a harsh indictment. Earlier in the article, Martinson had written, "With few and isolated exceptions, the rehabilitative efforts that have been reported so far have had no appreciable effect on recidivism" (p. 25).

The "nothing works" finding associated with Martinson was due partly to flaws in the studies he examined and partly to severe clinical blindness to the reported success of therapeutic methods, which were clearly effective for a clinical psychology clientele but did not produce the expected results when used with offenders. Martinson was the first to expose the major limitations of offender rehabilitation programs. He served as a conduit for a number of perspectives, some diametrically opposed to others, but all critical of rehabilitation programs.

Martinson's article sparked sometimes heated debate between advocates and opponents of such programs. At the time, evaluative methodology was having serious problems clearly defining the positive and negative effects of the programs,[1] so it was difficult to draw valid conclusions about their impact. Because of economic realities and budget priorities, many programs were too short-lived to bear fruit. They were at the mercy of changes in management and policy and were very often compromised by administrative and security priorities.[2]

The Punitive Post-Martinson Era

Proponents of punishment applauded Martinson's report, disseminating it widely in support of their tough-on-crime agenda. These law-and-order advocates claimed that it was impossible for offenders to change either their attitude or their behaviour and that harsh punishment for all criminals was the best way to protect society. Rehabilitation fell out of favour and was no longer the goal of the criminal justice system. Sentencing ceased to take into consideration the possibility of rehabilitation and was based solely on the severity of the crime.

Punishment was back in fashion. Courts imposed harsher and harsher sentences. American lawmakers believed that heavy prison sentences were the cure for all social ills.

Clinical criminologists, psychologists, psychosocial practitioners, doctors, and psychiatrists continued to believe that justice-involved and incarcerated individuals were entitled to the same health services as the rest of the population and that depriving them of psychological and physical care was out of the question. What to do? Did rejection of the rehabilitation model have to mean a wholesale takeover by punishment?

Martinson's conclusion that nothing worked to reduce recidivism spurred clinical criminology researchers to refine their methods and service providers to seek a better understanding of offenders' real needs and adapt their tools accordingly. Fortunately, the post-Martinson era was marked by a thorough re-examination of previous approaches and the implementation of what we now refer to as evidence-based practices.

The response from the field of clinical criminology was vigorous, methodical, and practical. In 1980, Ross and Gendreau published *Effective Correctional Treatment*, and Fréchette and LeBlanc's (1987) research on young offenders contributed a better understanding of delinquency issues that served as a foundation for better intervention.

"What Works?"

The "nothing works" way of thinking gradually gave way to a "What works?" movement (Cullen and Gendreau 2001) in search of promising approaches to offender rehabilitation. Central to the movement's theoretical underpinnings is the notion that correctional interventions must be science-based if they are to be effective, and that they must target the causes and factors that lead to recidivism (Lalande 2004). Studies show that positive, constructive approaches that promote the development of new skills and capitalize on the individual's strengths work because they target the problems at the root of criminal conduct (Andrews and Bonta 2006; Cullen and Gendreau 1989; McGuire 2004; Ward and Maruna 2007). According to Andrews and Bonta (1994), effective intervention to reduce recidivism must be based on three core principles: *risk, need,* and *responsivity.* The *risk* principle means "match[ing] the level of service to the offender's risk to re-offend" (Bonta and Andrews 2007, 1); that is, providing more services to higher-risk offenders and fewer or lower-intensity services to lower-risk offenders. The *need* principle involves "assess[ing] criminogenic needs [dynamic risk factors] and target[ing] them in treatment" (ibid.). The risk-need-responsivity model identifies seven major criminogenic risk/need factors, including drug dependence, that can be targeted in treatment (ibid.).

Lastly, the *responsivity* principle means that, in addition to the first two principles, intervention models must consider the offender's ability to participate in suitable programs and the non-criminogenic needs at the root of the behaviour (Kennedy 2000; Tellier and Serin 2000). The responsivity principle takes into account certain individual characteristics, including motivation to attend treatment, personality, and cognitive limitations. Meta-analyses have shown that, when correctional treatment is based on these principles, significant (around 10 percent) reductions in recidivism and parole revocations are observed (Andrews and Dowden 2006; Cortoni and Lafortune 2009; Hollin and Palmer 2006).

Treating Drug Dependence in Offenders

Over time, scientific discoveries have shown us that rehabilitation programs for drug-dependent offenders are economical and effective solutions that can be introduced at several points in the justice process. We will begin by looking at drug courts, which come into play between the time of arrest and sentencing. We will then examine post-sentencing treatment modalities available to offenders during incarceration, probation, and parole.

Drug Courts

In recent years, increasing awareness of the enormous cost of incarcerating drug-dependent individuals has resulted in growing enthusiasm for an alternative to incarceration: drug treatment courts (DTCs). This initiative, which is popular in North America, involves diverting individuals into drug treatment prior to sentencing. DTCs are not themselves treatment programs, but their personnel, including judges, play an active role in referring offenders to specialized drug rehabilitation services. The goal is to help the legal system and rehabilitation agencies work together to get offenders into treatment and off illicit drugs (Brochu and Landry 2010). Offenders who do not comply with the court's requirements are liable to sanctions ranging from official reprimands to prison sentences.

Despite the methodological weaknesses of research designed to evaluate the efficacy of DTCs (Gutierrez and Bourgon 2009; Slinger and Roesch 2010; Werb et al. 2007), data suggest that these services are promising and reduce criminal recidivism by about 10 percent (Bahr, Masters, and Taylor 2012; Belenko 2001; Brown 2010; Gutierrez and Bourgon 2009; Mitchell et al. 2012; Rempel, Green, and Kralstein, 2012; Werb et al. 2007; Wilson, Mitchell, and MacKenzie 2006). Programs targeting adolescents have smaller effects on recidivism (an odds ratio of 1.06, essentially null) (Mitchell et al. 2012, 64).

Courts with high completion rates that deal with non-violent offenders report greater success in terms of drug-related recidivism. According to Brown, Allison, and Nieto (2010), treatment failure is strongly associated with employability issues, low educational attainment, and polydrug use. Leukefeld et al. (2007) found evidence that participants in court-supervised drug treatment programs that included targeted employment interventions were more likely to find work. For example, those who remained in employment programs longer reported more positive effects on their drug use and criminality during follow-ups than those who left the program earlier or did not participate. Goyette et al. (2013) also showed that many studies found better recidivism reduction outcomes from DTCs that follow the risk-need-responsivity model (Bonta and Andrews 2007).

DTCs have come under fire, however. For one thing, they generally target addicts who are first-time offenders having committed non-violent crimes. In other words, DTCs deal primarily with people who would not be sentenced to imprisonment or who are low risk, which is contrary to risk-need-responsivity principles. For another, although some DTCs have experimented with a harm reduction approach, the emphasis on abstinence makes it difficult for therapists to talk about relapse prevention because, officially, relapse is not tolerated and can result in termination of the program and jail time. Offenders who agree to participate in a drug treatment program through a specialized court have to report on their progress to court authorities much more frequently and for a longer period of time than if they had gone through the regular judicial process (Werb et al. 2007).

Canada has far fewer DTCs than our neighbours to the south. In 2012, Quebec launched a program along similar lines but with some distinct features. Over a number of years, the Court of Quebec tried several initiatives that culminated in the Programme de traitement de la toxicomanie de la Cour du Québec (PTTCQ).[3] By the late 1970s, the Court of Quebec was already factoring successful completion of a treatment program into sentencing in order to promote offender rehabilitation and social reintegration. In 2008, the Centre de réadaptation en dépendance de Montréal – Institut universitaire[4] began working at the Montreal courthouse to evaluate potential risks of withdrawal, assess problems related to drug use intensity, and identify services required to treat the condition (Goyette et al. 2013). The enactment of the *Safe Streets and Communities Act* (Bill C-10) led to the creation of the PTTCQ in November 2012. It took several years to develop the program, the details of which were the subject of several recommendations and reports (Justice Québec 2014). Our team (Plourde et al. 2014) evaluated the implementation of this new initiative and found that one of the strengths of the PTTCQ is that its proposed approach is offender-centred. In addition to offering a personalized approach to participating offenders, it pays special attention to psychosocial elements and does not focus solely on the sentence. It addresses factors associated with maintenance of both delinquency and dependence. A unique feature of this Quebec program is that it is available to clients who have committed more serious crimes and present heavier drug use patterns than similar programs in the rest of Canada and the United States. The PTTCQ's harm reduction philosophy may surprise some and may require fine-tuning, but it is nevertheless commendable. That said, it is important to consider issues related to prolonging placement within the criminal justice system when participants who relapse are returned to the traditional justice system (i.e., transferring cases to a judge, which can lead to imprisonment), in which case the program becomes punitive (Plourde et al. 2014). At the time of writing, Canada does not have specialized DTCs for youth.

Post-sentencing Treatment

Adjudicated youth with substance use problems typically enter treatment by referral or by court order (Breda and Heflinger 2007; Diamond et al. 2006; Dow and Kelly 2013; Fickenscher, Novins, and Beals 2006; Wisdom, Manuel, and Drake 2011). Research on drug-dependent juvenile justice populations referred to treatment shows that, following treatment, they exhibit improvements in terms of both psychoactive substance use and delinquency, as well as in other spheres of their lives, such as their studies (Bergeron et al. 2009; Bertrand et al. 2009; Brunelle et al. 2010). It is important to note, however, that greater initial involvement in delinquent behaviour is associated with poorer drug treatment outcomes among youth (Brunelle et al. 2013). Studies of drug-dependent adolescents focus less on types of treatment received than on pinpointing factors that contribute to their success. We will take a closer look at those factors later in this chapter.

For adults sentenced to short jail terms, addiction treatment availability is relatively limited, considering the needs of the correctional population. Constraints unique to managing short sentences limit services available such that only a minority of inmates receive them (Arseneault, Plourde, and Alain 2014; Belenko and Houser 2012; Brochu and Plourde 2012; Grella et al. 2007; Kivivuori and Linderborg 2009; Stewart 2008; Webster et al. 2007). Conversely, in federal penitentiaries (sentences of two years or more), drug-dependent inmates in Canada have access to an intervention program comprising several stages, from initial assessment to post-treatment follow-up, based on the research and recommendations of an expert panel (Hume 2001; Matheson, Doherty, and Grant 2008). It incorporates cognitive behavioural, motivational, emotional/rational, problem-solving, and relapse prevention interventions. In addition, opiate-dependent inmates can receive methadone maintenance treatment and, as of 2002, can initiate this treatment while incarcerated (Plourde et al. 2005).

> I wanted to quit using heroin because I was so sick, it was killing me, but I wanted to keep using coke because there was no . . . no reason for me to stop until I was in jail and I did some programs and I felt better. Then I realized that it was ruining my life. (Jane)[5] (Plourde et al. 2007)

Some of the factors that lead to increased treatment participation are unique to offenders, but others are organizational and structural (Belenko and Houser 2012; Fletcher et al. 2009). The latter include:

(1) separate budget from host penitentiary administration;
(2) administrative independence;
(3) being somewhat isolated from the regular penitentiary environment to recreate a therapeutic environment;
(4) establishing a set of rules and consequences for breaking them;

(5) staff who act as positive role models for inmates and see themselves as therapists who care about the well-being of the participants rather than as officers responsible for security;

(6) encouraging participants to acquire new skills (that they can use in the job market or to resolve family problems);

(7) regular follow-ups with people who have completed the program; and

(8) using services provided by community resources.

Let us now take a more detailed look at the approaches that most treatments available to drug-dependent offenders are based on. Almost all the approaches or models are used within and outside of correctional institutions. Cognitive-behavioural programs and therapeutic communities are the primary intervention approaches in North American penal institutions.

Cognitive-Behavioural Programs

In addiction treatment, programs based on cognitive-behavioural theories view the development and continuation of drug use in certain contexts as classical or operant conditioning rooted in individual problems, which are themselves influenced by developmental, cognitive, and environmental factors (Deas and Thomas 2001; Waldron and Kaminer 2004). The goal of *cognitive-behavioural treatment* of addicted offenders is generally to define and modify stimuli associated with drug use, transform thoughts about drug use and delinquent behaviour, learn problem-solving techniques, and develop relapse prevention strategies (Blume 2005).

Studies on cognitive-behavioural programs for justice-involved individuals, including those convicted of drug-related crimes, have shown promising results with respect to the elements targeted in treatment, including drug use and criminal recidivism (Bahr, Masters, and Taylor 2012; Crane and Blud 2012; Easton et al. 2007; Moore et al. 2008; Roberts-Lewis et al. 2009). Nevertheless, as Comiskey, Stapleton, and Kelly (2012) observed, although this type of treatment has a positive effect on criminality, benefits may not last more than a few months.

Therapeutic Communities and Boot Camps

Therapeutic communities (TCs) are among the most stable correctional programs whose effects have been evaluated. In a prison setting, this type of intervention is one solution to *prisonization*,[6] a process by which inmates come to denigrate traditional social values (Peat and Winfree 1992). Participants often "receive a variety of treatment modalities, including cognitive therapy, individual counseling, group counseling, and 12-step programs" (Bahr, Masters, and Taylor 2012, 159). All TCs, whether they are inside or outside penal institutions, share certain basic principles, such as hierarchical community organization; confronting past values, attitudes, and behaviours; and the importance of community and peer support (Vandevelde et al. 2004). In hierarchical TCs, more senior members of the group show recruits and junior members the manual and psychological tasks to be done. Community life is an important element of these programs because it enables individuals to acquire social skills and show concern for other people. Participants confront individuals who exhibit an attitude or a behaviour that is against the community's values and try to persuade them to change the behaviour.

In TCs, individuals function as the main agents of their own change. Staff are, for the most part, former clients of the program. They keep domestic and therapeutic activities running smoothly and ensure that the community's values are upheld. When they intervene with community members, they do not adopt a client–counsellor approach (McCollister et al. 2003). The following characteristics are typical of the vast majority of TCs:

(1) in prison-based TCs, community members are relatively isolated from other inmates;

(2) activities are structured and regulated;

(3) privileges are earned gradually but are not irrevocable;[7]

(4) members must accept their personal and community responsibilities;

(5) members must make a constant effort to transform their values, change their lifestyle, and create an environment that supports the rehabilitation of all members;

(6) members must fit into a relatively rigid hierarchical structure;

(7) within that structure, more senior members act a role models for recruits;

(8) discipline is omnipresent, and failure to comply is punished severely; and

(9) members benefit from aftercare.

Despite the inherent limitations of evaluating treatment efficacy (Arseneault, Plourde, and Alain 2014), some of which have to do with challenges related to the prison environment, research on TCs has produced encouraging findings with respect to the rehabilitation of drug-dependent people in the criminal justice system. Hiller, Knight, and Simpson (2006) found that "a significantly smaller proportion of graduates were rearrested during the 2nd year after release compared to those who drop out of treatment or who do not receive treatment" (p. 230). They found no difference between the groups during the first year after treatment. In the vast majority of studies in the literature, two elements stand out as crucial to the success of these programs: treatment duration and therapeutic aftercare. We will take a closer look at these elements below.

In North America, more radical interpretations of TCs led to the development of *shock incarceration*, more widely known as *boot camp*. The first of these was set up in the United States in 1983,[8] and boot camps spread at a staggering pace. Despite ardent enthusiasm for the idea, it was not long before impact studies threw cold water on it (National Institute of Justice 2003b). At their peak, in the 1990s, there were seventy-five state and federal boot camps for adult offenders, thirty for juvenile offenders, and eighteen more in county prisons, with a total of nearly 10,000 participants (National Institute of Justice 1996, 2003b). In the 2000s, half were shut down, and the number of participants declined by a third. The programs have evolved somewhat, but the basic philosophy has not changed. Boot camp is physical and psychological intervention that lasts three to four months and is intended to instill strict discipline and bring about a radical lifestyle transformation (National Institute of Justice 2003b). This approach to rehabilitation employs some of the same techniques as TCs, but disciplinary measures are modelled after military boot camps. The idea is that individuals subjected to rigorous physical and psychological training will come to respect authority and embrace the values upheld by dominant social institutions. Although this military-style program aligns well with the American "war on drugs" mindset, studies show that it is not usually a winning strategy. Participants report positive attitude and behavioural changes in the short term, but these changes do not reduce recidivism (ibid.). However, more recent work suggests that boot camps can reduce recidivism among the highest-risk participants, especially if they include an aftercare component (Bahr, Masters, and Taylor 2012). These findings contrast with earlier research that deemed boot camps ineffective.

Peer Support and Twelve-Step Groups

Peer support movements (e.g., Alcoholics Anonymous, Narcotics Anonymous, Cocaine Anonymous) available to non-incarcerated individuals also have a strong presence in penal institutions. Members of these movements visit inmates regularly and base their interventions on the twelve-step model. They organize groups that encourage participants to share personal experiences and be abstinent.

Peer support movements view problematic substance use as a disease (Brown, Seraganian, and Tremblay 2001; Sheehan 2004) influenced by contextual factors. Offenders present drug-induced brain chemistry dysfunction that may interfere with their understanding of what is socially acceptable and, therefore, alter their behaviour (Sheehan 2004).

In the early 1990s, the National Institute on Alcohol Abuse and Alcoholism in the United States funded a research project that culminated in the *Twelve Step Facilitation Therapy Manual* (Nowinski, Baker, and Carroll 1992), standardizing the application of this treatment modality. To foster social skills, twelve-step programs are delivered in a group setting rather than on an individual basis (Sheehan 2004). The program employs various intervention strategies, including the following: (1) therapy that teaches new coping strategies and enhances motivation; (2) education about self-knowledge and social skills training; and (3) sponsorship by other program participants to provide social support.

According to Bahr, Masters, and Taylor (2012), "although 12-step programs are widely used, there has been . . . little . . . research evaluating their effectiveness . . . . Overall, the evidence suggests that 12-step programs are not as effective as other treatments in reducing drug use and recidivism" (p. 164).

Methadone Maintenance Programs

The most common pharmacological treatment available in prison is methadone, a synthetic opioid analgesic that enables opiate-dependent individuals to avoid withdrawal symptoms. It can be used as a replacement for opiate use or to help people stop using opiates entirely. According to Bahr, Masters, and Taylor (2012), "the objective is to . . . enable the addicts to live relatively normal lives." Despite some progress, methadone maintenance programs are still underutilized (Nunn et al. 2009), though they do exist in custody settings in Europe, the United States, Australia, and Canada.

Methadone maintenance programs have yielded positive results (Bahr, Masters, and Taylor 2012; Canadian HIV/AIDS Legal Network 2008; Gordon et al. 2008; Hedrich et al. 2011; Plourde et al. 2005; Stallwitz and Stöver 2007) for treatment recipients, including reductions in drug use, repeat incarcerations, and serious drug-related crimes. Other studies have found that high methadone doses (over 60 mg) can contribute to better health, social stabilization, greater health services take-up (Stallwitz and Stöver 2007), and reductions in associated risk behaviours (Hedrich et al. 2011). Methadone maintenance programs offered in custody and post-release reduce mortality risk significantly (Degenhardt et al. 2014; Larney et al. 2014). It is therefore important for such treatment to begin without delay in prison (Larney et al. 2014) and to continue post-release (Degenhardt et al. 2014; Gordon et al. 2008; Kinlock et al. 2007; Larney et al. 2012; MacSwain et al. 2014). People who begin treatment in prison are more likely to pursue treatment upon release (Kinlock et al. 2007, 2008, 2009; MacSwain et al. 2014). Continuity of treatment initiated during incarceration is also crucial. Interruption pre- or post-release is associated with an increase in risky injection behaviours, such as sharing needles, which increases the risk of hepatitis C and HIV infection (Hedrich et al. 2011; Stallwitz and Stöver 2007).

Although some of the challenges related to organizing methadone maintenance programs in correctional settings mirror realities on the outside, it goes without saying that, as Mužinić et al. (2011) point out, some issues are unique to treating opioid-dependent people in prison. Length of detention, which is often unknown or variable, is one issue that can influence the decision to initiate treatment. Misuse and trafficking, which are common on the outside, present challenges that penal institutions lack the resources to address and that can affect security (Plourde et al. 2012; Plourde et al. 2013; Stallwitz and Stöver 2006). Nevertheless, it is important to note that methadone maintenance programs reduce demand for illicit opiates in prisons (McMillan, Lapham, and Lackey 2008).

Motivational Interviewing

Motivational interviewing (MI) founders Miller and Rollnick define it as a directive, client-centred counselling style that strives to strengthen intrinsic motivation for change by exploring and resolving ambivalence (Miller and Rollnick 2002). MI is useful in all therapeutic contexts in which ambivalence and motivation are central to the desired change process.

According to Miller and Rollnick, client ambivalence is rooted in conflict between the pros and cons of various courses of action, which leads to an impasse regarding the possibility of change. MI practitioners view ambivalence as a normal process that can be resolved by exploring the client's values. MI guides help therapists work with clients to address their ambivalence (CSAT 1999; Miller and Rollnick 2002). One advantage of MI is its flexibility; it can be used together with other therapeutic modalities.

Studies of offenders with problem alcohol and cannabis use have shown that, in this context, MI is at least as effective as other types of addiction treatment if not more so, and is clearly better than no treatment at all. For individuals with problem use of other drugs, MI is more effective than no treatment and equal to other treatments for substance use (Lundahl and Burke 2009). One meta-analysis found that improvements associated with MI are maintained in the long term and that longer exposure to the approach has a positive influence on outcomes (ibid.). Another meta-analysis of MI with drug-dependent offenders showed that the approach "can lead to improved retention in treatment [and] enhanced motivation to change" (McMurran 2009, 83).

Co-occurring Mental Health and Substance Use Disorders

The presence of co-occurring disorders complicates treatment of drug-dependent offenders. Not all correctional institutions are equipped to provide the rehabilitation services this clientele needs (Chandler et al. 2004). Fletcher et al. (2007) profiled offenders who participated in the U.S. National Institute on Drug Abuse's Criminal Justice Drug Abuse Treatment Studies: 40 percent of the people in the sample reported serious depression, serious anxiety, or major concentration problems at some point in their lives. Mental health problems are also associated with heavier drug use. Hills (2000) identified the following principles that should be incorporated into treatment of offenders with co-occurring disorders no matter the treatment model employed:

(1) integrating treatment programming,
(2) simultaneously treating both disorders as primary,
(3) developing an individualized service plan to address specific symptoms and deficits,
(4) using medication when appropriate,
(5) tailoring intervention to the setting,
(6) continuing treatment when offenders return to the community, and
(7) providing support and self-help groups to assist reintegration into the community.

Cognitive-behavioural therapy and therapeutic communities are among the approaches that have been adapted to integrated treatment for individuals with co-occurring disorders (ibid.).

Integrated cognitive-behavioural therapy is especially suitable for individuals with a co-occurring psychotic disorder and sets out three primary objectives: (1) dispel misconceptions about psychoactive substances, (2) enable individuals to understand how drugs affect manifestations of their mental illness, and (3) help them recognize signs of psychosis relapse and find a solution to drug use (Rahioui and Karila 2006).

Personal reflections is a modified TC program delivered in a correctional setting for people with co-occurring disorders that addresses the individual's psychoactive substance use, criminal behaviours, and mental health disorders (Sacks et al. 2004). It includes cognitive-behavioural protocols, psychoeducational classes, and medication. Sacks and his collaborators (ibid.) found that this approach led to a reduction in criminal activity, particularly among those who receive aftercare.

Ingredients for Treatment Success

Studies of drug-dependent offender treatment have revealed key ingredients and characteristics for success. These include screening and assessment, personalized plans, relapse prevention, motivation, and judicial pressure.

Screening and Assessment

Screening for drug use problems is an important step in referring identified individuals for further assessment and placing them in a treatment program suited to their needs (CSAT 2005). Of course, addiction
treatment practices in Canada vary from one province to the next
with respect to screening, assessment, and treatment. In Quebec, the
most commonly used screening tool for adults is the Assessment and
Screening of Assistance Needs – Alcohol/Drugs (Tremblay, Rouillard,
and Sirois 2004).[9] The most popular screening instrument for youth is
the DEP-ADO (Germain et al. 2007).[10]

A greater understanding of the severity of problem drug use
requires an in-depth assessment of the substances used, along with
an assessment of several other dimensions, such as motivation to
change, resistance to treatment, criminal behaviour, health, the
presence of psychopathic and antisocial traits or psychiatric problems, and support network (CSAT 2005; CASA 2010). In the United
States, the Center for Substance Abuse Treatment, or CSAT, recommends using the Addiction Severity Index, a scientifically validated
instrument, to evaluate problem drug use in offenders (McLellan et
al. 1980). Another instrument, the Global Appraisal of Individual
Needs (GAIN) (Dennis, Feeney, and Titus 2013) is used to assess
an individual's biopsychosocial profile and is recommended by the
U.S. Substance Abuse and Mental Health Services Administration.
Motivation to change can also be assessed using the University of
Rhode Island Change-Assessment Scale (McConnaughy, Prochaska,
and Velicer 1983) or the TCU Treatment Motivation Scales (Simpson
1992).[11] Instruments used to assess antisocial or psychopathic person-
ality traits include the Psychopathy Checklist-Revised (PCL-R) (Hare
1991, 2003), the Millon Clinical Multiaxial Inventory-III (MCMI-III)
(Millon, Millon, and Davis 1996), and the Minnesota Multiphasic
Personality Inventory-2 (MMPI-2) (Butcher et al. 1989).

As mentioned above, assessment of problem drug use varies tre-
mendously across Canada. GAIN is becoming more popular in addiction rehabilitation facilities in Quebec and Ontario, but it is not used
consistently across jurisdictions. Correctional Service Canada uses the
Computerized Assessment of Substance Abuse for intake assessments
and as needed thereafter (Correctional Service Canada 2003). It com-
bines four instruments: the Alcohol Dependence Scale (ADS) (Skinner
and Horn 1984), the Drug Abuse Screening Test (DAST) (Skinner 1982),

the Michigan Alcoholism Screening Test (MAST) (Selzer 1981), and the Severity of Dependence Scale (SDS) (Gossop et al. 1995). Services correctionnels du Québec uses the Level of Service/Case Management Inventory (LS-CMI) to assess its clientele, although the use of this instrument is currently undergoing review (Andrews, Bonta, and Wormith 2004). The LS-CMI assesses a series of criminogenic needs, including substance misuse, and is used to develop correctional intervention plans.

An ethical analysis of certain aspects of these assessment tools is entirely appropriate. In some cases, a lawyer or judge may recommend treatment for an accused even if his or her problem and needs have not been carefully evaluated by an expert, and in others, justice-involved individuals may be subjected to an addiction assessment even if they do not want one.

Personalized Plans

After in-depth assessment of problem drug use, co-occurring mental disorders, antisocial traits, criminal attitudes, and motivation and readiness for change, the next step is treatment planning (CSAT 2005). The CSAT recommends that drug-dependent offenders be involved in every step of the process to ensure a comprehensive understanding of the circumstances surrounding their drug use and the full range of their needs to facilitate rehabilitation. If appropriate, treatment planning should also involve individuals from clients' social systems, such as family members and employers, as well as the full range of professionals involved, including those from the legal system. The CSAT (2005) also recommends that treatment plans be updated regularly. From a motivational perspective, treatment plans should be based on individuals' strengths rather than their weaknesses to reduce resistance and increase self-efficacy. Service intensity varies depending on several factors, such as the presence of psychopathic traits. Wanberg and Milkman (1998) identified some of the elements common to effective treatment plans: strategies that enhance motivation for treatment; and cognitive-behavioural methods, such as strengthening social-skills training, and developing coping strategies. Lastly, treatment plans must be informed by evidence-based practices (ACRDQ 2010; Blume 2005; CSAT 2005), some of which we discuss below.

Relapse Prevention

Canada's Department of Justice (2003) recommends incorporating relapse prevention into treatment of drug-dependent young offenders to reduce their rate of recidivism. Relapse prevention is a treatment modality that includes a range of elements inspired by the cognitive-behavioural approach and aims to maintain psychoactive substance use cessation (Lukasiewicz and Frenoy Peres 2006). It requires an assessment at the beginning of treatment to identify factors that could trigger a relapse. Clients are given an opportunity to observe their behaviours and thoughts to better understand their risk factors and to delve deeper into certain aspects, such as risky situations, expectations about the effects of drugs, periods of withdrawal, lifestyle, and coping strategies (ibid.). Therapists can also use the assessment period to inform and educate clients about various aspects of their drug use. Then they can help clients analyze their reactions and automatic thoughts in risk situations, acquire new coping strategies, and try to enhance self-efficacy. They can also work on distinguishing missteps from a relapse, which is important because if a person uses again it can trigger automatic thoughts and negative feelings of shame and guilt. These feelings can be recognized and reframed using cognitive-behavioural techniques (ibid.). Since relapse prevention is usually just one component of a larger program, it is difficult to assess the outcomes of this modality in isolation. Studies that assess the overall impact of this prevention model on recidivism are inconclusive. However, a meta-analysis by Dowden, Antonowicz, and Andrews (2003) showed that some parts of the model, such as training someone close to the client and understanding the offence chain, have a significant effect on reducing recidivism.

Motivation

People with a criminal record, or who have been referred for treatment through criminal proceedings, tend to have bad reputations with addiction treatment providers because clinicians often observe that they downplay their drug use problems. Acknowledging a problem is an indicator of motivation, one that addiction professionals associate with therapeutic success. According to many treatment providers, users who are aware of their problem and who feel affected by the consequences of drug use are more apt to take responsibility and change their behaviour. In contrast, they see clients who have little or no awareness of the consequences, who often participate in treatment solely to fulfil release conditions, as likely to abandon the process in the absence of judicial constraints.

Motivation plays a fundamental role in the addiction recovery process (Gregoire and Burke 2004; Simpson, Joe, and Brown 1997). "Although complicated by physiological and psychological dependence, an abuser's motivation and intentions represent a critical part of the process of recovery and healing" (DiClemente, Schlundt, and Gemmell 2004, 103). Motivation was long considered a relatively stable personality trait, but we now know that it is dynamic (Miller 1985).

The transtheoretical model of change (TMC) (DiClemente 2006; Prochaska, DiClemente, and Norcross 1992) is based on this idea and matches clients to five dynamic "stages of change." Clients at the *precontemplation* stage do not recognize that they have a problem or that they need treatment. Those at the *contemplation* stage are aware of the problems their substance use is causing. At the *preparation* stage, they begin to consider the possibility of change and assess their courses of action, and, at the *action* stage, they make changes to achieve the desired improvements. *Maintenance* is when they consolidate those improvements.

Motivation is a regulatory process that can be either intrinsic or extrinsic. "Intrinsically motivated behaviours are what people do by choice" (McMurran and Ward 2004, 303). For a person beginning therapy for drug dependence, intrinsic motivation may be expressed as interest and curiosity about the treatment process (Ryan and Deci 2008). "Extrinsically motivated behaviours are under external control and are performed to acquire rewards or avoid punishment" (McMurran and Ward 2004, 303). It is also important to distinguish between motivation for treatment and motivation for change. The first has to do with the individual's readiness to seek help and engage in therapeutic activities (DiClemente, Schlundt, and Gemmell 2004), while the second refers to the importance an individual attributes to his or her difficulties and how he or she views the possibility of change (Miller and Rollnick 2002; Rollnick, Mason, and Butler 1999). Many studies (Bergeron et al. 2009; Breda and Heflinger 2007; Fickenscher, Novins, and Beals 2006; Schroder et al. 2009; Wisdom et al. 2011) define motivation for treatment as a dynamic driver of positive drug treatment outcomes. Wisdom et al. (2011) also note that external factors, such as long waiting lists that delay access to specialized services, can enhance or detract from that motivation. In other words, both individual and organizational factors are involved. Unfortunately, these organizational factors are not accounted for in the majority of studies on this subject.

Some studies have focused on understanding the factors that boost motivation for treatment among youth. These include victimization, such as emotional abuse (Rosenkranz et al. 2012), and substance use severity upon entering treatment (Austin et al. 2010; Breda and Heflinger 2007; Rosenkranz et al. 2012). The most highly motivated young people are those who were victimized the most and who were the heaviest drug users. These characteristics are common to many youth in the criminal justice system. Austin and her co-investigators (2010) also showed that children perceive parents who use psychoactive drugs as providing less parental support, and less parental support is associated with lower motivation to change. Young people who perceive themselves as socially well integrated (sense of belonging to a group) at the end of treatment are more motivated to change their consumption habits or to maintain changes they have made (Wei et al. 2011).

Brunelle et al. (2010) reviewed the results of five Quebec studies of drug-dependent adolescents conducted in the 2000s and made the following observations regarding motivation for treatment and change: (1) youth are not very motivated to change their drug use (and still less to cease it entirely), (2) motivation increases over the course of treatment, and (3) many of them credit a good counsellor–client therapeutic alliance with improvements in both motivation and drug use.

Judicial Pressure

Very interestingly, research has shown that individuals who begin treatment by court order may reduce their psychoactive substance use as much as those who enter treatment voluntarily and that it may have a positive effect on both drug use and criminal recidivism (Landry et al. 2009; CASA 2010; Schaub et al. 2010).

Many people who work in criminal justice agree that, in court, the tacit threat of prison is the foremost motivator for drug-dependent people to agree to therapy. Brochu and his fellow researchers (2006) studied five Canadian addiction rehabilitation centres and found similar results, though they highlighted some important distinctions with respect to treatment retention and outcomes. Our results showed higher treatment retention among people who are awaiting charges, trial, or sentencing; who are under pressure to commit to treatment; and who have not yet entered the correctional system. It is therefore reasonable to conclude that the threat perceived by offenders has the impact desired by the courts in terms of diverting offenders toward therapy. It is important to note, however, that this impact is observed only at the pre-sentencing level. Probationers and parolees seem less fazed by the consequences of not participating in court-recommended treatment. All the same, treatment retention is not necessarily associated with improvements in substance use problems in this study, at least not with respect to drugs. We can assume that perceived judicial pressures have a positive effect on treatment initiation and retention for some offenders, but that does not necessarily translate into better outcomes vis-à-vis substance use problems. Pre-sentencing judicial pressure gives therapists an opportunity to initiate a therapeutic alliance, which is key to the offender participating in treatment in the absence of judicial constraints. Without a therapeutic alliance, offenders are highly likely to drop out. On the other end of the judicial or, rather, correctional spectrum, Tétrault and her collaborators (2007) observed especially high motivation for treatment and change among men in halfway houses or on parole.

Qualitative studies improve our understanding of what motivates offenders to accept addiction treatment. A Belgian study (Vandevelde et al. 2006) explored the expectations, needs, and motivations of incarcerated and released offenders. It identified both extrinsic and intrinsic motivations among participants. The most frequently reported extrinsic reasons for entering and remaining in treatment were hoping to be released sooner, not wanting to be sent back to prison for another drug crime, and social network pressures.

Intrinsic motivations included the desire to make something of their lives, to limit the impact of their actions on loved ones, and to improve their social network (ibid.). The qualitative component of a study by Stevens and his collaborators (2006) of people entering "quasi-compulsory treatment" (treatment for drug dependence ordered by the criminal justice system) in five European countries showed that this can be an opportunity for clients to engage with treatment services even if they might not have done so absent judicial pressure. Some of the participants had been waiting for treatment prior to their arrest; others did not perceive the coercive aspect and took ownership of the decision to begin treatment and their treatment goals. However, for clients with less favourable therapeutic outcomes, motivation seemed to have more to do with not being incarcerated than with intrinsic motivation for treatment. Treatment staff interviewed for the study talked about client ambivalence and the difficulty evaluating motivation because some clients choose to report intrinsic motivators even though their true motivators are extrinsic (Stevens et al. 2006). A qualitative study of twenty-seven Montreal child protection agency clients (Magrinelli Orsi 2011) showed that some perceived the controlled environment provided by the agency as a motivator to try to change drug use habits; others did not consider the environmental constraints to have affected them. Magrinelli Orsi (2011) suggested that it might be best to avoid labelling troubled youth as motivated or not motivated to change their drug use habits because perceptions about the need to make changes and the opportunity to do so vary so much from one youth to the next.

It appears that individuals compelled to be in treatment can reduce their drug use (Stevens et al. 2006), and that not everyone under judicial pressure feels forced to enter treatment (Brunelle et al. 2014; Magrinelli Orsi and Brochu, 2009). A court order to enter treatment does not necessarily mean involuntary participation. In fact, Fickenscher and her collaborators (2006) found that drug-dependent adolescents' degree of concern about legal pressure, not the presence of legal pressure itself, was related to treatment completion. Once again, we see that it is important to consider how social actors perceive their circumstances.

> Being here [in a treatment centre] was really good for me. . . . I was lucky to get in, and it helped me. . . . Personally, I've started working on myself. . . . I didn't even know I had all these tools. (Achille) (Brunelle et al. 2014)

Thus, we find no black or white here, only shades of grey. The good news is that motivation is flexible, mutable. Data suggest that pressure from the courts may be effective in eliciting sufficient extrinsic motivation for individuals to agree to treatment prior to sentencing. However, for offenders to remain in treatment beyond the first few sessions, therapists must form an alliance with them. This means that therapists have an important role to play in bringing about change in their clients' motivation.

The Therapeutic Relationship

We know that certain therapist characteristics influence the development of the relationship and the change process for people with dependencies. Therapists must have certain qualities identified by Rogers (1957), such as empathy, authenticity, warmth, and respect, to form a therapeutic alliance starting at the screening and referral stages (Arseneault 2009; Brunelle et al. 2015; Diamond et al. 2006; Hawley and Garland 2008; Mee-Lee, McLellan, and Miller 2010).

Therapeutic alliance means that the therapist and the client agree on treatment objectives and work well together (Wanberg and Milkman 1998). According to Fitzpatrick and Irannejad (2008), developing a personalized treatment plan and reviewing it periodically with the client is an important part of creating a therapeutic alliance. Bordin (1979) defines it as an emotional bond arising from active collaboration between the client and the therapist that includes agreeing on a change-focused goal and identifying tasks involved in achieving that goal. Thus, three key features must be present: the bond, the goals, and the tasks.

> Well, he [the caseworker involved in the referral] was always humane, he was understanding, and he suggested this [the treatment] to me, by sort of suggesting a decrease in my use, but not total abstinence. (Berthe) (Brunelle et al. 2015)

The first of these, the bond, involves the emotional aspect of the alliance, the client–counsellor relationship. Confidence, caring, and engagement are central to the relationship (Baillargeon and Puskas 2013). Full confidence and bonding are vital to gaining access to the client's inner experience (Bordin 1979). The second, goals, depends on mutual agreement and collaboration between the therapist and the client regarding treatment goals. The third, tasks, relates to treatment modalities and agreement between the client and the therapist about the steps to be taken. Baillargeon and Puskas (2013) explain that tasks must match the client's expectations, must not make the client uncomfortable, and must be related to the goals. These three key features of the therapeutic alliance are interdependent. A key finding of the literature review by Meier, Barrowclough, and Donmall (2005) is that early therapeutic alliance promotes subsequent engagement and retention in treatment. The therapeutic alliance is related to previous treatment experiences and the client's degree of motivation. For adolescents in substance abuse treatment, lack of social support and antisocial personality traits are associated with difficulty establishing a good therapeutic alliance (Garner, Godley, and Funk 2008). However, those with more severe drug use upon entering treatment develop a better therapeutic alliance during treatment (Bertrand et al. 2013a; Garner, Godley, and Funk 2008).

Literature about the therapeutic alliance for drug-dependent individuals in the criminal justice system is limited (Meier, Barrowclough, and Donmall 2005). Joe and his fellow researchers (2001) showed that the presence of a good therapeutic relationship, regardless of satisfaction with or duration of treatment, is related to lower rates of illegal activity and problem drug use. Cournoyer and his co-investigators (2007) separated individuals beginning drug treatment into three groups: those with criminal justice involvement, those with mental health problems, and those with neither. They found that people in the first group were more resistant and had a more negative attitude toward treatment than members of the other two groups, but that a therapeutic alliance with those in the first group was more likely to develop if the therapist was perceived as involved and understanding.

Adequate Treatment Duration

Several studies have shown that longer treatment duration for those who need it and treatment completion generally produce better outcomes (Best et al. 2008; Lang and Belenko 2000; Moos and Moos 2003; Zarkin et al. 2002). According to Laudet, Stanick, and Sands (2009), treatment retention "is associated with stabilization and/or improvement in protective resources that, in turn, bolster the long-term effects of treatment" (p. 182). Huebner and Cobbina (2007) analyzed the results of drug treatment given to probationers. Participants who completed treatment were less likely to reoffend than those who failed to complete treatment.

Certain factors may predict better treatment retention (Casares-López et al. 2013; Lang and Belenko 2000). These include a better social support network, fewer difficulties with loved ones in the months preceding arrest, intrinsic motivation, and few or no psychiatric problems or personality disorders. Individuals with aggressive-sadistic, narcissistic, or borderline personalities, or with hypomania, are more likely to drop out of treatment. Best and his collaborators (2008) showed that drug-dependent offenders with a history of heavier drug use prior to entering treatment and with fewer periods of incarceration were more likely to persevere.

We believe that accumulation of services for people with chronic dependence issues may satisfy the requirement for adequate exposure to treatment. A Quebec study of drug-dependent adults found that the cumulative effects of multiple treatment episodes had a positive impact on their rehabilitation trajectories, particularly for individuals recruited in courts (Brunelle et al. 2015).

Aftercare

It is well established that a transition between correctional programs and community-based aftercare is desirable and that service continuity promotes successful social reintegration and lower recidivism compared to prison-based treatment alone (Bahr, Masters, and Taylor 2012; Grella et al. 2007).

A number of studies have shown that offenders who participated in therapeutic community treatment while incarcerated reoffend less, and that post-release treatment continuation significantly improves their behaviour and the likelihood of successful social reintegration (Bahr, Masters, and Taylor 2012; Burdon et al. 2007).

Burdon's team examined whether post-prison treatment intensity affected therapeutic success. Their findings were interesting in that, contrary to what they expected, they observed that "subjects benefited equally from outpatient and residential aftercare, regardless of the severity of their [substance use] problem," although they did not define the intensity of either type of aftercare (Burdon et al. 2007). Their work indicates the need for a sophisticated assessment of the individual's needs and the treatment intensity level required, for an evaluation of services provided by treatment centres, and for a continuum of care that recognizes progress made in prison-based treatment.

According to the National Institute on Drug Abuse's thirteen principles of drug abuse treatment for criminal justice populations, community-based treatment is essential to sustaining gains achieved in prison (Fletcher and Chandler 2007). Bahr, Masters, and Taylor concur that "effective treatment programs . . . include an aftercare component" (2012, 155).

Extension of Social Control

Offering therapeutic services outside correctional settings may entail an extension of social control that treatment providers sometimes refuse to take on. In their regular practice, most of them are not in the habit of spying on their clients, and they have no intention of taking on a supervisory role for this population. When rehabilitation centres accept legally mandated clients, that is just one step removed from making participation in treatment mandatory or in addition to incarceration, or from making it a condition for release.

This raises the very real risk of blurring the line between punishment and rehabilitation. Rehabilitation becomes punishment, and the possibility of substantial extension of official control beyond what would otherwise exist emerges. This opens the door to punitive measures having less to do with offences committed than with the probability of reoffending. Can we in good conscience accept this?

For criminology researchers and practitioners, the discussion around drug treatment for the criminal justice population is a lively one that goes well beyond determining whether prison-based treatments are effective. Is it possible to truly assess drug dependence within that population? What limitations are there on the power and the right to intervene in a coercive environment? Would it not be best to wait until offenders have served their sentences and then recommend they sign up for a treatment program in their home community?

For people deprived of their liberty, a coercive environment is certainly not conducive to cooperating with those responsible for supervising them. In many cases, offenders may believe that their own interests clash with the goals of the criminal justice system (such as public safety and security).

Justice-involved individuals typically look for the best way to make the process as quick and painless as possible. Some try to convince judges that they are not fully responsible for their criminal actions because they have a serious drug problem. Their goal is to serve their sentence in a treatment centre where discipline is less harsh than in prison or to get a suspended sentence. Another strategy, which seems counterintuitive at first glance but actually makes sense for convicted offenders, is to deny the existence of a drug problem so as to be granted parole as soon as possible. Offenders understand that correctional authorities associate drug dependence with recidivism, so they try to avoid being labelled as addicts. Justice-involved individuals often feel the need to obfuscate and withhold full cooperation from those responsible for helping them.

The Real Client

Many other important questions bear asking. Who is the real client? To whom is the treatment provider accountable? The person in the provider's care or, as is often the case, the institution that refers the person for treatment? What drives intervention requests? A true desire for change or the desire to make the right impression on corrections officials and those responsible for granting parole? How should a treatment provider approach clients who were referred by prison officials and could be transferred or denied parole if they drop out of or fail treatment? Do providers have the right to exert pressure to elicit change, and what kind of pressure is appropriate? By whom and by what standards is change deemed positive? How should pressure be exerted? What tools should be used?

Do some prison-based therapeutic actions violate the individual's rights? Does a coercive setting taint interventions? Do some of the existing programs reinforce abuse of authority?

Can a person seeking treatment be denied it? Can providers abdicate their responsibility to offer suitable health care? To guard against offenders being forced to take steps toward change, should they bear full responsibility for their own lifestyle change with no therapeutic support whatsoever? Is there any reason to believe that offenders will maintain their desire for change post-release if no support was provided during incarceration? Will they have the determination to withstand the pressure of a new institution (a treatment centre) having recently regained their freedom?

It is also important to talk about what motivates treatment providers to work with people who have experienced prison socialization and who seem disinclined to help themselves. Some clients may try to recreate a known environment by reproducing elements of the prison code, which interferes with the traditional therapeutic process by discouraging people from opening up and accepting divergent viewpoints. This can affect the creation of a therapeutic alliance with the offender, which reduces the likelihood of positive treatment outcomes. Some clinicians even believe that admitting individuals from the criminal justice system, who may be recalcitrant and can have a negative impact on the group therapy environment, can obstruct the therapeutic process for all clients.

Boundaries and Bridges

Rigid boundaries between security and rehabilitation priorities and clear expectations on the part of everyone involved are key to preventing the aforementioned ethical issues from cropping up. Some professionals who work with drug-dependent criminal justice populations agree with the authorities not to write reports about their clients' progress. They do this in part because they do not want their clientele to be made up solely of individuals who just want to make a good impression on prison officials and in part because they want to provide some reassurance to clients who might hesitate to open up for fear that doing so could affect how long they remain under judicial supervision. This approach recognizes that offenders have a fundamental right to expect that information they disclose during the therapeutic process will be kept confidential. This is why, in some countries, public health intervention falls under the jurisdiction of health services, not corrections. Interdepartmental bureaucracy ensures the integrity of that boundary. On the surface, that integrity seems easier to ensure when the criminal justice system refers offenders to drug treatment centres located outside prison environments (Sullivan et al. 2007).

In this context, intervention must bridge the realm of criminal justice on the one hand and that of treatment on the other. Regardless of the services available to offenders while incarcerated, they must have every opportunity to use treatment services in the community. Bridging the criminal justice world and the health and social services arena reinforces the necessary boundaries between helping and controlling, roles that prison and penitentiary personnel are all too often expected to fulfil simultaneously. Collaborative initiatives such as the one between the Centre de détention de Québec[12] and the rehabilitation unit at the Centre intégré universitaire de santé et de services sociaux de la Capitale-Nationale,[13] which provides in-house services, seem to work very well (Arseneault 2014; Ferland et al. 2013; Plourde et al. 2015). Building these bridges takes work because criminal justice and health and social services are two separate worlds, each with their own culture. One is focused on public safety, and the other on health and personal development. One is naturally suspicious, while the other is more trusting. Nevertheless, dealing with a justice-involved drug-dependent individual calls for expertise from both worlds.

A recent American study (Friedmann et al. 2012) on the effectiveness of collaborative behavioural management (CBM) offers a concrete illustration of just how vital collaboration between criminal justice and addiction treatment partners is. The researchers observed a positive effect on both drug use and delinquency among cannabis users on probation. CBM involved an initial session between the drug-dependent offender and his or her parole officer and treatment counsellor, as well as twelve weekly sessions with the parole officer in which the treatment counsellor participated periodically. Sessions included a review of expectations and the consequences of failing to meet expectations, negotiation of a weekly behavioural contract (not socializing with drug-using friends, looking for work), reinforcers and incentives (verbal congratulations, gift certificates), and sanctions (more frequent reporting to parole officer) for failure to abide by the contract.

Healthy collaboration between the correctional system and treatment centres can be key to successful rehabilitation, but it comes with some major issues and challenges (Brunelle, Cousineau, and Ledoux 2012; Nissen 2006), such as clarifying the roles of custodial institution and treatment centre personnel, developing a prison-based psychoactive substance intervention philosophy that all staff understand and apply, and providing ongoing professional development for custodial institution and treatment centre staff (Brunelle, Cousineau, and Ledoux 2012). Healthy collaboration between the correctional and drug treatment systems rests on an agreement about the responsibilities of each, about the information to be shared, and about access to sensitive information (ibid.). One way to address confidentiality concerns is to have the drug-dependent offender sign a document detailing when and for what purpose information can be shared and whether the offender must be present at the time. It should also explain and remind clients of the limits of confidentiality (Brunelle and Bertrand 2010).

It is also important for all parties involved, including the client, to agree on what can be included in reports. All of the professionals working with the offender throughout the rehabilitation process should be able to decide what is relevant to the progress report and should notify the offender of any sensitive information to be included. All parties should sign a pre-treatment agreement specifying (1) at what point in the therapeutic process a report may be written, (2) for what purpose and for whom it will be written, and (3) which elements will be reported and how they will be reported. This protects the offenders' right to confidential treatment of what they say during therapeutic sessions, reduces the risk of seduction or rebellion in guard/inmate relationships, and encourages drug-dependent individuals to open up and work on the most difficult areas of their lives. Intervention in a criminal justice context involves erecting necessary boundaries and building appropriate bridges.

* * *

Problem substance use is prevalent within the criminal justice population because of drug laws and drug law enforcement, and because of crimes committed while intoxicated or to acquire drugs. The legal process provides a good opportunity to reach many people with drug dependence. They are entitled to the same health care services as the general population, so providing them with appropriate treatment is important. While this population presents complex cases, certain interventions do reduce criminal recidivism, which is a very good reason to provide addiction treatment services to offenders. As we have seen, effective practices exist and are well documented, but implementing them remains a challenge. In their study of how widespread evidence-based drug treatment practices are in the American justice system, Friedmann, Taxman, and Henderson (2007) found that fewer than 60 percent of the treatment modalities in most programs were best practices. Clearly, there is room for improvement.

All the approaches to rehabilitation and elements of effective treatment discussed in this chapter owe a significant measure of their success to good assessment of the client's situation, and to multi-modal service offerings matched to the individual's profile and needs. Interest in the role that motivation plays in the treatment of drug-dependent clients in the justice system is growing. Numerous intervention programs and techniques have been developed in the past two decades, and many of them include motivational interviewing. Even traditional treatments and those based on specific models, such as cognitive-behavioural approaches, include elements borrowed from motivational methods in their philosophy and techniques.

Now that we recognize the clinical importance of motivation, we can see how coerced intervention can have a downside. Motivation for change is a major issue for drug-dependent offenders participating in treatment under coercion. Nevertheless, studies have shown that even though intrinsic motivation seems to produce better clinical outcomes than extrinsic motivation, in some cases judicial constraint can create the right conditions for intrinsic motivation to develop and improve treatment retention. Judicial involvement in and of itself does not create ideal conditions for the therapeutic process, and offenders' immediate interests (avoiding conviction and sentencing, possibility of release) are not necessarily aligned with the goals of the criminal justice system (public safety and security). Even so, therapists who base their intervention on up-to-date knowledge about motivation for change can help clients progress regardless of the context. Therapeutic alliance is another factor strongly correlated to treatment success when relationships are built with clients themselves (justice-involved or incarcerated individuals) and the client behind the client (the legal and correctional system). Given that therapeutic alliance in drug treatment may be related to reduced problem drug use and criminal activity, more research on this approach and on other elements that have the potential to counter risk factors is in order.

As we have seen, for clients in a correctional context who are deprived of their liberty, treatment effects and efficacy criteria are not the only rehabilitation issues to consider. We must also consider the moral and ethical aspects of these interventions. One of the main issues we must contemplate in connection with drug treatment in legal and correctional contexts is the disconnect between the goals and priorities of the criminal justice system and those of drug rehabilitation. On the one hand, security is paramount, but on the other, the individual's right to optimal, confidential care is essential. The concept of coercion has highly subjective connotations, so giving due consideration to how it is used in treatment is important. One question remains at the end of this thought process: should treatment be provided by the criminal justice system, by specialized external organizations, or via an integrated shared services or co-intervention model involving judicial/correctional and treatment partners? One thing is clear: this management approach requires collaboration and alignment between two levels of service that have dramatically different philosophies.

Notes

1. Interventions were typically implemented without any evaluation component. In cases where evaluation was carried out, program implementation rarely allowed for the use of research designs appropriate to this context.
2. Ethical problems of all kinds, difficulty protecting confidentiality, administrative priorities that required transferring inmates before the end of treatment, lack of funding, difficulty complying with admission criteria, lack of program independence, and so on.
3. A Court of Quebec addiction treatment program.
4. In 2015, the centre (Montreal Addiction Rehabilitation Centre – University Institute) became part of the Centre intégré universitaire de santé et de services sociaux du Centre-Sud-de-l'Île-de-Montréal (South-Central Montreal Integrated University Health and Social Services Centre).
5. All names were changed.
6. See Vacheret and Lemire (2007) for a discussion of prisonization.
7. TCs make extensive use of positive reinforcement and punishment.
8. In Georgia.
9. DÉBA-Alcool and DÉBA-Drogues.
10. Detection of Alcohol and Drug Problems in Adolescents.
11. Texas Christian University.
12. A provincial prison in Quebec City.
13. Quebec City Integrated University Health and Social Services Centre.

Conclusion

Persistent myths and a heavy dose of sensationalism warp our understanding of issues related to illicit drugs. Too many people are under the impression that using psychoactive substances means surrendering to their tyrannical grip and allowing them to take total control of one's existence. Parents of teenagers believe that a deviant trajectory and a life of crime are the inevitable consequences of drug use. As we have shown, many attitudes about drugs and drug users are unfounded, simplistic, or based on stereotypes. That these fictions endure is probably due to their political expediency. It is true that, by definition, for people with dependencies, drugs are the focus of their existence, but dependence is not an issue for most illicit drug users around the world.

Throughout this book, we have attempted to show how and to what extent illicit drug use contributes to criminal behaviour, and vice versa. By examining scientific research, we have separated fact from fiction. Drugs and crime are related in some ways; prevalence studies reveal strong associations between the two in general. We have seen that a significant majority of offenders consume illicit psychoactive substances and that many drug-dependent people are involved in a large number of crimes, most of them lucrative. Regular and dependent users are more likely to turn to lucrative crime, which typically involves drug dealing, theft, and fraud. Variables modulating illegal activity include the user's income, the cost of drugs, and existing public safety policies, such as how forcefully drug trafficking is policed, basic income programs, and the availability of treatment services and drug substitution programs.

We have observed that violent crime is generally a product of the systemic criminality that is part and parcel of the illegal drug economy. It is more common in certain tough-on-crime cities and countries. Contrary to media messaging, people are rarely violent while high; those who are usually presented violent tendencies beforehand. Scientific studies have shown that psychoactive substances do not have the same effects on all intoxicated and dependent individuals. Context of use can also influence whether an individual resorts to crime. For some users, criminality depends on interactions among the drug, the person, and the context.

Consequently, the drug–crime dynamic cannot be reduced to linear causal relationships. Intervention strategies based on a proximate cause model are therefore doomed to fail. For a better understanding of the situation, we must look to various risk factors that can help us see how deviant attitudes and behaviours develop. Most importantly, our schema must account for idiosyncrasies and different drug use and delinquency pathways to contribute to that understanding and support intervention. The key notion here is that of *trajectory*, which conceptualizes the drug–crime relationship as evolving in accordance with a processual schema that represents the establishment of a lifestyle.

As a concept, *deviant lifestyle* is a convenient way to situate values, attitudes, and behaviours within an integrated whole. This schema both drives activities and explains their various dimensions. It bears repeating that the development of a lifestyle must be interpreted within a processual framework. The way we relate to life and other people, which is shaped by a set of attitudes, likes and dislikes, leads us to participate in some activities more than others, opening the door to possibilities and opportunities that would not otherwise be available. This applies to both deviant and socially integrated activities. Because of these inclinations and activities, and the extent to which we indulge and engage in them, we are drawn to one sort of lifestyle over another. By dint of repetition and symbolization, these behaviours crystallize into a way of life (Dérivois 2004). Lifestyles can undergo transformation. After all, nobody consciously pursues a deviant lifestyle in which withdrawal, overdose, debt, violence, victimization, stigmatization, and disease are everyday realities. The thing is, before those harsh realities set in, many users experience a period of good times, pleasure, living in the present (Cusson 1981), freedom, and intensity—a frenzied lifestyle of instant gratification and pleasure.

That is the fun part of the deviant lifestyle, but when people adopt it to make their unfulfilling lives and bleak prospects bearable or to mask deep-seated angst, when they party to hide their misery, the door to dependence eases open. The addict's lifestyle at the end of the dependence trajectory stands in stark contrast to the shiny happiness of the honeymoon period. Early on, drugs are but one of many features of the lifestyle. Further along the addictive trajectory, consequences begin to set in (job loss, social isolation, dependence, etc.) as drugs become the cornerstone of the user's way of life.

The Drug–Crime Relationship

Considering what we have learned, let us return to each of the questions we posed in the introduction to this book (Who? Why? What? How?) and answer them briefly in the hope of rooting out some stubborn prejudices.

Who?

Are all teenagers apt to engage in drug abuse and criminality? Adolescence is certainly a turbulent period of experimentation and identity formation. Teenagers are keenly aware that they are no longer children, as evidenced by their physical transformations, but as they are constantly reminded, they are not yet truly adults. As they make the transition from childhood to adulthood, teenagers become more critical of those who have influenced them thus far (to the dismay of parents and teachers), and friends become more central to their lives. Teenagers are thus seen as more vulnerable, having just begun to separate themselves from their family and with school no longer as dominant an influence. Parents worry about peers being a bad influence on their children, forgetting that those peers are themselves the sons and daughters of other concerned parents. We need to stop thinking of teenagers as members of a "social clientele" to be scrutinized. Most minors simply need love and enough freedom to flourish. It is worth remembering the upside to teenagers distancing themselves from their family and other childhood influences: the development of independent individuals who are not mere clones of their parents or exact replicas of their ancestors. We must reflect on the right of adolescents to rebel against society without being labelled marginal, delinquent, or addicted. Harmless escapades aside, most young people display a strong desire to be "normal." They want to pursue their studies, find a fulfilling job, and search for the perfect mate. They picture themselves enjoying a relatively stable future and contributing to society.

However, those in whom socialization institutions have not generated attachment to social values may gradually embark on a deviant trajectory. For some, it is but a brief foray; as they mature, they learn to manage their adjustment issues without pursuing their deviant trajectory. Only a minority plunge headlong into a lifestyle in which problem drug use and crime go hand in hand. These are the young people behind the statistics on problem drug use among offenders and the criminal activity of drug addicts. For them, using illicit psychoactive substances takes on a specific phenomenological meaning: the adoption of a deviant lifestyle.

Why?

A minority of those who consume illicit substances occasionally will undertake a life of crime. Many of the drug users on a criminal trajectory were exposed to a collection of risk factors during childhood, some of which affected them more deeply than others. Often, we can hear echoes of this in how people talk about their experiences with failure and rejection (family, school, economic, ethnic, etc.), and we can detect mangled self-esteem. Many people construct a lifestyle around their failures, and that lifestyle may become deviant. As their trajectory unfolds, progression and maintenance factors reinforce that lifestyle.

What?

Drug–crime relationships are highly variable and depend on individuals, the drugs they use, and their social context. They also change depending on where an individual is on his or her trajectory. For many people in the early stages of a deviant lifestyle, experiences with delinquency precede regular contact with drugs. Later, regular use of illicit psychoactive substances may be associated with dealing drugs, with systemic crime related to drug trafficking, and with deeper involvement in unlawful activities. At this stage, each spurs the other. Those who pursue this trajectory to the point of dependence begin to engage in economic-compulsive crime to meet their daily need for drugs.

Of course, only a small minority of users reach the economic-compulsive stage, not necessarily via a linear trajectory, but via one marked by periods of progression, maintenance, and interruption. Bit by bit, deviant attitudes and behaviours solidify into an identity in which drugs and crime become inseparable.

How Can Society Intervene?

The use and misuse of psychoactive substances and their links to criminal activity come down to an individual's dynamic relationship with his or her past (risk factors) and present (progression and interruption factors). As we have seen, the positivist paradigm and its simplistic conceptual models are incapable of accurately portraying this complex reality, and social policies based on this paradigm are doomed to fail.

What is the best way, under the circumstances, to intervene? There are two ways to loosen the bonds between drugs and crime: implement appropriate drug policies and provide suitable care to drug-dependent offenders.

Implementing Appropriate Policies

Misuse of psychoactive substances and criminality are as much a symptom of social problems and exclusion as a manifestation of individual problems, if not more. Our social structure marginalizes people and produces deviants; some of our laws, not least our drug laws, contribute significantly to this phenomenon.

We recognize the need for some measure of control over drug use. After all, we, as a society, control the legal distribution of tobacco and alcohol. What we must ask ourselves is whether criminalization of drugs that are currently illegal is really the best way to control them.

Lawmakers engage in endless debate about problems related to drug addiction and generally end up opting to strengthen police powers despite the fact that victory in the war on drugs remains elusive. Considering the high prevalence of illegal drug use in recent years and the astronomical cost of enforcing repressive drug laws, the contemporary approach to fighting drugs is clearly outdated, ineffective, and ridiculously expensive. We cannot continue to fund this repressive war for much longer without neglecting other priority public health needs associated with an aging population. Our existing drug policies subject us to an endless parade of legal lunacy in which law enforcement and paramilitary tactics are primarily responsible for the confrontations with drug users that distract us from effective public health approaches to curbing problems linked to excessive drug use. What is more, these repressive policies drive up the cost of drugs and put users from underprivileged social classes at an even greater disadvantage, essentially forcing them to resort to lucrative crime. Eradicating cocaine and heroin from the planet would in no way eliminate addiction problems and the profound angst of those dependent on drugs.

Portugal's decriminalization of all drugs and the legalization of recreational cannabis use in some U.S. states have added a new dimension to the prohibition–anti-prohibition debate, which is more a clash of paradigms than an informed discourse. The positivist paradigm and its emphasis on aggressive action against drug users is broadly based on a causal view of the drug–crime relationship. Individuals are seen as weak beings easily led astray by intoxication and addiction. Drugs rob them of their own will. The availability of drugs exposes them to risky use, abuse, and criminality. In contrast, the humanist paradigm holds that people are capable of thinking things through and acting to promote their own well-being as they interact with their environment, which influences them to some degree. From the humanist point of view, we should work to normalize social relationships with drug users.

Can the law force addicts to stop using drugs? Prohibiting drugs is too facile a solution. Instead, we must try to understand why the behaviour that some wish to forbid is so widespread. Can it be that the repression/marginalization/repression cycle is so overwhelming that it clouds judgment and obscures the very causes of marginalization? Prohibitionists justify criminalizing drug users on the grounds that they simply want to make sure users get appropriate treatment for their problem but, in so doing, they saddle users with a criminal record and rob them of their civil rights. Drug use and addiction are not legal problems; they are public health problems. We must replace the criminal justice response with a bona fide public health policy. Society is evolving. Canadians are increasingly in favour of decriminalizing cannabis. Governments must act accordingly. Senator Pierre-Claude Nolin's 2010 commentary in *Le Devoir* illustrated how perceptions of cannabis and the most appropriate responses to drugs have changed:

> We believe that education, therapy, and prevention—not prohibi-
> tion and criminalization—are our best weapons against problems
> arising from the use of tobacco, alcohol, and cannabis. If you are
> trying to convince your children not to use drugs, our report will
> be extremely helpful. . . .
> We believe that Canadians are capable of making an enlightened
> decision about cannabis. I hope our report will continue to sup-
> ply the information and ideas Canada needs to develop a new
> policy that champions healing and dignity over the degradation
> and despair of its current repressive policy.[1]

Providing Suitable Care

Toward the end of the twentieth century in North America, drug users were being incarcerated or placed under the care of psychologists, doctors, and social workers in record numbers. Prisons were crammed with people convicted of drug crimes, and with the advent of drug courts, legally mandated clients flooded drug treatment centres.

Drug rehabilitation services are an integral part of an effective crime prevention strategy that tends to have fewer undesirable effects than incarceration. Despite some drawbacks, judicial pressure can actually function as a lever of intervention and change for drug-using offenders. There is a caveat, however. While treatment may hold more appeal than incarceration (both philosophically and in terms of the impact on relapse and recidivism), the intervention strategies have their limitations: they reach only a minority of drug users, address certain crucial problems (e.g., re-entry into the workforce, chronic debt) only indirectly, and, most importantly, come much too late in the marginalization process.

While the impact of a program is a relevant consideration, it is also important to examine the moral and ethical dimensions of a given intervention. Therapists who work with drug-dependent offenders must be very persuasive if they are to convince their clients that they want what is best for them, create a healthy therapeutic alliance, and help their clients find the motivation to engage in a program essen-tially imposed by the system that is punishing them. By simultane-ously offering help and imposing control, the criminal justice context can all too easily undermine the founding premise of a therapeutic relationship based on voluntary participation. When the criminal justice system is involved in treating drug-dependent offenders, its purpose is no longer just to punish those who break the law, but also to shape offenders' conduct and get them to behave more "normally."

Incarceration and rehabilitation do not necessarily go hand in hand. For treatment to be truly effective, it must be integrated into the individual's natural environment (e.g., family, school, work). At the very least, treatment for criminal-justice clients must be examined closely to ensure that it is provided in a respectful manner.

Over the past twenty years, we have refined our understanding of the drug–crime relationship through new studies that focus on drug users' stories, experiences, and perceptions, but much work remains to be done. We need to keep listening to social actors themselves, because their points of view reveal a reality that standardized questionnaires and tests are not designed to measure. We must find better ways to correlate the results of quantitative and qualitative studies to achieve a thorough understanding of the relationship and how it evolves.

Here is our hope for the future: may those who read this book become champions of policies that help people break with difficult life trajectories rather than sink deeper into marginalization and deviance.

Note

1. Translation of "Nous croyons que l'éducation, les thérapies et la prévention – non pas la prohibition et la criminalisation – sont les meilleures armes contre les problèmes que peut occasionner la consommation de tabac, d'alcool ou de cannabis. Par conséquent, si vous vous efforcez de convaincre vos enfants de ne pas consommer de drogues, notre rapport se révélera d'une aide précieuse […] Nous croyons que les Canadiens sont en mesure de prendre une décision éclairée au sujet du cannabis. J'espère que notre rapport continuera de fournir les renseignements et les idées dont le Canada a besoin pour formuler une nouvelle politique qui favorise la guérison et la dignité au lieu de la dégradation et du désespoir qu'entraîne notre politique répressive actuelle."

References

ACRDQ. *See* Association des centres de réadaptation en dépendance du Québec.

Afifi, Tracie O., Christine A. Henriksen, Gordon J.G. Asmundson, and Jitender Sareen. 2012. "Victimization and Perpetration of Intimate Partner Violence and Substance Use Disorders in a Nationally Representative Sample." *Journal of Nervous and Mental Disease* 200 (8): 684–91.

Ahmad, Affizal, and Nurul Hazrina Mazlan. 2014. "Substance Abuse and Childhood Trauma Experiences: Comparison between Incarcerated and Non-incarcerated Youth." *Procedia–Social and Behavioral Sciences* 113: 161–70.

Aldridge, Judith, and David Décary-Hétu. 2016. "Cryptomarkets and the Future of Illicit Drug Markets." In *The Internet and Drug Markets*, European Monitoring Centre for Drugs and Drug Addiction: Insights 21, 23–30. Luxembourg: Publications Office of the European Union. Accessed July 29, 2017. http://www.emcdda.europa.eu/system/files/publications/2155/TDXD16001ENN_FINAL.pdf.

Alexander, Bruce K. 1994. "L'héroïne et la cocaïne provoquent-elles la dépendance? Au carrefour de la science et des dogmes établis." In *L'usage des drogues et la toxicomanie: un phénomène multiple*, second edition, edited by P. Brisson, 3–30. Boucherville, QC: Gaëtan Morin Éditeur.

Andia, Jonny F., Sherry Deren, Rafaela R. Robles, Sung-Yeon Kang, Héctor M. Colón, Denise Oliver-Velez, and Ann Finlinson. 2005. "Factors Associated with Injection and Noninjection Drug Use During Incarceration Among Puerto Rican Drug Injectors in New York and Puerto Rico." *Prison Journal* 85 (3): 329–42.

Andrews, Donald A., and James Bonta. 1994. *The Psychology of Criminal Conduct*. Cincinnati, OH: Anderson.

———. 2006. *The Psychology of Criminal Conduct*. 4th edition. Cincinnati, OH: Anderson.

Andrews, Donald A., James L. Bonta, and J. Stephen Wormith. 2004. *The Level of Service/Case Management Inventory (LS/CMI)*. Toronto: Multi-Health Systems.

Andrews, Donald A., and Craig Dowden. 2006. "Risk Principle of Case Classification in Correctional Treatment: A Meta-Analytic Investigation." *International Journal of Offender Therapy and Comparative Criminology* 50 (1): 88–100.

Arseneault, Catherine. 2009. "Points de vue de jeunes sur leur passage dans une unité spécialisée en toxicomanie en centre jeunesse." Master's thesis, Université du Québec.

———. 2015. "Évaluation des effets du programme d'intervention en toxicomanie offert par le Centre de réadaptation en dépendance de Québec à l'Établissement de détention de Québec." Doctoral dissertation, Université de Québec à Trois-Rivières.

Arseneault, Catherine, Chantal Plourde, and Marc Alain. 2014. "Les défis de l'évaluation d'un programme d'intervention en contexte carcéral." *Canadian Journal of Program Evaluation/Revue canadienne d'évaluation de programme* 29 (2): 21–47. Accessed June 25, 2017. https://evaluationcanada.ca/system/files/cjpe-entries/29-2-021.pdf.

Association des centres de réadaptation en dépendance du Québec. 2010. *Les services de réadaptation en toxicomanie auprès des adultes dans les centres de réadaptation en dépendance. Guide de pratique et offre de services de base*. Montreal: ACRDQ.

Austin, Ashley, Michelle Hospital, Eric F. Wagner, and Staci Leon Morris. 2010. "Motivation for Reducing Substance Use Among Minority Adolescents: Targets for Intervention." *Journal of Substance Abuse Treatment* 39 (4): 399–407.

Bahr, Stephen J., Amber L. Masters, and Bryan M. Taylor. 2012. "What Works in Substance Abuse Treatment Programs for Offenders?" *Prison Journal* 92 (2): 155–74.

Baillargeon, Pierre, and Daniel Puskas. 2013. "L'alliance thérapeutique: conception, pratique." *Défi jeunesse* 19 (3): 4–9.

Beauchesne, Line 1991. "Consommation: le débat sur la légalisation." In *Géopolitique de la drogue*, edited by Guy Delbrel, 253–70. Paris: La Découverte.

Beauchesne, Line. 2011. "Setting Public Policy on Drugs: A Choice of Social Values." In *The Real Dope: Social, Legal, and Historical Perspectives on the Regulation of Drugs in Canada*, edited by Edgar-André Montigny, 25–28. Toronto: University of Toronto Press.

Becker, Howard S. 1963. *Outsiders: Studies in the Sociology of Deviance.* New York: Free Press.

Beirness, Douglas J., and Erin E. Beasley. 2010. "A Roadside Survey of Alcohol and Drug Use Among Drivers in British Columbia." *Traffic Injury Prevention* 11 (3): 215–21.

Belackova, Vendula, and Christian Alexander Vaccaro. 2013. "'A Friend with Weed is a Friend Indeed': Understanding the Relationship Between Friendship Identity and Market Relations Among Marijuana Users." *Journal of Drug Issues* 43 (3): 289–313.

Belenko, Steven. 2001. *Research on Drug Courts: A Critical Review 2001 Update.* Columbia University: Than National Center on Addiction and Substance Abuse. Accessed June 24, 2017. http://www.drugpolicy.org/docUploads/2001drugcourts.pdf.

——. 2006. "Assessing Released Inmates for Substance-Abuse-Related Service Needs." *Crime & Delinquency* 52 (1): 94–113.

Belenko, Steven, and Kimberly A. Houser. 2012. "Gender Differences in Prison-Based Drug Treatment Participation." *International Journal of Offender Therapy and Comparative Criminology* 56 (5): 790–810.

Bell, Richard. 1991. "Prohibition des stupéfiants, l'histoire de la législation." *Revue internationale de police criminelle* 432, 2–6.

Bellot, Céline, Isabelle Raffestin, Marie-Noële Royer, and Véronique Noël. 2005. *Judiciarisation et criminalisation des populations itinérantes à Montréal.* Research report for Canada's National Secretariat on Homelessness. Accessed June 15, 2017. http://www.cremis.ca/sites/default/files/rapports-de-recherche/bellot-et-al-judiciarisation-2005.pdf.

Ben Amar, Mohamed. 2007. "Les psychotropes criminogènes." *Criminologie* 40 (1): 11–30.

Ben Amar, Mohamed, and Louis Léonard. 2002. *Les psychotropes. Pharmacologie et toxicomanie.* Les Presses de l'Université de Montréal.

Benavie, Arthur. 2009. *Drugs: America's Holy War.* New York: Routledge.

Benda, Brent B., Robert Flynn Corwyn, and Nancy J. Toombs. 2001. "Recidivism Among Adolescent Serious Offenders: Prediction of Entry Into the Correctional System for Adults." *Criminal Justice and Behavior* 28 (95): 588–613.

Bennett, Trevor, Katy Holloway, and David Farrington. 2008. "The Statistical Association Between Drug Misuse and Crime: A Meta-Analysis." *Aggression and Violent Behavior* 13 (2): 107–18.

Bergeron, Jacques, Pierre Joly, Isabelle Richer, and Guillaume Théorêt. 2007. "Cannabis au volant versus alcool au volant: Études sur la perception des risques." In *Proceedings of the Canadian Multidisciplinary Road Safety Conference XVII*, edited by Michel Gou and Érick Abraham, 1–18.

Bergeron, Jacques, Joël Tremblay, Louis-Georges Cournoyer, Serge Brochu, and Michel Landry. 2009. "Consommation de cannabis et utilisation des

techniques de l'Entretien Motivationnel dans les programmes de traitement pour adolescents." *RISQ-INFO* 17 (1): 5–8.

Bertrand, Karine, Natacha Brunelle, Isabelle Richer, Isabelle Beaudoin, Annie
Lemieux, and Jean-Marc Ménard. 2013a. "Assessing Covariates of Drug
Use Trajectories Among Adolescents Admitted to a Drug Addiction
Centre: Mental Health Problems, Therapeutic Alliance and Treatment
Persistence." *Substance Use & Misuse* 48 (1–2): 117–28.

Bertrand, Karine, Natacha Brunelle, J.-M. Ménard, Isabelle Richer, A. Lemieux,
and Cinthia Ledoux. 2009. *Étude évaluative auprès d'adolescents en traitement de la toxicomanie (partie 1): suivis trois mois et six mois.* Final report to
the Ministère de la Santé et des Services Sociaux.

Bertrand, Karine, and Louise Nadeau. 2006. "Toxicomanie et inadaptation
sociale grave: perspectives subjectives de femmes en traitement quant
à l'initiation et la progression de leur consommation." *Drogues, santé et
société* 5 (1): 9–44.

Best, David, Ed Day, Saffron Homayoun, Hannah Lenton, Robert Moverley,
and Mark Openshaw. 2008. "Treatment Retention in the Drug
Intervention Programme: Do Primary Drug Users Fare Better than
Primary Offenders?" *Drugs: Education, Prevention and Policy* 15 (2):
201–9.

*Bill C-17, An Act to Amend the Contraventions Act and the Controlled Drugs and
Substances Act.* 2004. 1st Reading Nov. 1, 2004, 38th Parliament, 1st ses-
sion. Accessed May 28, 2017. http://www.ourcommons.ca/Content/
Bills/381/Government/C-17/C-17_1/C-17_1.PDF.

Blume, Arthur W. 2005. *Treating Drug Problems.* Chichester, UK: John Wiley
& Sons.

Boles, Sharon M., and Karen Miotto. "Substance Abuse and Violence: A
Review of the Literature." *Aggression and Violent Behavior* 8 (2): 155–74.

Bonta, James, and Donald A. Andrews. 2003. "A Commentary on Ward and
Stewart's Model of Human Needs." *Psychology, Crime & Law* 9 (3):
215–18.

———. 2007. *Risk-Need-Responsivity Model for Offender Assessment and
Rehabilitation.* Ottawa: Public Safety Canada. Accessed June 24, 2017.
https://www.publicsafety.gc.ca/cnt/rsrcs/pblctns/rsk-nd-rspnsvty/rsk-
nd-rspnsvty-eng.pdf.

Bonta, James, Julie Blais, and Holly A. Wilson. 2013. "The Prediction of Risk for
Mentally Disordered Offenders: A Quantitative Synthesis." Corrections
Research, Public Safety Canada. Accessed May 27, 2017. https://www.
publicsafety.gc.ca/cnt/rsrcs/pblctns/prdctn-rsk-mntlly-dsrdrd/index-
en.aspx.

Bordin, Edward S. 1979. "The Generalizability of the Psychoanalytic Concept
of the Working Alliance." *Psychotherapy: Theory, Research & Practice* 16
(3): 252–60.

Born, Michel, and Sylvie Boët. 2005. "La résilience hors la loi." In *La résilience: le réalisme de l'espérance*, edited by Fondation pour l'enfance, 223–39. Ramonville: Éditions Érès.

Bouhnik, Patricia. 1996. "Système de vie et trajectoires de consommateurs d'héroïne en milieu urbain défavorisé." *Communications* 62 (1): 241–56.

Boys, Annabel, John Marsden, and John Strang. 2001. "Understanding Reasons for Drug Use Amongst Young People: A Functional Perspective." *Health Education Research* 16 (4): 457–69.

Brady, Sonya S., Jeanne M. Tschann, Lauri A. Pasch, Elena Flores, and Emily J. Ozer. 2008. "Violence Involvement, Substance Use, and Sexual Activity Among Mexican-American and European-American Adolescents." *Journal of Adolescent Health* 43 (3): 285–95.

Brain, Kevin, Howard Parker, and Tim Bottomley. 1998. *Evolving Crack Cocaine Careers: New Users, Quitters and Long Term Combination Drug Users in N.W. England*. University of Manchester. doi=10.1.1.624.7018&rep=rep 1&type=pdf.

Braithwaite, Ronald L., Rhonda C. Conerly, Alyssa G. Robillard, Torrance T. Stephens, and Tammy Woodring. 2003. "Alcohol and Other Drug Use Among Adolescent Detainees." *Journal of Substance Use* 8 (2): 126–31.

Breda, Carolyn S., and Craig Anne Heflinger. 2007. "The Impact of Motivation to Change on Substance Use Among Adolescents in Treatment." *Journal of Child & Adolescent Substance Abuse* 16 (3): 106–24.

Brisson, Pierre. 1997. *L'approche de réduction des méfaits: sources, situation, pratiques*. Gouvernement du Québec. Ministère de la Santé et des Services sociaux. Comité permanent de lutte à la toxicomanie.

——. 1995. *Drogue et criminalité: une relation complexe*. Les Presses de l'Université de Montréal.

——. 2006. *Drogue et criminalité: une relation complexe* (2e édition). Les Presses de l'Université de Montréal.

Brochu, Serge, Candido da Agra, and Marie-Marthe Cousineau. 2002. *Drugs and Crime Deviant Pathways*. London: Ashgate Publishing.

Brochu, Serge, Jacques Bergeron, Michel Landry, Michel Germain, and Pascal Schneeberger. 2002. "The Impact of Treatment on Criminalized Substance Addicts." *Journal of Addictive Diseases* 21 (3): 23–41.

Brochu, Serge, and Natacha Brunelle. 1997. "Toxicomanie et délinquance. Une question de style de vie?" *Psychotropes* 3 (4): 107–25.

Brochu, Serge, Louis-Georges Cournoyer, Joël Tremblay, Jacques Bergeron, Natacha Brunelle, and Michel Landry. 2006. "Understanding Treatment Impact on Drug-Addicted Offenders." *Substance Use & Misuse* 41 (14): 1937–49.

Brochu, Serge, Marie-Marthe Cousineau, Sun Fu, Kai Pernanen, Louis-Georges Cournoyer, Mélanie Desrosiers. 2001. "Estimation statistique des liens entre alcool/drogues et crimes chez les détenus fédéraux." *Revue Internationale de Police Technique et Scientifique* 54 (3): 318–33.

Brochu, Serge, Marie-Marthe Cousineau, Chloé Provost, Patricia Erickson, and Sun Fu. 2010. "Quand drogues et violence se rencontrent chez les jeunes: un cocktail explosif?" *Drogues, santé et société* 9 (2): 149–78.

Brochu, Serge, Cameron Duff, Mark Asbridge, and Patricia Gail Erickson. 2011. "There's What's on Paper and Then There's What Happens, Out on the Sidewalk: Cannabis Users' Knowledge and Opinion of Canadian Drug Laws." *Journal of Drug Issues* 41 (1): 95–115.

Brochu, Serge, Louise Guyon, and Lyne Desjardins. 2001. "Trajectoires de délinquance et de consommation de substances chez des hommes et des femmes en détention." *Canadian Journal of Criminology*, 43 (2): 173–96.

Brochu, Serge, and Michel Landry. 2010. "Les tribunaux spécialisés dans le traitement de la toxicomanie au Québec." *RISQ-Info* 18 (1): 1–3.

Brochu, Serge, Michel Landry, Karine Bertrand, and Natacha Brunelle. 2014. *À la croisée des chemins: trajectoires addictives et trajectoires de services. La perspective des personnes toxicomanes*. Quebec City: Presses de l'Université Laval.

Brochu, Serge, and Mylène Magrinelli-Orsi. 2008. "Les substances psychoactives au Canada: Historique de leur criminalisation et développements récents." *Déviance et société* 32 (3): 363–76.

Brochu, Serge, and Isabelle Parent. 2005. *Les flambeurs: trajectoires d'usagers de cocaïne*. Ottawa: University of Ottawa Press.

Brochu, Serge, Isabelle Parent, Anne Chamandy, and Lyne Chayer. 1997. "Victimisation et style de vie parmi un échantillon de toxicomanes incarcérés." *Annales internationales de criminologie* 35 (1–2): 131–54.

Brochu, Serge, and Chantal Plourde. 2012. "L'offre de services aux adultes toxicomanes sous le coup de mesures judiciaires: un jeu de murs et de ponts [The range of services to adult drug addicts within the scope of judicial measures: A set of walls and bridges]." In *L'intégration des services en toxicomanie*, edited by Michel Landry, Serge Brochu, and Catherine Patenaude, 107–130. Quebec City: Presses de l'Université Laval.

Brook, Judith S., Jung Yeon Lee, Stephen J. Finch, and David W. Brook. 2014. "Developmental Trajectories of Marijuana Use from Adolescence to Adulthood: Relationship with Using Weapons Including Guns." *Aggressive Behavior* 40 (3): 229–37.

Brown, B. Bradford, and James Larson. 2009. "Peer Relationships in Adolescence." In *Handbook of Adolescent Psychology, Volume 2: Contextual Influences on Adolescent Development*, 3rd edition, edited by Richard M. Lerner and Laurence Steinberg, 74–103. Hoboken, NJ: John Wiley & Sons.

Brown, Randall T. 2010. "Associations with Substance Abuse Treatment Completion Among Drug Court Participants." *Substance Use & Misuse* 45 (12): 1874–91.

Brown, Randall T., Paul A. Allison, and F. Javier Nieto. 2010. "Impact of Jail Sanctions During Drug Court Participation upon Substance Abuse Treatment Completion." *Addiction* 106 (1): 135–42.

Brown, Thomas G., Peter Seraganian, and Jacques Tremblay. 2001. "Postcure dans le traitement des problèmes d'abus de substances." In *Impact du traitement en alcoolisme et toxicomanie: Études québécoises*, edited by Michel Landry, Louise Guyon, and Serge Brochu, 17–44. Quebec City: Les Presses de l'Université Laval.

Brunelle, Natacha. 1994. "Analyse biopsychosociale de personnes admises en traitement pour la toxicomanie." Master's thesis, Université de Montréal.

———. 2001. "Trajectoires déviantes à l'adolescence: usage de drogues illicites et délinquance." PhD dissertation, Université de Montréal.

Brunelle, Natacha, and Karine Bertrand. 2010. "Trajectoires déviantes et trajectoires de rétablissement à l'adolescence: typologie et leviers d'intervention." *Criminologie* 43 (2): 373–99.

Brunelle, Natacha, Karine Bertrand, Isabelle Beaudoin, Cinthia Ledoux, Annie Gendron, and Catherine Arseneault. 2013. "Drug Trajectories Among Youth Undergoing Treatment: The Influence of Psychological Problems and Delinquency." *Journal of Adolescence* 36 (4): 705–16.

Brunelle, Natacha, Karine Bertrand, Jorge Flores-Aranda, Catherine Patenaude, Michel Landry, Joanie Lafontaine, and Serge Brochu. 2014. "Trajectoires de consommation: les influences du point de vue des personnes toxicomanes." In *À la croisée des chemins: trajectoires addictives et trajectoires de services, la perspective des personnes toxicomanes*, edited by Serge Brochu, Michel Landry, Karine Bertrand, Natacha Brunelle, and Catherine Patenaude, 113–50. Quebec City: Les Presses de l'Université Laval.

Brunelle, Natacha, Karine Bertrand, Michel Landry, Jorge Flores-Aranda, Catherine Patenaude, and Serge Brochu. 2015. "Recovery from Substance Use: Drug-Dependent People's Experiences with Sources that Motivate them to Change." *Drugs: Education, Prevention and Policy* 22 (3): 301–7.

Brunelle, Natacha, Karine Bertrand, Joël Tremblay, Catherine Arseneault, Michel Landry, Jacques Bergeron, and Chantal Plourde. 2010. "Impact des traitements et processus de rétablissement chez les jeunes toxicomanes québécois." *Drogues, santé et société* 9 (1): 211–47.

Brunelle, Natacha, Serge Brochu, and Marie-Marthe Cousineau. 1998. "Des cheminements vers un style de vie déviant: adolescents des centres jeunesse et des centres pour toxicomanes." *Les Cahiers de recherches criminologiques*, no. 27. Montreal: Centre international de criminologie comparée. Accessed June 11, 2017. https://depot.erudit.org/bitstream/001000dd/1/CRC_1998_N27.pdf.

———. 2000. "Drug–Crime Relations Among Drug-Consuming Juvenile Delinquents: A Tripartite Model and More." *Contemporary Drug Problems* 27 (4): 835–66.

———. 2005. "Des jeunes se racontent : le point sur leurs trajectoires d'usage de drogues et de délinquance." In *Les jeunes et les drogues. Usages et dépendances*, edited by Louise Guyon, Serge Brochu, and Michel Landry, 279–319. Quebec City: Les Presses de l'Université Laval.

Brunelle, Natacha, Marie-Marthe Cousineau, and Serge Brochu. 2002a. "Deviant Youth Trajectories: Adoption, Progression and Regression of Deviant Lifestyles." In *Drugs and Crime Deviant Pathways*, edited by Serge Brochu, Candido da Agra, and Marie-Marthe Cousineau, 115–35. London: Ashgate Publishing.

———. 2002b. "Trajectoires types de déviance juvénile: un regard qualitatif." *Revue canadienne de criminologie* 44 (1): 2–32.

———. 2005. "Juvenile Drug Use and Delinquency: Youths' Accounts of their Trajectories." *Substance Use & Misuse* 40 (5): 721–34.

Brunelle, Natacha, Marie-Marthe Cousineau, and Cinthia Ledoux. 2012. "Toxico-justice: l'intégration des services offerts aux jeunes." In *L'intégration des services en toxicomanie*, edited by Michel Landry, Serge Brochu, and Catherine Patenaude, 81–106. Quebec City: Les Presses de l'Université Laval.

Bryan, Michael, and Patrick Crawshaw. 1988. "Politiques internationales et législation canadienne en matière de drogues." In *L'usage des drogues et la toxicomanie: un phénomène multiple*, edited by Pierre Brisson, 105–23. Boucherville, QC: Gaëtan Morin Éditeur.

Burdon, William M., Jeff Dang, Michael L. Prendergast, Nena P. Messina, and David Farabee. 2007. "Differential Effectiveness of Residential versus Outpatient Aftercare for Parolees from Prison-Based Therapeutic Community Treatment Programs." *Substance Abuse Treatment, Prevention, and Policy* 2 (16).

Butcher, James N., John. R. Graham, Auke Tellegen, and Beverly Kaemmer. 1989. *Manual for the restandardized Minnesota Multiphasic Personality Inventory: MMPI-2.* Minneapolis: University of Minnesota Press.

Butler, Tony, Michael Levy, Kate Dolan, and John Kaldor. 2003. "Drug Use and Its Correlates in an Australian Prisoner Population." *Addiction Research & Theory* 11 (2): 89–101.

Butler, Tony, Eva Malacova, Juliet Richters, Lorraine Yap, Luke Grant, Alun Richards, Anthony M. A. Smith, and Basil Donovan. 2013. "Sexual Behaviour and Sexual Health of Australian Prisoners." *Sexual Health* 10 (1): 64–73.

Buu, Anne, Cydney DiPiazza, Jing Wang, Leon I. Puttler, Hiram E. Fitzgerald, and Robert A. Zucker. 2009. "Parent, Family, and Neighborhood Effects on the Development of Child Substance Use and Other Psychopathology from Preschool to the Start of Adulthood." *Journal of Studies on Alcohol and Drugs* 70 (4): 489–98.

Canadian HIV/AIDS Legal Network. 2008. *HIV and Hepatitis C in Prisons: Info Sheets*. Canadian HIV/AIDS Legal Network. Accessed June 27, 2017. http://www.aidslaw.ca/site/hiv-and-hepatitis-c-in-prisons/?lang=en.

CASA. *See* National Centre on Addiction and Substance Abuse at Columbia University.

Casanueva, Cecilia, Leyla Stambaugh, Matthew Urato, Jenifer Goldman Fraser, and Jason Williams. 2014. "Illicit Drug Use from Adolescence to Young Adulthood Among Child Welfare-Involved Youths." *Journal of Child & Adolescent Substance Abuse* 23 (1): 29–48.

Casares-López, Maria José, Ana González-Menéndez, David S. Festinger, Paula Fernández-Garcia, José Ramón Fernández-Hermida, Roberto Secades, and Jason Matejkowski. 2013. "Predictors of Retention in a Drug-Free Unit/Substance Abuse Treatment in Prison." *International Journal of Law and Psychiatry* 36 (3–4): 264–72.

Casavant, Lyne, and Chantal Collin. 2001. *Illegal Drug Use and Crime: A Complex Relationship*. Library of Parliament, Political and Social Affairs Division. Accessed May 20, 2017. https://sencanada.ca/content/sen/committee/371/ille/library/collin-e.htm.

Cascini, Fidelia, Carola Aiello, and GianLuca Di Tanna. 2012. "Increasing Delta-9-Tetrahydrocannabinol (Δ-9-THC) Content in Herbal Cannabis Over Time: Systematic Review and Meta-Analysis." *Current Drug Abuse Reviews* 5 (1): 32–40.

Castel, R. 1992. *Les sorties de la toxicomanie*. Paris: Grass-Mire.

Castellanos-Ryan, Natalie, Maeve O'Leary-Barrett, and Patricia J. Conrod. 2013. "Substance-Use in Childhood and Adolescence: A Brief Overview of Developmental Processes and their Clinical Implications." *Journal of the Canadian Academy of Child and Adolescent Psychiatry* 22 (1): 41–46.

Caulkins, Jonathan P., and Rosalie Liccardo Pacula. 2006. "Marijuana Markets: Inferences from Reports by the Household Population." *Journal of Drug Issues* 36 (1): 173–200.

Cazale, Linda, Claire Fournier, and Gaëtane Dubé. 2009. "Consommation d'alcool et de drogues." In *Enquête québécoise sur le tabac, l'alcool, la drogue et le jeu chez les élèves du secondaire, 2008*, edited by Gaëtane Dubé, Monique Bordeleau, Linda Cazale, Claire Fournier, Issouf Traoré, Nathalie Plante, Robert Courtemanche, and Jocelyne Camirand, 91–147. Quebec City: Institut de la statistique du Québec. Accessed May 26, 2017. http://www.stat.gouv.qc.ca/statistiques/sante/enfants-ados/alcool-tabac-drogue-jeu/tabac-alcool-drogue-jeu-2008.pdf.

Centre for Addiction and Mental Health. 2014. *Cannabis Policy Framework*. Accessed July 29, 2017. http://www.camh.ca/en/hospital/

about_camh/influencing_public_policy/Documents/
CAMHCannabisPolicyFramework.pdf.

Center for Substance Abuse Treatment. 1999. *Enhancing Motivation for Change in Substance Abuse Treatment.* Treatment Improvement Protocol (TIP) Series no. 35. U.S. Department of Health and Human Services Administration, Substance Abuse and Mental Health Services Administration. Accessed June 27, 2017. https://store.samhsa.gov/shin/content/SMA13-4212/ SMA13-4212.pdf.

Center for Substance Abuse Treatment. 2005. *Substance Abuse Treatment for Adults in the Criminal Justice System.* Treatment Improvement Protocol (TIP) Series no. 44. U.S. Department of Health and Human Services Administration, Public Health Service, Substance Abuse and Mental Health Services Administration. Accessed June 27, 2017. http://store.samhsa.gov/product/ TIP-44-Substance-Abuse-Treatment-for-Adults-in-the-Criminal-Justice-System/SMA13-4056.

Centre Québécois de lutte aux dépendances. 2006. *Drogues: savoir plus, risquer moins.* Montreal: Centre Québécois de lutte aux dépendances.

Chandler, Redonna K., Bennett W. Fletcher, and Nora D. Volkow. 2009. "Treating Drug Abuse and Addiction in the Criminal Justice System: Improving Public Health and Safety." *Journal of the American Medical Association* 301 (2): 183–90.

Chandler, Redonna K., Roger H. Peters, Gary Field, and Denise Jubilano-Bult. 2004. "Challenges in Implementing Evidence-Based Treatment Practices for Co-Occurring Disorders in the Criminal Justice System." *Behavioral Sciences & the Law* 22 (4): 431–48.

Chassin, Laurie, George Knight, Delfino Vargas-Chanes, Sandra H. Losoya, and Diana Naranjo. 2009. "Substance Use Treatment Outcomes in a Sample of Male Serious Juvenile Offenders." *Journal of Substance Abuse Treatment* 36 (2): 183–94.

Cheung, Nicole W. T., and Yuet W. Cheung. 2006. "Is Hong Kong Experiencing Normalization of Adolescent Drug Use? Some Reflections on the Normalization Thesis." *Substance Use & Misuse* 41 (14): 1967–90.

Chouvy, Pierre-Arnaud. 2014. "Contrôle politico-territorial et culture illégale de plantes à drogue." In *Dossier Illégalité et gouvernement des territoires, Annales de géographie* 700:1359–80.

Cloutier, Karine. 2014. "Les parcours professionnels de toxicomanes ayant été victimes d'abus physiques ou sexuels durant l'enfance." Master's thesis, Université Laval.

Cobbina, Jennifer E., and Sharon S. Oselin. 2011. "It's Not Only for the Money: An Analysis of Adolescent versus Adult Entry into Street Prostitution." *Sociological Inquiry* 81 (3): 310–32.

Comiskey, Catherine M., Robert Stapleton, and Paul A. Kelly. 2012. "Ongoing Cocaine and Benzodiazepine Use: Effects on Acquisitive

Crime Committal Rates Amongst Opiate Users in Treatment." *Drugs: Education, Prevention and Policy* 19 (5): 406–14.

Commission of Inquiry into the Non-Medical Use of Drugs. 1972. *Cannabis: A Report of the Commission of Inquiry into the Non-Medical Use of Drugs.* Ottawa: Information Canada. Accessed June 9, 2017. http://www.drug-library.org/schaffer/library/studies/ledain/ldctoc.html.

Commission of Inquiry into the Non-Medical Use of Drugs. 1973. *Final Report of the Commission of Inquiry into the Non-Medical Use of Drugs.* Ottawa: Information Canada. Accessed June 9, 2017. http://publications.gc.ca/collections/collection_2014/sc-hc/H21-5370-2-1-eng.pdf.

Cope, Nina. 2000. "Drug Use in Prison: The Experience of Young Offenders." *Drugs: Education, Prevention and Policy* 7 (4): 355–66.

Copes, Heith, Andy Hochstetler, and Sveinung Sandberg. 2015. "Using a Narrative Framework to Understand the Drugs and Violence Nexus." *Criminal Justice Review* 40 (1): 32–46.

Cormier, Dollard. 1993. *Toxicomanies: styles de vie.* Montreal: Éditions du Méridien.

Correctional Service Canada. 2003. *Offender Intake Assessment and Correctional Planning, Standard Operating Practices 700-04.* Ottawa: Correctional Service Canada.

Cortoni, Franca, and Denis Lafortune. 2009. "Le traitement correctionnel fondé sur des données probantes: une recension." *Criminologie* 42 (1): 61–90.

Corwyn, Robert Flynn, and Brent B. Benda. 2002. "The Relationship Between Use of Alcohol, Other Drugs, and Crime Among Adolescents: An Argument for a Delinquency Syndrome." *Alcoholism Treatment Quarterly* 20 (2): 35–49.

Cournoyer, Louis-Georges, Serge Brochu, Michel Landry, and Jacques Bergeron. 2007. "Therapeutic Alliance, Patient Behaviour and Dropout in a Drug Rehabilitation Programme: The Moderating Effect of Clinical Subpopulations." *Addiction* 102 (12): 1960–70.

Couvrette, Amélie. 2014. "L'influence de la maternité dans la trajectoire de consommation et de criminalité de femmes toxicomanes judiciarisées." Doctoral dissertation, Université de Montréal. Accessed June 7, 2017. https://papyrus.bib.umontreal.ca/xmlui/bitstream/handle/1866/10503/Couvrette_Amelie_2013_These.pdf?sequence=8&isAllowed=y.

Crane, Cory A., Caroline J. Easton, and Susan Devine. 2013. "The Association Between Phencyclidine Use and Partner Violence: An Initial Examination." *Journal of Addictive Diseases* 32 (2): 150–57.

Crane, Mark A. J., and Linda Blud. 2012. "The Effectiveness of Prisoners Addressing Substance Related Offending (P-ASRO) Programme: Evaluating the Pre and Post Treatment Psychometric Outcomes in an Adult Male Category C Prison." *British Journal of Forensic Practice* 14 (1): 49–59.

CSAT. *See* Center for Substance Abuse Treatment.

Cullen, Francis T., and Paul Gendreau. 1989. "Assessing Correctional Rehabilitation: Policy, Practice, and Prospects." In *Policies, Processes, and Decisions of the Criminal Justice System*, edited by Julie Horney, vol. 3 of *Criminal Justice 2000*, 109–75. Washington, DC: National Institute of Justice, U.S. Department of Justice.

———. 2001. "From Nothing Works to What Works: Changing Professional Ideology in the 21st Century." *Prison Journal* 81 (3): 313–38.

Cusson, Maurice. 1981. *Délinquant pourquoi?* Montreal: Hurtubise HMH.

———. 2005. *La délinquance, une vie choisie. Entre plaisir et crime*. Montreal: Éditions Hurtubise inc.

da Agra, Candido. 1986. "Science, maladie mentale et dispositifs de l'enfance: du paradigme biologique au paradigme systémique." Doctoral dissertation, Instituto Nacional de Investigaçao Cientifica, Lisbon.

———. 1999. "Drogue et Crime: l'expérience Portugaise." *Toxicodependencias* 5 (3): 25–34.

———. 2002. "The Complex Structures, Processes and Meanings of the Drug/ Crime Relationship." In *Drugs and Crime: Deviant Pathways*, edited by Serge Brochu, Candido da Agra, and Marie-Marthe Cousineau, 9–32. London: Ashgate Publishing.

———. 2005. "Postface." In *Trajectoires de déviance juvénile: les éclairages de la recherche qualitative*, edited by Natacha Brunelle and Marie-Marthe Cousineau, 209–12. Presses de l'Université du Québec.

Dafters, Richard I. 2006. "Impulsivity, Inhibition and Negative Priming in Ecstasy Users." *Addictive Behaviors* 31 (8): 1436–41.

D'Amico, Elizabeth J., Maria Orlando Edelen, Jeremy N. V. Miles, and Andrew R. Morral. 2008. "The Longitudinal Association Between Substance Use and Delinquency Among High-Risk Youth." *Drug and Alcohol Dependence* 93 (1–2): 85–92.

Darke, Shane, Johan Duflou, and Michelle Torok. 2009. "Drugs and Violent Death: Comparative Toxicology of Homicide and Non-Substance Toxicity Suicide Victims." *Addiction* 104 (6): 1000–1005.

Deas, Deborah, and Suzanne E. Thomas. 2001. "An Overview of Controlled Studies of Adolescent Substance Abuse Treatment." *American Journal on Addictions* 10 (2): 178–89.

DeBeck, Kora, Kate Shannon, Evan Wood, Kathy Li, Julio Montaner, and Thomas Kerr. 2007. "Income Generating Activities of People Who Inject Drugs." *Drug and Alcohol Dependence* 91 (1): 50–56.

De Choiseul-Praslin, Charles-Henri. 1991. *La drogue, une économie dynamisée par la répression*. Paris: Presses du CNRS.

Decorte, Tom. 2000. *The Taming of Cocaine: Cocaine Use in European and American Cities*. Amsterdam: VUB University Press.

———. 2002. "Mécanismes d'autorégulation chez les consommateurs de drogues illégales. Étude ethnographique sur des consommateurs de cocaïne et de crack à Anvers (Belgique)." In *Société avec drogues. Enjeux et limites*, edited by Claude Faugeron and Michel Kokoreff, 35–62. Paris: Éditions Érès.

Degenhardt, Louisa, and Wayne Hall. 2012. "Extent of Illicit Drug Use and Dependence, and their Contribution to the Global Burden of Disease." *The Lancet* 379 (9810): 55–70.

Degenhardt, Louisa, Sarah Larney, Jo Kimber, Natasa Gisev, Michael Farrell, Timothy Dobbins, Don J. Weatherburn et al. 2014. "The Impact of Opioid Substitution Therapy on Mortality Post-release from Prison: Retrospective Data Linkage Study." *Addiction* 109 (8): 1306–17.

Dennis, Michael L., Tim Feeney, and Janet C. Titus. 2013. *Global Appraisal of Individual Needs-Short Screener (GAIN-SS): Administration and Scoring Manual (Version 3)*. Normal, IL: Chestnut Health Systems. Accessed June 27, 2017. https://chestnut.app.box.com/v/GAIN-SS-Materials/file/63780162801.

Dennis, Michael L., Susan H. Godley, Guy Diamond, Frank M. Tims, Thomas Babor, Jean Donaldson, Howard Liddle et al. 2004. "The Cannabis Youth Treatment (CYT) Study: Main Findings from Two Randomized Trials." *Journal of Substance Abuse Treatment* 27 (3): 197–213.

Denton, Barbara, and Pat O'Malley. 2001. "Property Crime and Women Drug Dealers in Australia." *Journal of Drug Issues* 31 (2): 465–86.

Department of Justice Canada. 2007. *Drugs and Driving: A Compendium of Research Studies*. Traffic Injury Research Foundation and Sherilyn A. Palmer. Accessed July 29, 2017. http://www.justice.gc.ca/eng/rp-pr/csj-sjc/crime/rr06_8/rr06_8.pdf.

Department of Justice Canada. 2003. *The Effectiveness of Substance Abuse Treatment with Young Offenders*. Ottawa: Department of Justice Canada, Youth Justice Research. Accessed June 28, 2017. http://www.justice.gc.ca/eng/rp-pr/cj-jp/yj-jj/rr03_yj1-rr03_jj1/rr03_yj1.pdf.

Dérivois, Daniel. 2004. *Psychodynamique du lien drogue-crime à l'adolescence: Répétition et symbolisation*. Paris: L'Harmattan.

Desjardins, Norm, and Tina Hotton. 2004. "Trends in Drug Offences and the Role of Alcohol and Drugs in Crime." *Juristat* 24 (1): 1–24. Statistics Canada – Catalogue no. 85-002-XPE. Accessed June 3, 2017. http://publications.gc.ca/collections/Collection-R/Statcan/85-002-XIE/0010485-002-XIE.pdf.

Diamond, Guy S., Howard A. Liddle, Matthew B. Wintersteen, Michael L. Dennis, Susan H. Godley, and Frank Tims. 2006. "Early Therapeutic Alliance as a Predictor of Treatment Outcome for Adolescent Cannabis Users in Outpatient Treatment." *American Journal on Addictions* 15 (s1): s26–s33.

DiClemente, Carlo C. 2006. *Addiction and Change: How Addictions Develop and Addicted People Recover*. New York: The Guilford Press.

DiClemente, Carlo C., Debra Schlundt, and Leigh Gemmell. 2004. "Readiness and Stages of Change in Addiction Treatment." *American Journal on Addictions* 13 (2): 103–19.

Doherty, Elaine Eggleston, Kerry M. Green, and Margaret E. Ensminger. 2008. "Investigating the Long-Term Influence of Adolescent Delinquency on Drug Use Initiation." *Drug and Alcohol Dependence* 93 (1–2): 72–84.

Domosławski, Artur. 2011. *Drug Policy in Portugal: The Benefits of Decriminalizing Drug Use*. New York: Open Society Foundations. Accessed May 22, 2017. https://www.opensocietyfoundations.org/sites/default/files/drug-policy-in-portugal-english-20120814.pdf.

Donovan, John E., Richard Jessor, and Frances M. Costa. 1999. "Adolescent Problem Drinking: Stability of Psychosocial and Behavioral Correlates Across a Generation." *Journal of Studies on Alcohol* 60 (3): 352–61.

Dow, Sarah J., and John F. Kelly. 2013. "Listening to Youth: Adolescents' Reasons for Substance Use as a Unique Predictor of Treatment Response and Outcome." *Psychology of Addictive Behaviors* 27 (4): 1122–231.

Dowden, Craig, Daniel Antonowicz, and D. A. Andrews. 2003. "The Effectiveness of Relapse Prevention with Offenders: A Meta-Analysis." *International Journal of Offender Therapy and Comparative Criminology* 47 (5): 516–28.

Dowden, Craig, and S. L. Brown. 2002. "The Role of Substance Abuse Factors in Predicting Recidivism: A Meta-Analysis." *Psychology, Crime & Law* 8 (3): 243–64.

Duff, Cameron. 2005. "Party Drugs and Party People: Examining the "Normalization" of Recreational Drug Use in Melbourne, Australia." *International Journal of Drug Policy* 16 (3): 161–70.

Duff, Cameron, Mark Asbridge, Serge Brochu, Marie-Marthe Cousineau, Andrew D. Hathaway, David Marsh, and Patricia G. Erickson. 2012. "A Canadian Perspective on Cannabis Normalization Among Adults: Has all the Stigma Gone?" *Addiction Research and Theory* 20 (4): 271–83.

Dufour, Céline. 2004. "Étude sur le rôle des substances psychoactives en lien avec les manifestations de comportements violents chez les jeunes contrevenants de la région de Montréal." Master's thesis, Université de Montréal. Accessed May 29, 2017. https://papyrus.bib.umontreal.ca/xmlui/bitstream/handle/1866/14371/Dufour_Celine_2004_memoire.pdf?sequence=1&isAllowed=y.

Dufour, Stéphanie. 2014. "Les facteurs de protection et leurs implications pour le traitement des délinquants sexuels." Master's thesis, Université de Montréal. Accessed June 5, 2017. https://papyrus.bib.umontreal.ca/xmlui/bitstream/handle/1866/12169/Dufour_Stephanie_2014_rapport-destage.pdf?sequence=1&isAllowed=y.

Duprez, Dominique, and Michel Kokoreff. 2000. *Les mondes de la drogue: Usages et trafics dans les quartiers*. Paris: Odile Jacob.

Easton, Caroline J., Dolores L. Mandel, Karen A. Hunkele, Charla Nich, Bruce J. Rounsaville, and Kathleen M. Carroll. 2007. "A Cognitive Behavioral Therapy for Alcohol-dependent Domestic Violence Offenders: An Integrated Substance Abuse-Domestic Violence Treatment Approach (SADV)." *American Journal on Addictions* 16 (1): 24–31.

The Economist. 2014a. "The Amazons of the Dark Net." November 1. Accessed May 27, 2017. http://www.economist.com/news/international/21629417-business-thriving-anonymous-internet-despite-efforts-law-enforcers.

——. 2014b. "The Silk Road, Reborn." February 15. Accessed May 27, 2017. http://www.economist.com/news/international/21596561-it-still-possible-get-line-online-silk-road-reborn.

Ellickson, Phyllis, Hilary Saner, and Kimberly A. McGuigan. 1997. "Profiles of Violent Youth: Substance Use and Other Concurrent Problems." *American Journal of Public Health* 87 (6): 985–91.

EMCDDA. *See* European Monitoring Centre for Drugs and Drug Addiction.

Erickson, Patricia G. 2005. "Alternative Sanctions for Cannabis Use and Possession." In *Substance Abuse in Canada: Current Challenges and Choices*, 39–43. Ottawa: Canadian Centre on Substance Abuse. Accessed June 9, 2017. http://www.ccsa.ca/Resource%20Library/ccsa-004032-2005.pdf.

Erickson, Patricia G., Jennifer Butters, Patti McGillicuddy, and Ase Hallgren. 2000. "Crack and Prostitution: Gender, Myths, and Experiences." *Journal of Drug Issues* 30 (4): 767–88.

Erickson, Patricia G., Mark Van Der Maas, and Andrew D. Hathaway. 2013. "Revisiting Deterrence: Legal Knowledge, Use Context and Arrest Perception for Cannabis." *Sociologický časopis/Czech Sociological Review* 49 (3): 427–48.

European Monitoring Centre for Drugs and Drug Addiction. 2001. *Annual report on the state of the drugs problem in the European Union 2001*. Luxembourg: Office for Official Publications of the European Communities. Accessed July 7, 2017. http://www.emcdda.europa.eu/system/files/publications/200/ar01_en_69624.pdf.

——. 2002. *2002 Annual report on the state of the drugs problem in the European Union and Norway*. Luxembourg: Office for Official Publications of the European Communities. Accessed July 7, 2017. http://www.emcdda.europa.eu/system/files/publications/167/2002_0458_EN_69588.pdf.

——. 2004. *Annual report 2004: the state of the drugs problem in the European Union and Norway*. Luxembourg: Office for Official Publications of the European Communities. Accessed July 7, 2017. http://www.emcdda.europa.eu/system/files/publications/923/ar2004-en1_69524.pdf.

——. 2011. "Drug Policy Profiles—Portugal." EMCDDA Papers. Lisbon: Publications Office of the European Union. Accessed May 27, 2017. http://www.emcdda.europa.eu/system/files/publications/642/PolicyProfile_Portugal_WEB_Final_289201.pdf.

———. 2015. "Alternatives to Punishment for Drug-Using Offenders." EMCDDA Papers. Luxembourg: Publications Office of the European Union. Accessed May 27, 2017. http://www.emcdda.europa.eu/system/files/publications/1020/TDAU14007ENN.pdf.

Evans, Rhonda D., Craig J. Forsyth, and DeAnn K. Gauthier. 2002. "Gendered pathways into and experiences within crack cultures outside of the inner city." *Deviant Behavior* 23 (6): 483–510.

Falls, Benjamin J., Eric D. Wish, Laura M. Garnier, Kimberly M. Caldeira, Kevin E. O'Grady, Kathryn B. Vincent, and Amelia M. Arria. 2011. "The Association Between Early Conduct Problems and Early Marijuana Use in College Students." *Journal of Child Adolescent Substance Abuse* 20 (3): 221–36.

Fallu, Jean-Sébastien, Frédéric N. Brière, Frank Vitaro, Stéphane Cantin, and Anne I. H. Borge. 2011. "The Influence of Close Friends on Adolescent Substance Use: Does Popularity Matter?" In *Jahrbuch Jugendforschung, volume 10*, edited by Angela Ittel, Hans Merkens, and Ludwig Stecher, 235–62. VS Verlag für Sozialwissenschaften.

Farrell, Shanna, Jonathan Ross, Marguerite Ternes, and Dan Kunic. 2010. "Prevalence of Injection Drug Use among Male Offenders." Research Snippet 10-2. Addiction Research Centre, Correctional Service Canada. Accessed May 27, 2017. http://www.csc-scc.gc.ca/research/005008-rs10-02-eng.shtml.

Farrington, David P., Rolf Loeber, and Maria M. Ttofi. 2012. "Risk and Protective Factors for Offending." In *The Oxford Handbook of Crime Prevention*, edited by Brandon C. Welsh and David P. Farrington, 46–69. New York: Oxford University Press.

Faupel, Charles E. 1991. *Shooting Dope: Career Patterns of Hard-Core Heroin Users*. Gainesville: University of Florida Press.

Fazel, Seena, Parveen Bains, and Helen Doll. 2006. "Substance Abuse and Dependence in Prisoners: A Systematic Review." *Addiction* 101 (2): 181–91.

Felson, Richard B., and Luke Bonkiewicz. 2013. "Guns and Trafficking in Crack-Cocaine and Other Drug Markets." *Crime and Delinquency* 59 (3): 319–43.

Fergusson, David M., Richie Poulton, Paul F. Smith, and Joseph M. Boden. 2006. "Drugs: Cannabis and Psychosis." *British Medical Journal* 332 (7534): 172–75.

Ferland, Francine, Nadine Blanchette-Martin, Catherine Arseneault, Isabelle Jacques, Céline Desbiens, and Nancy Émond. 2013. "Programme Toxico-Justice: le département spécialisé en toxicomanie en milieu carcéral." In *Sortir des sentiers battus: Pratiques prometteuses auprès d'adultes dépendants*, edited by Chantal Plourde, Myriam Laventure, Michel Landry, and Catherine Arseneault, 211–27. Quebec City: Les Presses de l'Université Laval.

Ferner, Matt. 2014. "Colorado Recreational Weed Sales Top $14 Million in First Month." *Huffington Post*, March 10. Accessed July 29, 2017. http://www.huffingtonpost.ca/entry/colorado-marijuana-tax-revenue_n_4936223.

Fickenscher, Alexandra, Douglas K. Novins, and Janette Beals. 2006. "A Pilot Study of Motivation and Treatment Completion Among American Indian Adolescents in Substance Abuse Treatment." *Addictive Behaviors* 31 (8): 1402–14.

Fleetwood, Jennifer. 2014. "Keeping Out of Trouble: Women Crack Cocaine Dealers in England." *European Journal of Criminology* 11 (1): 91–109.

Fletcher, Bennett W., and Redonna K. Chandler. 2007. *Principles of Drug Abuse Treatment for Criminal Justice Populations: A Research-Based Guide*. National Institute on Drug Abuse. Accessed July 3, 2017. http://www.nationaltasc.org/wp-content/uploads/2012/11/Principles-for-Drug-Abuse-Treatment-for-Criminal-Justice-Populations-NIDA.pdf.

Fletcher, Bennett W., Wayne E. K. Lehman, Harry K. Wexler, and Gerald Melnick. 2007. "Who participates in The Criminal Justice Drug Abuse Treatment Studies (CJ-DATS)?" *Prison Journal* 87 (1): 25–57.

Fletcher, Bennett W., Wayne E. K. Lehman, Harry K. Wexler, Gerald Melnick, Faye S. Taxman, and Douglas W. Young. 2009. "Measuring Collaboration and Integration Activities in Criminal Justice and Substance Abuse Treatment Agencies." *Drug and Alcohol Dependence* 103 (1): 191–201.

Forsyth, Alasdair J. M., Furzana Khan, and Bill Mckinlay. 2011. "Diazepam, Alcohol Use and Violence Among Male Young Offenders: 'The Devil's Mixture.'" *Drugs: Education, Prevention and Policy* 18 (6): 468–76.

Fortin-Dufour, Isabelle, Marc Alain, Julie Marcotte, and Marie-Pierre Villeneuve. 2015. "La sentence de la 'dernière chance': un aperçu des jeunes soumis à une ordonnance différée de placement et de surveillance au Québec." In *Intervenir auprès des adolescents contrevenants au Québec: dix ans d'expérience et de défis sous la LSJPA*, edited by Marc Alain and Sylvie Hamel, 135–56. Québec: Presses de l'Université du Québec.

Fothergill, Kate E., and Margaret E. Ensminger. 2006. "Childhood and Adolescent Antecedents of Drug and Alcohol Problems: A Longitudinal Study." *Drug and Alcohol Dependence* 82 (1): 61–76.

Frappier, Jean-Yves, Manon Duchesne, Yves Lambert, and Ronald Chartrand. 2015. *Santé des adolescent(e)s hébergé(e)s en centres de réadaptation des centres jeunesse au Québec*. Rapport de recherche. Montreal: Association des centres jeunesse du Québec et Hôpital Sainte-Justine. Accessed May 26, 2017. http://www.centrejeunessemonteregie.qc.ca/wp-content/uploads/2015/04/rapport-sante-des-ados-en-cr-des-cj2015-3-14.pdf.

Fréchette, Marcel, and Marc LeBlanc. 1987. *Délinquances et délinquants*. Chicoutimi, QC: Gaëtan Morin Éditeur.

Fridell, Mats, Morten Hesse, Mads Meier Jæger, and Eckart Kühlhorn. 2008. "Antisocial Personality Disorder as a Predictor of Criminal Behaviour in a Longitudinal Study of a Cohort of Abusers of Several Classes of Drugs: Relation to Type of Substance and Type of Crime." *Addictive Behaviors* 33 (6): 799–811.

Friedman, Alfred S., Arlene Terras, and Kimberly Glassman. 2003. "The Differential Disinhibition Effect of Marijuana Use on Violent Behavior: A Comparison of this Effect on a Conventional, Non-Delinquent Group Versus a Delinquent or Deviant Group." *Journal of Addictive Diseases* 22 (3): 63–78.

Friedmann, Peter D., Faye S. Taxman, and Craig E. Henderson. 2007. "Evidence-Based Treatment Practices for Drug-Involved Adults in the Criminal Justice System." *Journal of Substance Abuse Treatment* 32 (3): 267–77.

Friedmann, Peter D., Traci C. Green, Faye S. Taxman, Magdalena Harrington, Anne G. Rhodes, Elizabeth Katz, Daniel O'Connell et al. 2012. "Collaborative Behavioral Management Among Parolees: Drug Use, Crime and Re-Arrest in the Step'n Out Randomized Trial." *Addiction* 107 (6): 1099–108.

Garner, Bryan R., Susan H. Godley, and Rodney R. Funk. 2008. "Predictors of Early Therapeutic Alliance Among Adolescents in Substance Abuse Treatment." *Journal of Psychoactive Drugs* 40 (1): 55–65.

Gendreau, Paul, and Robert R. Ross. 1987. "Revivification of Rehabilitation: Evidence from the 1980s." *Justice Quarterly* 4 (3): 349–407.

Germain, Michel, Louise Guyon, Michel Landry, Joël Tremblay, Natacha Brunelle, and Jacques Bergeron. 2007. *DEP-ADO Detection of Alcohol and Drug Problems in Adolescents*, version 3.2. Recherche et intervention sur les substances psychoactives – Québec (RISQ). Accessed June 27, 2017. https://oraprdnt.uqtr.uquebec.ca/pls/public/docs/GSC4242/F463443489_DEP_ADO_ang_V3_2.pdf.

Gillet, Michaël, and Serge Brochu. 2005. "Institutionnalisation des stratégies de réduction des méfaits au sein de l'agenda politique canadien: les enjeux et les limites de la conceptualisation actuelle." *Drogues, santé et société* 4 (2): 79–139.

Gillies, Donna, Stephanie Sampson, Alison Beck, and John Rathbone. 2013. "Benzodiazepines for Psychosis-Induced Aggression or Agitation." *Cochrane Database of Systematic Reviews* issue 9.

Goldstein, A. P., 1998. *Drug Abuse and Violence*, Washington, DC: United States Sentencing Commission.

Goldstein, Paul J. 1987. "Impact of Drug-Related Violence." *Public Health Reports* 102 (6): 625–27.

———. 1985. "The Drugs/Violence Nexus: A Tripartite Conceptual Framework." *Journal of Drug Issues* 15 (4): 493–506.

Goode, Erich. 1999. "Drugs and Crime and Violence." In *Drugs in American Society*, 5th edition, edited by Erich Goode, 144–72.

Gordon, Michael S., Timothy W. Kinlock, Robert P. Schwartz, and Kevin E. O'Grady. 2008. "A Randomized Clinical Trial of Methadone Maintenance for Prisoners: Findings at 6 Months Post-Release." *Addiction* 103 (8): 1333–42.

Gossop, Michael, Shane Darke, Paul Griffiths, Julie Hando, Beverly Powis, Wayne Hall, and John Strang. 1995. "The Severity of Dependence Scale (SDS): Psychometric Properties of the SDS in English and Australian Samples of Heroin, Cocaine and Amphetamine Users." *Addiction* 90 (5): 607–14.

Government of Canada. 2015. *Cocaine and Crack*. Accessed May 19, 2017. https://www.canada.ca/en/health-canada/services/substance-abuse/controlled-illegal-drugs/cocaine-crack.html.

———. 1996. *Controlled Drugs and Substances Act* (CDSA). (S.C. 1996, c. 19). Accessed May 19, 2017. http://laws-lois.justice.gc.ca/eng/acts/c-38.8/.

Goyette, Mathieu, Rachel Charbonneau, Chantal Plourde, and Serge Brochu. 2013. "Conjuguer réadaptation et justice: un défi possible." In *Sortir des sentiers battus: Pratiques prometteuses auprès d'adultes dépendants*, edited by Chantal Plourde, Myriam Laventure, Michel Landry, and Catherine Arseneault, 75–96. Quebec City: Les Presses de l'Université Laval.

Grapendaal, Martin, Ed Leuw, and Hans Nelen. 1995. *A World of Opportunities. Life-Style and Economic Behavior of Heroin Addicts in Amsterdam*. Albany: State University of New York Press.

Greenberg, Stephanie W. 1976. "The Relationship Between Crime and Amphetamine Abuse: An Empirical Review of the Literature." *Contemporary Drug Problems* 5 (2): 101–29.

Greenwald, Glenn. 2009. *Drug Decriminalization in Portugal: Lessons for Creating Fair and Successful Drug Policies*. Washington: Cato Institute. Accessed July 29, 2017. https://object.cato.org/sites/cato.org/files/pubs/pdf/greenwald_whitepaper.pdf.

Gregoire, Thomas K., and Anna Celeste Burke. 2004. "The Relationship of Legal Coercion to Readiness to Change Among Adults with Alcohol and Other Drug Problems." *Journal of Substance Abuse Treatment* 26 (1): 35–41.

Grella, Christine E., Lisa Greenwell, Michael Prendergast, David Farabee, Elizabeth Hall, Jerome Cartier, and William Burdon. 2007. "Organizational Characteristics of Drug Abuse Treatment Programs for Offenders." *Journal of Substance Abuse Treatment* 32 (3): 291–300.

Gretton, Heather M., and Robert J.W. Clift. "The Mental Health Needs of Incarcerated Youth in British Columbia, Canada." *International Journal of Law and Psychiatry* 34 (2): 109–15.

Gutierrez, Leticia, and Guy Bourgon. 2009. *Drug Treatment Courts: A Quantitative Review of Study and Treatment Quality*. Ottawa: Public Safety Canada. Accessed June 24, 2017. https://www.securitepublique.gc.ca/cnt/rsrcs/pblctns/2009-04-dtc/2009-04-dtc-eng.pdf.

Hare, Robert D. 1991. Hare Psychopathy Checklist-Revised. Toronto: Multi-Health Systems.

——. 2003. Hare Psychopathy Checklist–Revised: 2nd Edition Manual. Toronto: Multi-Health Systems.

Harrison, Lana D. 1994. "Cocaine Using Careers in Perspective." *Addiction Research* 2 (1): 1–20.

Hartwell, Karen J., Sudie E. Back, Aimee L. McRae-Clark, Stephanie R. Shaftman, and Kathleen T. Brady. 2012. "Motives for Using: A Comparison of Prescription Opioid, Marijuana and Cocaine Dependent Individuals." *Addictive Behaviors* 37 (4): 373–78.

Hathaway, Andrew D., Patricia G. Erickson, and Philippe Lucas. 2007. "Canadian Public Opinion on Cannabis How Far Out of Step With It Is The Existing Law?" *Canadian Review of Social Policy* 59: 44–55.

Haug, Severin, Carla López-Núñez, Julia Becker, Gerhard Gmel, and Michael P. Schaub. 2014. "Predictors of Onset of Cannabis and Other Drug Use in Male Young Adults: Results from a Longitudinal Study." *BMC Public Health* 14 (1202): 1–15.

Havnes, Ingrid Amalia. 2015. "Violence and Diversion of Prescribed Opioids Among Individuals in Opioid Maintenance Treatment: A Complementary Methods Study of Violent Crime Convictions in a National Cohort and Qualitative Interviews Among Prisoners." Doctoral dissertation, Norwegian Centre for Addiction Research, Institute of Clinical Medicine, Faculty of Medicine, University of Oslo. Accessed May 29, 2017. https://www.duo.uio.no/bitstream/handle/10852/42124/PhD-Havnes-DUO.pdf?sequence=1&isAllowed=y.

Hawley, Kristin M., and Ann F. Garland. 2008. "Working Alliance in Adolescent Outpatient Therapy: Youth, Parent and Therapist Reports and Associations with Therapy Outcomes." *Child & Youth Care Forum* 37 (2): 59–74.

Health Canada. 2005. *Canadian Addiction Survey (CAS): A National Survey of Canadians' Use of Alcohol and Other Drugs: Prevalence of Use and Related Harms: Detailed Report*. Canadian Centre on Substance Abuse. Accessed June 5, 2017. http://www.ccsa.ca/Resource%20Library/ccsa-004028-2005.pdf.

——. 2008. *Canadian Alcohol and Drug Use Monitoring Survey (CADUMS): Detailed Tables for 2007*. Office of Research and Surveillance, Controlled Substances and Tobacco Directorate.

——. 2009. *Canadian Alcohol and Drug Use Monitoring Survey (CADUMS): Detailed Tables for 2008*. Office of Research and Surveillance, Controlled Substances and Tobacco Directorate.

——. 2010a. *Canadian Alcohol and Drug Use Monitoring Survey (CADUMS): Summary of Results for 2009*. Office of Research and Surveillance, Controlled Substances and Tobacco Directorate.

——. 2010b. *Canadian Alcohol and Drug Use Monitoring Survey (CADUMS): Detailed Tables for 2009*. Office of Research and Surveillance, Controlled Substances and Tobacco Directorate.

——. 2011a. *Canadian Alcohol and Drug Use Monitoring Survey (CADUMS): Detailed Tables for 2010*. Office of Research and Surveillance, Controlled Substances and Tobacco Directorate.

——. 2011b. *Canadian Alcohol and Drug Use Monitoring Survey (CADUMS): Summary of Results for 2010*. Office of Research and Surveillance, Controlled Substances and Tobacco Directorate. Accessed May 16, 2017. http://www.hc-sc.gc.ca/hc-ps/drugs-drogues/stat/_2010/summary-sommaire-eng.php.

——. 2012. *Canadian Alcohol and Drug Use Monitoring Survey: Detailed Tables for 2011*. Office of Research and Surveillance, Controlled Substances and Tobacco Directorate. Accessed July 29, 2017. https://www.canada.ca/en/health-canada/services/health-concerns/drug-prevention-treatment/drug-alcohol-use-statistics/canadian-alcohol-drug-use-monitoring-survey-tables-2011.html.

——. 2013a. *Information for Health Care Professionals: Cannabis (marihuana, marijuana) and the cannabinoids*. Accessed May 16, 2017. http://www.hc-sc.gc.ca/dhp-mps/alt_formats/pdf/marihuana/med/infoprof-eng.pdf.

——. 2013b. "Ecstasy." Accessed May 16, 2017. https://www.canada.ca/en/health-canada/services/substance-abuse/controlled-illegal-drugs/ecstasy.html.

——. 2013c. *Canadian Alcohol and Drug Use Monitoring Survey (CADUMS): Detailed Tables for 2012*. Office of Research and Surveillance, Controlled Substances and Tobacco Directorate. Accessed May 16, 2017. http://www.hc-sc.gc.ca/hc-ps/drugs-drogues/stat/_2012/tables-tableaux-eng.php#t1.

Hedrich, Dagmar, Paula Alves, Michael Farrell, Heino Stöver, Lars Møller, and Soraya Mayet. 2012. "The Effectiveness of Opioid Maintenance Treatment in Prison Settings: A Systematic Review." *Addiction* 107 (3): 501–17.

Henry, Kimberly L., Kelly E. Knight, and Terence P. Thornberry. 2012. "School Disengagement as a Predictor of Dropout, Delinquency, and Problem Substance Use during Adolescence and Early Adulthood." *Journal of Youth and Adolescence* 41 (2): 156–66.

Hiller, Matthew L., Kevin Knight, and D. Dwayne Simpson. 2006. "Recidivism Following Mandated Residential Substance Abuse Treatment for Felony Probationers." *Prison Journal* 86 (2): 230–41.

Hills, Holly A., 2000. *Creating Effective Treatment Programs for Persons with Co-Occurring Disorders in the Justice System*. Delmar, New York: The GAINS Center.

Hoaken, Peter N.S., and Sherry H. Stewart. 2003. "Drugs of Abuse and the Elicitation of Human Aggressive Behavior." *Addictive Behaviors* 28 (9): 1533–54.

Hollin, Clive R., and Emma J. Palmer. 2006. *Offending Behaviour Programmes: Development, Application and Controversies*. Chichester, UK: John Wiley & Sons.

Hser, Yih-Ing, Christine E. Grella, Robert L. Hubbard, Shih-Chao Hsieh, Bennett W. Fletcher, Barry S. Brown, and M. Douglas Anglin. 2001. "An Evaluation of Drug Treatments for Adolescents in 4 US Cities." *Archives of General Psychiatry* 58 (7): 689–95.

Hser, Yih-Ing, M. Douglas Anglin, Christine Grella, Douglas Longshore, and Michael L. Prendergast. 1997. "Drug Treatment Careers: A Conceptual Framework and Existing Research Findings." *Journal of Substance Abuse Treatment* 14 (6): 543–58.

Huebner, Beth M., and Jennifer Cobbina. 2007. "The Effect of Drug Use, Drug Treatment Participation, and Treatment Completion on Probationer Recidivism." *Journal of Drug Issues* 37 (3): 619–42.

Hughes, Caitlin, and Alex Stevens. 2007. "The Effects of Decriminalization of Drug Use in Portugal." Beckley Foundation Drug Policy Programme briefing paper no. 14.

———. 2010. "What Can We Learn From the Portuguese Decriminalization of Illicit Drugs?" *British Journal of Criminology* 50 (6): 999–1022.

Hume, Lucy. 2001. *Substance Abuse Programming: A Proposed Structure*. Addiction Research Centre, Correctional Service Canada discussion paper no. R-120. Accessed June 25, 2017. http://publications.gc.ca/collections/collection_2010/scc-csc/PS83-3-120-eng.pdf.

Hunt, Dana E. 1990. "Drugs and Consensual Crimes: Drug Dealing and Prostitution." In *Crime and Justice 13: Drugs and Crime*, edited by Michael Tonry and James Q. Wilson, 159–202. Chicago: University of Chicago Press.

———. 1991. "Stealing and Dealing: Cocaine and Property Crimes." In *The Epidemiology of Cocaine Use and Abuse*, edited by Susan Schober and Charles Schade, 139–150. U.S. Department of Health and Human Services, Public Health Service, National Institutes of Health, National Institute on Drug Abuse research monograph no. 110. Accessed July 6, 2017. https://archives.drugabuse.gov/pdf/monographs/110.pdf.

INCB. *See* International Narcotics Control Board.

International Narcotics Control Board. 2015. Report of the International Narcotics Control Board for 2014. Vienna: United Nations Office. Accessed May 27, 2017. https://www.incb.org/documents/Publications/AnnualReports/AR2014/English/AR_2014.pdf.

Jacobs, Bruce A., and Jody Miller. 1998. "Crack Dealing, Gender, and Arrest Avoidance." *Social Problems* 45 (4): 550–69.

Jacobs, Bruce A., Volkan Topalli, and Richard Wright. 2000. "Managing Retaliation: Drug Robbery and Informal Sanction Threats." *Criminology* 38 (1): 171–98.

Jacques, Scott, and Danielle M. Reynald. 2011. "The Offenders' Perspective on Prevention: Guarding Against Victimization and Law Enforcement." *Journal of Research in Crime and Delinquency* 49 (2): 269–94.

Jacques, Scott, Andrea Allen, and Richard Wright. 2014. "Drug Dealers' Rational Choices on Which Customers to Rip-Off." *International Journal of Drug Policy* 25 (2): 251–56.

Jacques, Scott, and Richard Wright. 2008. "The Relevance of Peace Studies of Drug Market Violence." *Criminology* 46 (1): 221–54.

Jadidi, Nadjme, and Nouzar Nakhaee. 2014. "Etiology of Drug Abuse: A Narrative Analysis." *Journal of Addiction*, 1–6.

Jennings, Wesley G., Alex R. Piquero, David P. Farrington, Maria M. Ttofi, Rebecca V. Crago, and Delphine Theobald. 2016. "The Intersections of Drug Use Continuity with Nonviolent Offending and Involvement in Violence Over the Life Course: Findings from the Cambridge Study in Delinquent Development." *Youth Violence and Juvenile Justice* 14 (2): 95–109.

Joe, George W., D. Dwayne Simpson, Donald F. Dansereau, and Grace A. Rowan-Szal. 2001. "Relationships Between Counseling Rapport and Drug Abuse Treatment Outcomes." *Psychiatric Services* 52 (9): 1223–29.

Johnson, Bruce D., Andrew Golub, and Jeffrey Fagan. 1995. "Careers in Crack, Drug Use, Drug Distribution, and Nondrug Criminality." *Crime and Delinquency* 41 (3): 275–95.

Johnson, Bruce D., Paul J. Goldstein, Edward Preble, James Schmeidler, Douglas S. Lipton, Barry Spunt, and Thomas Miller. 1985. *Taking Care of Business: The Economics of Crime by Heroin Abusers*. Toronto: D.C. Heath and Company.

Johnson, Holly. 2006. "Drug Use by Incarcerated Women Offenders." *Drug and Alcohol Review* 25 (5): 433–37.

Jones, Katy A., Suzanne Nielsen, Raimondo Bruno, Matthew Frei, and Dan I. Lubman. 2011. "Benzodiazepines: Their Role in Aggression and Why GPs Should Prescribe with Caution." *Australian Family Physician* 40 (11): 862–65.

Justice Québec. 2014. Québec court-supervised drug treatment program. Accessed June 24, 2017. http://www.justice.gouv.qc.ca/english/programmes/traitement_toxicomanie-a.htm.

Kaplan, Howard B. 1995. "Contemporary Themes and Emerging Directions in Longitudinal Research on Deviant Behavior." In *Drugs, Crime, and Other Deviant Adaptations: Longitudinal Studies*, edited by Howard B. Kaplan, 233–41. New York: Plenum Press.

Kennedy, Sharon M. 2000. "Treatment Responsivity: Reducing Recidivism by Enhancing Treatment Effectiveness." In *Compendium 2000 on Effective Correctional Programming*, edited by Laurence L. Motiuk and Ralph C. Serin, ch. 5. Ottawa: Correctional Service Canada. Accessed June 24,

2017. http://www.csc-scc.gc.ca/005/008/compendium/2000/chap_5-eng. shtml.

Kinlock, Timothy W., Michael S. Gordon, Robert P. Schwartz, Kevin O'Grady, Terrence T. Fitzgerald, and Monique Wilson. 2007. "A Randomized Clinical Trial of Methadone Maintenance for Prisoners: Results at One-Month Post-Release." *Drug and Alcohol Dependence* 91 (2): 220–27.

Kinlock, Timothy W., Michael S. Gordon, Robert P. Schwartz, and Kevin E. O'Grady. 2008. "A Study of Methadone Maintenance for Male Prisoners: 3 Month Post-Release Outcomes." *Criminal Justice and Behavior* 35 (1): 34–47.

Kinlock, Timothy W., Michael S. Gordon, Robert P. Schwartz, Terrence T. Fitzgerald, and Kevin E. O'Grady. 2009. "A Randomized Clinical Trial of Methadone Maintenance for Prisoners: Results at 12 Months Post-Release." *Journal of Substance Abuse Treatment* 37 (3): 277–85.

Kivivuori, Janne, and Henrik Linderborg. 2009. *Short-term Prisoners in Finland: A Study of Their Living Conditions and Criminality, Summary.* Helsinki: National Research Institute of Legal Policy, The Criminal Sanctions Agency.

Kliewer, Wendy, and Lenn Murrelle. "Risk and Protective Factors for Adolescent Substance Use: Findings from a Study in Selected Central American Countries." *Journal of Adolescent Health* 40 (5): 448–55.

Kokoreff, Michel. 2005. "Toxicomanie et trafics de drogues. Diversité des cheminements et effets de génération au sein des milieux populaires en France." In *Trajectoires de déviance juvénile: les éclairages de la recherche qualitative,* edited by Natacha Brunelle and Marie-Marthe Cousineau, 31–70. Sainte-Foy: Presses de l'Université de Québec.

Kokoreff, Michel, and Claude Faugeron. 2002. *Société avec drogues. Enjeux et limites.* Paris: Éditions Érès.

Kolb, Lawrence. 1925. "Drug Addiction and Its Relation to Crime." *Mental Hygiene* 9:74–89.

Konopka, Anna, Justyna Pełka-Wysiecka, Anna Grzywacz, Jerzy Samochowiec. 2013. "Psychosocial characteristics of benzodiazepine addicts compared to not addicted benzodiazepine users." *Progress in Neuro-Psychopharmacology & Biological Psychiatry* 10 (40): 229–35.

Krank, Marvin, Sherry H. Stewart, Roisin O'Connor, Patricia B. Woicik, Anne-Marie Wall, and Patricia J. Conrod. 2011. "Structural, Concurrent, and Predictive Validity of the Substance Use Risk Profile Scale in Early Adolescence." *Addictive Behaviors* 36 (1–2): 37–46.

Kuhns, Joseph B., David B. Wilson, Edward R. Maguire, Stephanie A. Ainsworth, and Tammatha A. Clodfelter. 2009. "A Meta-Analysis of Marijuana, Cocaine and Opiate Toxicology Study Findings Among Homicide Victims." *Addiction* 104 (7): 1122–31.

Kunic, Dan, and Brian A. Grant. 2006. *The Computerized Assessment of Substance Abuse (CASA): Results from the Demonstration Project.* Addictions

Research Centre, Research Branch, Correctional Service of Canada. Accessed May 27, 2017. http://www.csc-scc.gc.ca/research/r173-eng. shtml.

Lacharité-Young, Elisabeth, Natacha Brunelle, Michel Rousseau, Iris Bourgault-Bouthillier, Danielle Leclerc, Marie-Marthe Cousineau, Joël Tremblay, and Magali Dufour. 2017. "Liens drogue-délinquance lucrative chez les adolescents." *Criminologie* 501: 263–85.

Lader, Malcolm. 2011. "Benzodiazepines Revisited—Will We Ever Learn?" *Addiction* 106 (12): 2086–109.

Lalande, Pierre. 2004. "Punir ou réhabiliter les contrevenants ? "Du 'Nothing Works' au 'What Works' (Montée, déclin et retour de l'idéal de réhabilitation)." In *La sévérité pénale à l'heure du populisme*, edited by Pierre Lalande and Olivier Lamalice, 30–77. Québec: Ministère de la Sécurité publique, Gouvernement du Québec. Accessed June 24, 2017. http://www.securitepublique.gouv.qc.ca/fileadmin/Documents/services_correctionnels/publications/severite_penale/severite_penale.pdf.

Lambert, Gilles, Nancy Haley, Sandrine Jean, Claude Tremblay, Jean-Yves Frappier, Joanne Otis, and Élise Roy. 2012. *Sexe, drogue et autres questions de santé: Étude sur les habitudes de vie et les comportements associés aux infections transmissibles sexuellement chez les jeunes hébergés dans les centres jeunesse du Québec.* Agence de la santé et des services sociaux de Montréal, Direction de santé publique. Accessed May 26, 2017. https://publications.santemontreal.qc.ca/uploads/tx_asssmpublications/978-2-89673-134-3.pdf.

Lanctôt, Nadine, Mélanie Bernard, and Marc Le Blanc. 2002. "Le début de l'adolescence: une période critique pour l'éclosion des conduites déviantes des adolescents." *Criminologie* 35 (1): 69–88.

Landry, Pierre, Maryse Gervais, and Kieron P. O'Connor. 2008. "Mise à jour sur les considérations pharmacocinétiques, pharmacodynamiques et les interactions médicamenteuses dans le choix d'une benzodiazépine." *Annales Médico-Psychologiques* 166 (7): 585–94.

Lang, Michelle A., and Steven Belenko. 2000. "Predicting Retention in a Residential Drug Treatment Alternative to Prison Program." *Journal of Substance Abuse Treatment* 19 (2): 145–60.

Laprise, Patrick, Hélène Gagnon, Pascale Leclerc, and Linda Cazale. 2012. "Consommation d'alcool et de drogues." In *L'Enquête québécoise sur la santé des jeunes du secondaire 2010-2011, TOME 1, Le visage des jeunes d'aujourd'hui: leur santé physique et leurs habitudes de vie*, edited by Lucille A. Pica, Issouf Traoré, Francine Bernèche, Patrick Laprise, Linda Cazale, Hélène Camirand, Mikaël Berthelot, and Nathalie Plante, 169–207. Quebec City: Institut de la statistique du Québec. Accessed May 26, 2017. http://www.stat.gouv.qc.ca/statistiques/sante/enfants-ados/alimentation/sante-jeunes-secondaire1.pdf.

Laqueur, Hannah. 2014. "Uses and Abuses of Drug Decriminalization in Portugal." *Law & Social Inquiry* 40 (3): 746–81.

Larney, Sarah, Barbara Toson, Lucy Burns, and Kate Dolan. "Effect of Prison-Based Opioid Substitution Treatment and Post-Release Retention in Treatment on Risk of Re-Incarceration." *Addiction* 107 (2): 372–80.

Larney, Sarah, Natasa Gisev, Michael Farrell, Timothy Dobbins, Lucinda Burns, Amy Gibson, Jo Kimber, and Louisa Degenhardt. 2014. "Opioid Substitution Therapy as a Strategy to Reduce Deaths in Prison: Retrospective Cohort Study." *Drug and Alcohol Dependence* 146: e168.

Lasnier, Benoit, Serge Brochu, Neil Boyd, and Benedikt Fisher. 2010. "A Heroin Prescription Trial: Case Studies from Montreal and Vancouver on Crime and Disorder in the Surrounding Neighbourhoods." *International Journal of Drug Policy* 21 (1): 28–35.

La Tribune. 2013. "La Chine et la malédiction de l'opium." August 18. Accessed July 29, 2017. http://www.latribune.fr/journal/edition-du-1908/opinions/779527/la-chine-et-la-malediction-de-l-opium.html.

Laudet, Alexandre B., Virginia Stanick, and Brian Sands. 2009. "What Could the Program Have Done Differently? A Qualitative Examination of Reasons for Leaving Outpatient Treatment." *Journal of Substance Abuse Treatment* 37 (2): 182–90.

Laventure, Myriam, Michèle Déry, and Robert Pauzé. 2008. "Profils de consommation d'adolescents, garçons et filles, desservis par des centres jeunesse." *Drogues, santé et société* 7 (2): 9–45.

Lee, Juliet P., Robynn S. Battle, Brian Soller, and Naomi Brandes. 2011. "Thizzin'—Ecstasy use contexts and emergent social meanings." *Addiction Research & Theory* 19 (6): 528–41.

Légaré-Tremblay, Jean-Frédéric. 2014. "Narcotrafic: une violence glorifiée gangrène le Mexique." *Le Devoir*, March 26. Accessed July 29, 2017. http://www.ledevoir.com/international/actualites-internationales/403594/narcotrafic-une-violence-glorifiee-gangrene-le-mexique.

Léonard, Louis, and Mohamed Ben Amar. 2000. "Classification, caractéristiques et effets généraux des substances psychotropes." In *L'usage des drogues et la toxicomanie: un phénomène multiple*, edited by P. Brisson, 121–74. Boucherville, QC: Gaëtan Morin Éditeur.

Logan, T. K., and Carl Leukefeld. 2000. "Sexual and Drug Use Behaviors Among Female Crack Users: A Multi-Site Sample." *Drug and Alcohol Dependence* 58 (3): 237–45.

Lovell, Julia. 2011. *The Opium War: Drugs, Dreams and the Making of China.* Basingstoke/Oxford, UK: Picador.

Lukasiewicz, Michael, and Magali Frenoy Peres. 2006. "Prévention de la rechute." In Thérapies cognitives et comportementales et addictions, edited by Hassan Rahioui and Michel Reynaud, 40–48. Paris: Flammarion.

Lundahl, Brad, and Brian L. Burke. 2009. "The Effectiveness and Applicability of Motivational Interviewing: A Practice-Friendly Review of Four Meta-Analyses." *Journal of Clinical Psychology* 65 (11): 1232–45.

Lundholm, Lena, Ulrika Haggård, Jette Möller, Johan Hallqvist, and Ingemar Thiblin. 2013. "The Triggering Effect of Alcohol and Illicit Drugs on Violent Crime in a Remand Prison Population: A Case Crossover Study." *Drug and Alcohol Dependence* 129 (1–2): 110–15.

MacCoun, Robert, and Peter Reuter. 1992. "Are the Wages of Sin $30 an Hour? Economic Aspects of Street-Level Drug Dealing." *Crime & Delinquency* 38 (4): 477–91.

Macdonald, Scott, P. Erickson, S. Wells, A. Hathaway, and B. Pakula. 2008. "Predicting Violence Among Cocaine, Cannabis, and Alcohol Treatment Clients." *Addictive Behaviors* 33 (1): 201–5.

MacSwain, Mary-Ann, Shanna Farrell-MacDonald, Madelon Cheverie, and Benedikt Fischer. 2014. "Assessing the Impact of Methadone Maintenance Treatment (MMT) on Post-Release Recidivism Among Male Federal Correctional Inmates in Canada." *Criminal Justice and Behavior* 41 (3): 380–94.

Magrinelli Orsi, Mylène. 2011. "Consommation de substances psychoactives, motivation et ouverture envers l'intervention des adolescents placés en centre de réadaptation." Doctoral dissertation, Université de Montréal.

Magrinelli Orsi, Mylène, and Serge Brochu. 2009a. "Du sable dans l'engrenage: la motivation des clients sous contrainte judiciaire dans les traitements pour la toxicomanie." *Drogues, santé et société* 8 (2): 141–85.

——. 2009b. "La place des programmes d'échange de seringues parmi les stratégies de réduction des méfaits dans les pénitenciers canadiens." *Canadian Journal of Public Health* 100 (1): 29–31.

Makkai, Toni, and Jason Payne. 2003. *Drugs and Crime: A Study of Incarcerated Male Offenders*. Australian Institute of Criminology, Research and Public Policy Series no. 52. Accessed May 20, 2017. http://www.aic.gov.au/media_library/publications/rpp/52/rpp052.pdf.

Manzoni, Patrik, Benedikt Fischer, and Jürgen Rehm. 2007. "Local Drug–Crime Dynamics in a Canadian Multi-Site Sample of Untreated Opioid Users." *Canadian Journal of Criminology and Criminal Justice* 49 (3): 341–73.

Manzoni, Patrik, Serge Brochu, Benedikt Fischer, and Jürgen Rehm. 2006. "Determinants of Property Crime Among Illicit Opiate Users Outside of Treatment Across Canada." *Deviant Behavior* 27 (3): 351–76.

Marsh, Amélie. 2002. "La trajectoire des femmes contrevenantes consommatrices régulières de cocaïne." PhD dissertation, Université de Montréal.

Martinson, Robert M. 1974. "What Works? Questions and Answers About Prison Reform." *Public Interest* (Spring): 22–54. Accessed June 21, 2017. https://www.nationalaffairs.com/public_interest/detail/what-works-questions-and-answers-about-prison-reform.

Mason, W. Alex, Julia E. Hitchings, and Richard L. Spoth. 2007. "Emergence of Delinquency and Depressed Mood Throughout Adolescence as Predictors of Late Adolescent Problem Substance Use." *Psychology of Addictive Behaviors* 21 (1): 13–24.

Matheson, Flora I., Sherri Doherty, and Brian A. Grant. 2008. *Women Offender Substance Abuse Programming & Community Reintegration.* Research Branch, Correctional Service Canada research report no. R-202. Accessed June 25, 2017. http://publications.gc.ca/collections/collection_2010/scc-csc/PS83-3-202-eng.pdf.

Maxwell, Sheila R., and Christopher D. Maxwell. 2000. "Examining the "Criminal Careers" of Prostitutes Within the Nexus of Drug Use, Drug Selling, and Other Illicit Activities." *Criminology* 38 (3): 787–809.

McCollister, Kathryn E., Michael T. French, James A. Inciardi, Clifford A. Butzin, Steven S. Martin, and Robert M. Hooper. 2003. *Journal of Quantitative Criminology* 19 (4): 389–407.

McConnaughy, Eileen A., James O Prochaska, and Wayne F. Velicer. 1983. "Stages of Change in Psychotherapy: Measurement and Sample Profiles." *Psychotherapy: Theory, Research and Practice* 20 (3): 368–75.

McGuire, James. 2004. "Commentary: Promising Answers, and the Next Generation of Questions." *Psychology, Crime & Law* 10 (3): 335–45.

McIntosh, James, Michael Bloor, and Michele Robertson. 2007. "The Effect of Drug Treatment upon the Commission of Acquisitive Crime." *Journal of Substance Use* 12 (5): 375–84.

McLellan, A. Thomas, Lester Luborsky, George Woody, and Charles O'Brien. 1980. "An Improved Diagnostic Evaluation Instrument for Substance Abuse Patients: The Addiction Severity Index." *Journal of Nervous and Mental Disease* 168 (1): 26–33.

McMillan, Garnett P., Sandra Lapham, and Michael Lackey. 2008. "The Effect of a Jail Methadone Maintenance Therapy (MMT) Program on Inmate Recidivism." *Addiction* 103 (12): 2017–23.

McMurran, Mary. 2009. "Motivational Interviewing with Offenders: A Systematic Review." *Legal and Criminal Psychology* 14 (1): 83–100.

McMurran, Mary, and Tony Ward. 2004. "Motivating Offenders to Change in Therapy: An Organizing Framework." *Legal and Criminological Psychology* 9 (2): 295–311.

McVie, Fraser. 2001. "Drugs in Federal Corrections—The Issues and Challenges." *Forum on Corrections Research* 13 (3): 7–9. Accessed May 27, 2017. http://www.csc-scc.gc.ca/research/forum/e133/133c_e.pdf.

Mee-Lee, David, A. Thomas McLellan, and Scott D. Miller. 2010. "What Works in Substance Abuse and Dependence Treatment." In *The Heart and Soul of Change, Second Edition: Delivering What Works in Therapy*, edited by Barry L. Duncan, Scott D. Miller, Bruce E. Wampold, and Mark A. Hubble, 393–417. Washington, DC: American Psychological Association.

Meier, Petra S., Christine Barrowclough, and Michael C. Donmall. 2005. "The Role of the Therapeutic Alliance in the Treatment of Substance Misuse: A Critical Review of the Literature." *Addiction* 100 (3): 304–16.

Menard, Scott, Sharon Mihalic, and David Huizinga. 2001. "Drugs and Crime Revisited." *Justice Quarterly* 18 (2): 269–99.

Mercier, Céline, and Sophie Alarie. 2002. "Pathways Out of Deviance: Implications for Programs Evaluation." In *Drugs and Crime Deviant Pathways*, edited by Serge Brochu, Candido da Agra, and Marie-Marthe Cousineau, 229–40. London: Ashgate Publishing.

Miller, Norman S. 1991. *The Pharmacology of Alcohol and Drugs of Abuse and Addiction*. New York: Springer-Verlag.

Miller, William R. 1985. "Motivation for Treatment: A Review with Special Emphasis on Alcoholism." *Psychological Bulletin* 98 (1): 84–107.

Miller, William R., and Stephen Rollnick. 2002. *Motivational Interviewing: Preparing People for Change*, 2nd edition. New York: Guilford Publications.

———. 2006. *L'entretien Motivationnel: Aider la personne à engager le changement*. 2nd edition. Paris: InterÉditions.

Millon, Theodore, Carrie Millon, and Roger Davis. 1997. MCMI-III: Millon Clinical Multiaxial Inventory-III Manual. Minneapolis, MN: National Computer Systems.

Miron, Jeffrey A. 2001. "Violence, Guns, and Drugs: A Cross-Country Analysis." *Journal of Law and Economics* 44 (S2): 615–33.

Mitchell, Ojmarrh, David B. Wilson, Amy Eggers, and Doris L. MacKenzie. 2012. "Assessing the Effectiveness of Drug Courts on Recidivism: A Meta-Analytic Review of Traditional and Non-Traditional Drug Courts." *Journal of Criminal Justice* 40 (19): 60–71.

Moeller, F. Gerard, Donald M. Dougherty, Ernest S. Barratt, Victor Oderinde, Charles W. Mathias, R. Andrew Harper, and Alan C. Swann. 2002. "Increased Impulsivity in Cocaine Dependent Subjects Independent of Antisocial Personality Disorder and Aggression." *Drug and Alcohol Dependence* 68 (1): 105–11.

Moeller, Kim, and Sveinung Sandberg. 2015. "Credit and Trust: Management of Network Ties in Illicit Drug Distribution." *Journal of Research in Crime and Delinquency* 52 (5): 691–716.

Moffitt, Terrie E. 1993. "Adolescence-Limited and Life-Course-Persistent Antisocial Behavior: A Developmental Taxonomy." *Psychological Review* 100 (4): 674–701.

Moffitt, Terrie E., Avshalom Caspi, Honalee Harrington, and Barry J. Milne. 2002. "Males on the Life-Course-Persistent and Adolescence-Limited Antisocial Pathways: Follow-Up at Age 26 Years." *Development and Psychopathology* 14 (1): 179–207.

Monahan, Kathryn C., Isaac C. Rhew, J. David Hawkins, and Eric C. Brown. 2014. "Adolescent Pathways to Co-Occurring Problem Behavior: The

Effects of Peer Delinquency and Peer Substance Use." *Journal of Research on Adolescence* 24 (4): 630–45.

Montingy, Edgar-André. 2011. "Introduction." In *The Real Dope: Social, Legal, and Historical Perspectives on the Regulation of Drugs in Canada*, edited by Edgar-André Montigny, 3–24. Toronto: University of Toronto Press.

Moore, Kathleen A., Melissa Harrison, M. Scott Young, and Ezra Ochshorn. 2008. "A Cognitive Therapy Treatment Program for Repeat DUI Offenders." *Journal of Criminal Justice* 36 (6): 539–45.

Moos, Rudolph H., and Bernice S. Moos. 2003. "Long-Term Influence of Duration and Intensity of Treatment on Previously Untreated Individuals with Alcohol Use Disorders." *Addiction* 98 (3): 325–37.

Motiuk, Larry L., and Ben Vuong. 2006. "Re-profiling the Drug Offender Population in Canadian Federal Corrections." *Forum on Corrections Research* 18 (1): 27–33. Accessed May 21, 2017. http://www.csc-scc.gc.ca/recherche/forum/e181/e181f-eng.shtml.

Mužinić, Lana, Zvonimir Penić, Ljiljana Vukota, and Tija Žarković Palijan. 2011. "The Treatment of Drug Addicts in the Prison System." *Alcoholism: Journal on Alcoholism and Related Addictions* 47 (2): 111–26.

Nadelmann, Ethan A. 1990. "Global Prohibition Regimes: The Evolution of Norms in International Society." *International Organization* 44 (4): 479–526.

Nadelmann, Ethan A., and Xenia Schiray. 1992. "Régimes globaux de prohibition et trafic international de drogue." *Revue Tiers Monde* 33 (131): 538–52.

Nancy, Dominique. 2015. "L'achat de stupéfiants en ligne explose." *Forum*, April 20. Accessed July 29, 2017. http://nouvelles.umontreal.ca/article/2015/04/20/lachat-de-stupefiants-en-ligne-explose/.

Nasr, Wren, and Karin Phillips. 2014. *Current Issues in Mental Health in Canada: Directions in Federal Substance Abuse Policy.* Ottawa: Library of Parliament, Parliamentary Information and Research Service, Legal and Social Affairs Division publication no. 2014-06-E. Accessed May 28, 2017. http://www.bdp.parl.gc.ca/Content/LOP/ResearchPublications/2014-06-e.pdf.

National Centre on Addiction and Substance Abuse at Columbia University. 2010. *Behind Bars: Substance Abuse and America's Prison Population.* New York: The National Center on Addiction and Substance Abuse at Columbia University. Accessed June 27, 2017. https://www.centeronaddiction.org/addiction-research/reports/behind-bars-ii-substance-abuse-and-america's-prison-population.

National Institute of Justice. 1996. *Boot Camp Research and Evaluation for Fiscal Year 1996.* Washington, DC: National Institute of Justice. Accessed July 29, 2017. https://babel.hathitrust.org/cgi/pt?id=pur1.32754066644497;view=1up;seq=3.

——. 2003a. *2000 Arrestee Drug Abuse Monitoring (ADAM): Annual Report.* Washington, DC: U.S. Department of Justice, Office of Justice Programs. Accessed June 26, 2017. https://www.ncjrs.gov/pdffiles1/nij/193013.pdf.

——. 2003b. *Correctional Boot Camps: Lessons From a Decade of Research.* Washington, DC.: U.S. Department of Justice, Office of Justice Programs. Accessed July 4, 2017. https://www.ncjrs.gov/pdffiles1/nij/197018.pdf.

National Institute on Drug Abuse. 2012. *Spice ("Synthetic Marijuana")* National Institutes of Health, U.S. Department of Health and Human Services. Accessed November 16, 2017. https://www.drugabuse.gov/sites/default/files/drugfacts_spice.pdf.

——. 2015. "Synthetic Cannabinoids." National Institutes of Health, U.S. Department of Health and Human Services. Accessed May 16, 2017. https://www.drugabuse.gov/publications/drugfacts/synthetic-cannabinoids.

National Treatment Agency for Substance Misuse. 2012. *Estimating the Crime Reduction Benefits of Drug Treatment and Recovery.* London: National Health Service. Accessed July 29, 2017. http://www.nta.nhs.uk/uploads/vfm2012.pdf.

Neff, Joan L., and Dennis E. Waite. 2007. "Male Versus Female Substance Abuse Patterns Among Incarcerated Juvenile Offenders: Comparing Strain and Social Learning Variables." *Justice Quarterly* 24 (1): 106–32.

Negrusz, Adam, and R. E. Gaensslen. 2003. "Analytical Developments in Toxicological Investigation of Drug-Facilitated Sexual Assault." *Analytical and Bioanalytical Chemistry* 376 (8): 1192–97.

NIDA. *See* National Institute on Drug Abuse.

Nissen, Laura B. 2006. Bringing Strength-Based Philosophy to Life in Juvenile Justice." *Reclaiming Children and Youth: The Journal of Strength-Based Interventions* 15 (1): 40–46. Accessed July 29, 2017. https://lauraburneynissenlovessocialwork.files.wordpress.com/2012/03/bringing-strength-based-philosophy-to-life-in-juvenile-justice-settings.pdf.

Nolin, Pierre-Claude. 2010. "Le sénateur Nolin s'explique – Drogues: un rapport mal compris." *Le Devoir* August 30, 2010. Accessed July 17, 2017. http://www.ledevoir.com/non-classe/10597/le-senateur-nolin-s-explique-drogues-un-rapport-mal-compris.

Nowinski, Joseph, Stuart Baker, and Kathleen Carroll. 1992. *Twelve Step Facilitation Therapy Manual: A Clinical Research Guide for Therapists Treating Individuals with Alcohol Abuse and Dependence.* Rockville, MD: National Institute on Alcohol Abuse and Alcoholism. Accessed June 27, 2017. https://pubs.niaaa.nih.gov/publications/projectmatch/match01.pdf.

Nunn, Amy, Nickolas Zaller, Samuel Dickman, Catherine Trimbur, Ank Nijhawan, and Josiah D. Rich. 2009. "Methadone and Buprenorphine

Prescribing and Referral Practices in US Prison Systems: Results from a Nationwide Survey." *Drug and Alcohol Dependence* 105 (1–2): 83–88.

Obradovic, Ivana. 2011. "Législations relatives à l'usage et à la détention de cannabis: définitions et état des lieux en Europe." Observatoire français des drogues et des toxicomanies, no. 2011-19. Accessed July 29, 2017. http://www.ofdt.fr/BDD/publications/docs/eisxiow3.pdf.

Odgers, Candice L., Terrie E. Moffitt, Jonathan M. Broadbent, Nigel Dickson, Robert J. Hancox, Honalee Harrington, Richie Poulton et al. 2008. "Female and Male Antisocial Trajectories: From Childhood Origins to Adult Outcomes." *Development and Psychopathology* 20 (2): 673–716.

Oesterle, Sabrina, J. David Hawkins, Majone Steketee, Harrie Jonkman, Eric C. Brown, Marit Moll, and Kevin P. Haggerty. 2012. "A Cross-national Comparison of Risk and Protective Factors for Adolescent Drug Use and Delinquency in the United States and the Netherlands." *Journal of Drug Issues* 42 (4): 337–57.

Office of National Drug Control Policy. 2014. *2013 Annual Report, Arrestee Drug Abuse Monitoring Program II.* Washington, DC: Executive Office of the President. Accessed May 27, 2017. https://obamawhitehouse. archives.gov/sites/default/files/ondcp/policy-and-research/adam_ ii_2013_annual_report.pdf.

O'Keefe, Maureen L., and Marissa J. Schnell. "Offenders with Mental Illness in the Correctional System." *Journal of Offender Rehabilitation* 45 (1–2): 81–104.

ONDCP. *See* Office of National Drug Control Policy.

Ostrowsky, Michael K. 2011. "Does Marijuana Use Lead to Aggression and Violent Behavior?" *Journal of Drug Education* 41 (4): 369–89.

Ousey, Graham C., and Matthew R. Lee. 2007, "Homicide Trends and Illicit Drug Markets: Exploring Differences Across Time." *Justice Quarterly* 24 (1): 48–79.

Oviedo-Joekes, Eugenia, Bohdan Nosyk, Suzanne Brissette, Jill Chettiar, Pascal Schneeberger, David C. March, Michael Krausz, Aslam Anis, and Martin T. Schechter. 2008. "The North American Opiate Medication Initiative (NAOMI): Profile of Participants in North America's First Trial of Heroin-Assisted Treatment." *Journal of Urban Health* 85 (6): 812–25.

Palamar, Joseph J. 2014. "Predictors of Disapproval toward "Hard Drug" Use among High School Seniors in the US." *Prevention Science* 15 (5): 725–35.

Pardini, Dustin, Helene Raskin White, and Magda Stouthamer-Loeber. 2007. "Early Adolescent Psychopathology as a Predictor of Alcohol Use Disorders by Young Adulthood." *Drug and Alcohol Dependence* 88 (Supplement 1): S38–S49.

Pardini, Dustin, Jordan Bechtold, Rolf Loeber, and Helene White. 2015. "Developmental Trajectories of Marijuana Use among Men: Examining

Linkages with Criminal Behavior and Psychopathic Features into the Mid-30s." *Journal of Research in Crime and Delinquency* 52 (6): 797–828.

Parent, Isabelle, and Serge Brochu. 2002. "Drug/Crime Pathways Among Cocaine Users." In *Drugs and Crime: Deviant Pathways*, edited by Serge Brochu, Candido da Agra, and Marie-Marthe Cousineau, 139–53. London: Ashgate Publishing.

Parker, Howard. 2005. "Normalization as a Barometer: Recreational Drug use and the Consumption of Leisure by Younger Britons." *Addiction Research & Theory* 13 (3): 205–15.

Parker, Howard, Judith Aldridge, and Fiona Measham. 1998. *Illegal Leisure: The Normalization of Adolescent Recreational Drug Use*. Hove, UK: Routledge.

Parker, Howard, Lisa Williams, and Judith Aldridge. 2002. "The Normalization of 'Sensible' Recreational Drug Use: Further Evidence from the North West England Longitudinal Study." *Sociology* 36 (4): 941–64.

Parrott, Andrew C. 2013. "Human Psychobiology of MDMA or 'Ecstasy': An Overview of 25 Years of Empirical Research." *Human Psychopharmacology: Clinical and Experimental* 28 (4): 289–307.

Passarotti, A. M., Natania A. Crane, Donald Hedeker, and Robin J. Mermelstein. "Longitudinal Trajectories of Marijuana Use from Adolescence to Young Adulthood." *Addictive Behaviors* 45:301–08.

Payne, Jason, and Antonette Gaffney. 2012. "How Much Crime is Drug or Alcohol Related? Self-Reported Attributions of Police Detainees." *Trends & Issues in Crime and Criminal Justice* no. 439. Canberra: Australian Institute of Criminology. Accessed May 31, 2017. http://www.aic.gov.au/publications/current%20series/tandi/421-440/tandi439.html.

Pearson, Geoffrey, and Dick Hobbs. 2001. "Middle Market Drug Distribution." Home Office Research Study 227, Development and Statistics Directorate, London. Accessed May 21, 2017. https://core.ac.uk/download/pdf/94137.pdf.

Peat, Barbara J., and L. Thomas Winfree Jr. 1992. "Reducing the Intra-Institutional Effects of 'Prisonization': A Study of a Therapeutic Community for Drug-Using Inmates." *Criminal Justice and Behavior* 19 9(2): 206–25.

Pedersen, Willy, and Torbjørn Skardhamar. 2010. "Cannabis and Crime: Findings from a Longitudinal Study." *Addiction* 105 (1): 109–18.

Pepler, Debra J., Depeng Jiang, Wendy M. Craig, and Jennifer Connolly. 2010. "Developmental Trajectories of Girls' and Boys' Delinquency and Associated Problems." *Journal of Abnormal Child Psychology* 38 (7): 1033–44.

Pernanen, Kai. 2001. "What is Meant by 'Alcohol-Related' Consequences?" In *Mapping the Social Consequences of Alcohol Consumption*, edited by Harald Klingemann and Gerhard Gmel, 21–31. Dordrecht, NL: Kluwer Academic Publishers.

Pernanen, Kai, Marie-Marthe Cousineau, Serge Brochu, and Fu Sun. 2002. *Proportions of Crimes Associated with Alcohol and Other Drugs in Canada.* Ottawa: Canadian Centre on Substance Abuse. Accessed May 29, 2017. http://www.ccsa.ca/Resource%20Library/ccsa-009105-2002.pdf.

Pflieger, Christophe. 2005. "Les flashbacks induits par les psychodysleptiques hallucinogènes." *Psychotropes* 11 (1): 9–32.

Piza, Eric L., and Victoria A. Sytsma. 2015. "Exploring the Defensive Actions of Drug Sellers in Open-Air Markets: A Systematic Social Observation." *Journal of Research in Crime and Delinquency* 53 (1): 36–65.

Plourde, Chantal. 2002. "Consumption of Psychoactive Substances in Quebec Prisons." Forum on Corrections Research 14 (1): 16–18. Accessed May 27, 2017. http://www.csc-scc.gc.ca/research/forum/e141/141d_e.pdf.

Plourde, Chantal, and Serge Brochu. 2002. "Drogue et alcool durant l'incarcération: examen de la situation des pénitenciers fédéraux québécois." *Revue canadienne de criminologie* 44 (2): 209–40.

Plourde, Chantal, Serge Brochu, and Guy Lemire. 2001. "Drogues et prison: faits et enjeux actuels." *Revue internationale de criminologie et de police technique et scientifique* 54 (2): 197–220.

Plourde, Chantal, Catherine Arseneault, Francine Ferland, Nadine Blanchette-Martin, Marc Alain, Renée-Claude Roy, and Pascal Garceau. 2015. *Évaluation des effets du programme d'intervention en toxicomanie offert par le Centre de réadaptation en dépendance de Québec à l'Établissement de détention de Québec.* Université du Québec à Trois-Rivières, final research report. Accessed July 29, 2017. http://www.securitepublique.gouv.qc.ca/fileadmin/Documents/services_correctionnels/publications/chercheurs_partenaires/RAPPORT_DE_RECHERCHE_1.pdf.

Plourde, Chantal, Mathieu Goyette, Serge Brochu, Marc Alain, Sophie Alarie, and Julie Bélanger. 2014. *Évaluation d'implantation du Programme de traitement de la toxicomanie de la Cour du Québec (PTTCQ), Rapport de recherche final.*

Plourde, Chantal, Serge Brochu, Né Djawn White, and Amélie Couvrette. 2005. "La réduction des méfaits en contexte carcéral québécois et canadiens: tour d'horizon des pratiques connues." *Revue de psychoéducation* 34 (2): 287–300.

Plourde, Chantal, Natasha Dufour, Serge Brochu, and Annie Gendron. 2013. "Medication Use, Substance Use, and Psychological Conditions of Female Inmates in Canadian Federal Prisons." *International Annals of Criminology* 50 (1–2): 23–37.

Plourde, Chantal, Serge Brochu, Annie Gendron, and Natacha Brunelle. 2012. "Pathways of Substance Use Among Female and Male Inmates in Canadian Federal Settings." *Prison Journal* 92 (4): 506–24.

Plourde, Chantal, Serge Brochu, Amélie Couvrette, and Annie Gendron. 2007. "Points de vue de femmes incarcérées dans des établissements fédéraux concernant les impacts du contexte carcéral sur leur trajectoire de consommation de drogues." *Criminologie* 40 (1): 105–34.

Poikolainen, Kari. 2002. "Antecedents of Substance Use in Adolescence." *Current Opinion in Psychiatry* 15 (3): 241–45.

Poirier, Andrée-Anne. 2011. "La trajectoire des jeunes adultes qui ont une consommation problématique de drogues illicites aux Îles de la Madeleine." Master's thesis, Université Laval. Accessed June 7, 2017. http://theses.ulaval.ca/archimede/meta/28499.

Polet, François. 2013a. "Politique de drogues: l'émancipation latino-américaine." CETRI (Centre Tricontinental), Narcotrafic. Accessed June 7, 2017. http://www.cetri.be/Politique-de-drogues-l?lang=fr.

——. 2013b. "Ravages du narcotrafic, naufrage de la 'guerre aux drogues'." CETRI (Centre Tricontinental), Alternatives Sud. Accessed June 7, 2017. http://www.cetri.be/Ravages-du-narcotrafic-naufrage-de.

Prisciandaro, James J., Jeffrey E. Korte, Aimée L. McRae-Clark, and Kathleen T. Brady. "Associations Between Behavioral Disinhibition and Cocaine Use History in Individuals with Cocaine Dependence." *Addictive Behaviors* 37 (10): 1185–88.

Prochaska, James O., Carlo C. DiClemente, and John C. Norcross. 1992. "In Search of How People Change: Applications to Addictive Behaviors." *American Psychologist* 47 (9): 1102–14.

Quintas, Jorge. 2011. *Regulação legal do consumo de drogas: impactos da experiência portuguesa da descriminalização* [Regulating drug use: The impact of the Portuguese decriminalization experience]. Porto, PT: Fronteira do Caos Editores.

Quirion, Bastien. 2002. "Réduction des méfaits et gestion des risques: les frontières normatives entre les différents registres de régulation de la pratique psychotrope." *Déviance et société* 26 (4): 479–95.

Rahioui, Hassan, and Laurent Karila. 2006. "Thérapies cognitives et comportementales adaptées aux comorbidités: troubles schizophréniques et usage de drogues." In *Thérapies cognitives et comportementales et addictions*, edited by Hassan Rahioui and Michel Reynaud, 79–83. Paris: Flammarion.

Rainone, Gregory A., James W. Schmeidler, Blanche Frank, and Robinson Bevin Smith. 2006. "Violent Behavior, Substance Use, and Other Delinquent Behaviors Among Middle and High School Students." *Youth Violence and Juvenile Justice* 4 (3): 247–65.

Ramaekers, Johannes G., G. Berghaus, Margriet van Laar, and Olaf H. Drummer. "Dose related risk of motor vehicle crashes after cannabis use." *Drug and Alcohol Dependence* 73 (2): 109–19.

Rapin, Ami-Jacques. 2013. *Du madat au chandu: Histoire de la fumée d'opium.* Paris: Harmattan.

RCMP. *See* Royal Canadian Mounted Police.

Rehn, Jürgen, William Gnam, Svetlana Popova, Dolly Baliunas, Serge Brochu, Benedikt Fischer, Jayadeep Patra et al. 2007. "The Costs of Alcohol, Illegal Drugs, and Tobacco in Canada, 2002." *Journal of Studies on Alcohol and Drugs* 68 (6): 886–95.

Rehm, Jürgen., Dolly Baliunas, Serge Brochu, Benedikt Fischer, William Gnam, Jayadeep Patra, Svetlana Popova et al. 2006. *The Costs of Substance Abuse in Canada 2002*. Ottawa: Canadian Centre on Substance Abuse. Accessed July 29, 2017. http://www.ccsa.ca/Resource%20Library/ccsa-011332-2006.pdf.

Reid, Lesley Williams, Kirk W. Elifson, and Claire E. Sterk. 2007. "Hug Drug or Thug Drug? Ecstasy Use and Aggressive Behavior." *Violence and Victims* 22 (1): 104–19.

Rempel, Michael, Mia Green, and Dana Kralstein. 2012. "The Impact of Adult Drug Courts on Crime and Incarceration: Findings from a Multi-Site Quasi-Experimental Design." *Journal of Experimental Criminology* 8 (2): 165–92.

Resignato, Andrew J. 2000. "Violent Crime: A Function of Drug Use or Drug Enforcement?" *Applied Economics* 32 (6): 681–88.

Reynolds, Maureen D., Ralph E. Tarter, Levent Kirisci, and Duncan B. Clark. 2011. "Marijuana but not Alcohol Use During Adolescence Mediates the Association Between Transmissible Risk for Substance Use Disorder and Number of Lifetime Violent Offenses." *Journal of Criminal Justice* 39 (3): 218–23.

Roberts, Bryan R., and Yu Chen. 2013. "Drugs, Violence, and the State." *Annual Review of Sociology* 39: 105–25.

Roberts-Lewis, Amelia C., Sharon Parker, Chiquitia Welch, Ariana Wall, and Pam Wiggins. 2009. "Evaluating the Cognitive and Behavioral Outcomes of Incarcerated Adolescent Females Receiving Substance Abuse Treatment: A Pilot Study." *Journal of Child & Adolescent Substance Abuse* 18 (2): 157–71.

Robitaille, Clément, Jean-Pierre Guay, and Caroline Savard. 2002. *Portrait de la clientèle correctionnelle du Québec, 2001*. Direction générale des services correctionnels du Ministère de la Sécurité publique du Québec. Accessed May 27, 2017. http://www.securitepublique.gouv.qc.ca/fileadmin/Documents/services_correctionnels/publications/portrait_2001/version_integrale.pdf.

Rogers, Carl R. 1957. "The Necessary and Sufficient Conditions of Therapeutic Personality Change." *Journal of Consulting Psychology* 21: 95–103.

Rollnick, Stephen, Pip Mason, and Chris Butler. 1999. *Health Behavior Change*. London: Churchill Livingstone.

Rollnick, Stephen, and William R. Miller. 1995. "What is Motivational Interviewing?" *Behavioural and Cognitive Psychotherapy* 23 (4): 325–34.

Room, Robin. 2014. "Legalizing a Market for Cannabis for Pleasure: Colorado, Washington, Uruguay and Beyond." *Addiction* 109 (3): 345–51.

Rosenkranz, Susan E., Joanna L. Henderson, Robert T. Muller, and Ilana R. Goodman. 2012. "Motivation and Maltreatment History Among Youth Entering Substance Abuse Treatment." *Psychology of Addictive Behaviors* 26 (1): 171–77.

Ross, Robert R., and Paul Gendreau, eds. 1980. *Effective Correctional Treatment.* Toronto: Butterworths.

Rouillard, Claude. 2003. *Ecstasy et drogues de synthèse. Le point sur la question.* Montreal: Comité permanent de lutte à la toxicomanie. Accessed June 6, 2017. http://metadame.org/documentation/Ecstasy%20et%20 drogue%20de%20synthese.pdf.

Royal Canadian Mounted Police. 2015. "Drogues et nouvelles tendances." Drug and Organized Crime Awareness Service. Magdala Turpin. Accessed May 17, 2017. http://reseauintersection.ca/data/reseauintersection/files/file/seminaire2015/atelier4turpingrc21mai.pdf.

Rozier, Marielle, at Valérie Vanasse. 2000. "Les mesures de réduction des méfaites: entre cadre pénal et pratiques d'intervention." In *L'errance urbaine,* edited by Danielle Laberge, 417–32. Sainte-Foy: Les Éditions MultiMondes.

Rubington, Earl. 1967. "Drug Addiction as a Deviant Career." *International Journal of the Addictions* 2 (1): 3–20.

Ryan, Richard M., and Edward L. Deci. 2008. "A Self-Determination Theory Approach to Psychotherapy: The Motivational Basis for Effective Change." *Canadian Psychology* 49 (3): 186–93.

Sacks, Stanley, JoAnn Y. Sacks, Karen McKendrick, Steven Banks, and Joe Stommel. 2004. "Modified TC for MICA Offenders: Crime Outcomes." *Behavioral Sciences & the Law* 22 (4): 477–501.

Saïas, T., and T. Gallarda. 2008. "Réactions d'aggressivité sous benzodiazépines: une revue de la littérature." *L'encéphale* 34 (4): 330–36.

Schaub, Michael, Alex Stevens, Daniele Berto, Neil Hunt, Victoria Kerschi, Tim McSweeney, Kerrie Oeuvray et al. 2010. "Comparing Outcomes of 'Voluntary' and 'Quasi-Compulsory' Treatment of Substance Dependence in Europe." *European Addiction Research* 16 (1): 53–60.

Schroder, Ria, Doug Sellman, Chris Frampton, and Daryle Deering. 2009. "Youth Retention: Factors Associated with Treatment Drop-Out from Youth Alcohol and Other Drug Treatment." *Drug and Alcohol Review* 28 (6): 663–68.

Seal, David W., Lisa Belcher, Kathleen Morrow, Gloria Eldridge, and Diane Binson. 2004. "A Qualitative Study of Substance Use and Sexual Behavior Among 18- to 29-Year-Old Men While Incarcerated in the United States." *Health Education & Behavior* 31 (6): 775–89.

Seddon, Toby. 2000. "Explaining the Drug–Crime Link: Theoretical, Policy and Research Issues." *Journal of Social Policy* 29 (1): 95–107.

Sedlak, Andrea J., and Karla S. McPherson. 2010. "Youth's Needs and Services: Findings from the Survey of Youth in Residential Placement." *Juvenile*

Justice Bulletin (April). U.S. Department of Justice, Office of Justice Programs, Office of Juvenile Justice and Delinquency Prevention. Accessed May 26, 2017. https://www.ncjrs.gov/pdffiles1/ojjdp/227728.pdf.

Selzer, Melvin L. 1971. "The Michigan Alcoholism Screening Test: The Quest for a New Diagnostic Instrument." *American Journal of Psychiatry* 127 (12): 1653–58.

Senate of France. 2002. "La dépénalisation de la consommation du cannabis."

Senate Special Committee on Illegal Drugs. 2002. *Cannabis: Our Position for a Canadian Public Policy*. Ottawa: Senate of Canada. Accessed June 9, 2017. https://sencanada.ca/content/sen/committee/371/ille/rep/summary-e. pdf.

Sheehan, Timothy. 2004. "Twelve Step Facilitation: A Necessary Treatment for Offenders." *Journal of Forensic Psychology Practice* 4 (3): 71–81.

Simons-Morton, Bruce, William Pickett, Will Boyce, Tom F. M. ter Bogt, and Wilma Vollebergh. 2010. "Cross-national Comparison of Adolescent Drinking and Cannabis Use in the United States, Canada, and the Netherlands." *International Journal of Drug Policy* 21 (1): 64–69.

Simpson, D. Dwayne. 1992. *TCU Forms Manual: Drug Abuse Treatment for AIDS-Risks Reduction (DATAR)*. Fort Worth: Institute of Behavioral Research, Texas Christian University.

Simpson, D. Dwayne, George W. Joe, and Barry S. Brown. 1997. "Treatment Retention and Follow-Up Outcomes in the Drug Abuse Treatment Outcome Study (DATOS)." *Psychology of Addictive Behaviors* 11 (4): 294–307.

Simpson, Mark. 2003. "The Relationship Between Drug Use and Crime: A Puzzle Inside an Enigma." *International Journal of Drug Policy* 14 (4): 307–19.

Sinha, Jay. 2001. *The History and Development of the Leading International Drug Control Conventions*, report prepared for the Senate Special Committee on Illegal Drugs. Library of Parliament, Law and Government Division. Accessed July 29, 2017. https://sencanada.ca/content/sen/committee/ 371/ille/library/history-e.htm.

Skinner, Harvey A. 1982. "The Drug Abuse Screening Test." *Addictive Behaviors* 7: 363–71.

Skinner, Harvey A., and John L. Horn.1984. *Alcohol Dependence Scale (ADS) User's Guide*. Toronto: Addiction Research Foundation.

Slinger, Emily, and Ronald Roesch. 2010. "Problem-Solving Courts in Canada: A Review and a Call for Empirically-Based Evaluation Methods." *International Journal of Law and Psychiatry* 33 (4): 258–64.

Small, Will, S. Kain, Nancy Laliberte, Martin T. Schechter, Michael V. O'Shaughnessy, and Patricia M. Spittali. 2005. "Incarceration, Addiction and Harm Reduction: Inmates Experience Injecting Drugs in Prison. *Substance Use & Misuse*. 40 (6): 831–43.

Small, Will, Lisa Maher, Jeff Lawlor, Evan Wood, Kate Shannon, and Thomas Kerr. 2013. "Injection drug users' involvement in drug dealing in the downtown eastside of Vancouver: Social organization and systemic violence." *International Journal of Drug Policy* 24 (5): 479–87.

Small, Will, Tim Rhodes, Evan Wood, and Thomas Kerr. 2007. "Public Injection Settings in Vancouver: Physical Environment, Social Context and Risk." *International Journal of Drug Policy* 18 (1): 27–36.

Smith, Philip H., Gregory G. Homish, Kenneth E. Leonard, and Jack R. Cornelius. 2012. "Intimate Partner Violence and Specific Substance Use Disorders: Findings from the National Epidemiologic Survey on Alcohol and Related Conditions." *Psychology of Addictive Behaviors*. 26 (2): 236–45.

Sommers, Ira, Deborah Baskin, and Jeffrey Fagan. 1996. "The Structural Relationship between Drug Use, Drug Dealing, and other Income Support Activities among Women Drug Sellers." *Journal of Drug Issues* 26 (4): 975–1006.

Spaderna, Max, Peter H. Addy, and Deepak Cyril D'Souza. 2013. "Spicing Things Up: Synthetic Cannabinoids." *Psychopharmacology* 228 (4): 525–40.

Special Committee on Non-Medical Use of Drugs. 2002. *Policy for the New Millennium: Working Together to Redefine Canada's Drug Strategy.* Ottawa: House of Commons. Accessed June 9, 2017. http://www.parl.gc.ca/content/hoc/Committee/372/SNUD/Reports/RP1032297/snudrp02/snudrp02-e.pdf.

Stallwitz, Anke, and Heino Stöver. 2007. "The Impact of Substitution Treatment in Prisons: A Literature Review." *International Journal of Drug Policy* 18 (6): 464–74.

Statistics Canada. 1998. "Canadian Crime Statistics, 1997." *Juristat* 18 (11): 1–22. Accessed July 29, 2017. http://www.statcan.gc.ca/pub/85-002-x/85-002-x1998011-eng.pdf.

——. 1999. "Crime Statistics in Canada, 1998." *Juristat* 19 (9): 1–25. Accessed July 29, 2017. http://www.statcan.gc.ca/pub/85-002-x/85-002-x1999009-eng.pdf.

——. 2000. "Crime Statistics in Canada, 1999." *Juristat* 20 (5): 1–24. Accessed July 29, 2017. http://www.statcan.gc.ca/pub/85-002-x/85-002-x2000005-eng.pdf.

——. 2001. "Crime Statistics in Canada, 2000." *Juristat* 21 (8): 1–22. Accessed July 29, 2017. http://www.statcan.gc.ca/pub/85-002-x/85-002-x2001008-eng.pdf.

——. 2002. "Crime Statistics in Canada, 2001." *Juristat* 22 (6): 1–22. Accessed July 29, 2017. http://www.statcan.gc.ca/pub/85-002-x/85-002-x2002006-eng.pdf.

——. 2003. "Crime Statistics in Canada, 2002." *Juristat* 23 (5): 1–25. Accessed July 29, 2017. http://www.statcan.gc.ca/pub/85-002-x/85-002-x2003005-eng.pdf.

——. 2004. "Crime Statistics in Canada, 2003." *Juristat* 24 (6): 1–26. Accessed July 29, 2017. http://www.statcan.gc.ca/pub/85-002-x/85-002-x2004006-eng.pdf.

——. 2005. "Crime Statistics in Canada, 2004." *Juristat* 25 (5): 1–23. Accessed July 29, 2017. http://www.statcan.gc.ca/pub/85-002-x/85-002-x2005005-eng.pdf.

——. 2006. "Crime Statistics in Canada, 2005." *Juristat* 26 (4): 1–23. Accessed July 29, 2017. http://www.statcan.gc.ca/pub/85-002-x/85-002-x2006004-eng.pdf.

——. 2007. "Crime Statistics in Canada, 2006." *Juristat* 27 (5): 1–15. Accessed July 29, 2017. http://www.statcan.gc.ca/pub/85-002-x/85-002-x2007005-eng.pdf.

——. 2008. "Crime Statistics in Canada, 2007." *Juristat* 28 (7): 1–17. Accessed July 29, 2017. http://www.statcan.gc.ca/pub/85-002-x/85-002-x2008007-eng.pdf.

——. 2009a. "Police-Reported Crime Statistics in Canada, 2008." *Juristat* 29 (3): 1–37. Accessed July 29, 2017. http://www.statcan.gc.ca/pub/85-002-x/2009003/article/10902-eng.pdf.

——. 2009b. "Trends in Police-Reported Drug Offences in Canada." *Juristat* 29 (2): 1–25. Accessed July 29, 2017. http://www.statcan.gc.ca/pub/85-002-x/2009002/article/10847-eng.pdf.

——. 2010. "Police-Reported Crime Statistics in Canada, 2009." *Juristat* 30 (2): 1–37. Accessed July 29, 2017. http://www.statcan.gc.ca/pub/85-002-x/2010002/article/11292-eng.pdf.

——. 2011. "Police-Reported Crime Statistics in Canada, 2010." *Juristat*. Accessed July 29, 2017. http://www.statcan.gc.ca/pub/85-002-x/2011001/article/11523-eng.pdf.

——. 2012a. "Police-Reported Crime Statistics in Canada, 2011." *Juristat*. Accessed July 29, 2017. http://www.statcan.gc.ca/pub/85-002-x/2012001/article/11692-eng.pdf.

——. 2012b. "Canadian Community Health Survey, Mental Health, 2012."

——. 2013a. "Table 252-0056 - Adult Criminal Courts, Guilty Cases by Type of Sentence, annual (number)." CANSIM (database). Accessed May 8, 2017, http://www5.statcan.gc.ca/cansim/a26?lang=eng&id=2520056.

——. 2013b. "Homicide in Canada, 2012." *Juristat* 33 (1): 1-37. Accessed July 29, 2017. http://www.statcan.gc.ca/pub/85-002-x/2013001/article/11882-eng.pdf.

——. 2013c. "Table 109-5335 - Estimates of population (2006 Census and administrative data), by age group and sex for July 1st, Canada, provinces, territories, health regions (2013 boundaries) and peer groups, annual (number)." CANSIM (database). Accessed May 10, 2017. http://www5.statcan.gc.ca/cansim/a26?lang=eng&retrLang=eng&id=10953 25&&pattern=&stByVal=1&p1=1&p2=-1&tabMode=dataTable&csid=.

——. 2013d. "Table 109-5335 - Estimates of population (2011 Census and administrative data), by age group and sex for July 1st, Canada, provinces, territories, health regions (2013 boundaries) and peer groups, annual (number)." CANSIM (database). Accessed May 10, 2017. http://www5. statcan.gc.ca/cansim/a26?id=1095335&pattern=&p2=-1&tabMode= dataTable&p1=1&stByVal=1&csid=&retrLang=eng&lang=eng.

——. 2013e. "Police-Reported Crime Statistics in Canada, 2012." *Juristat.* Accessed July 29, 2017. http://www.statcan.gc.ca/pub/85-002-x/2013001/ article/11854-eng.pdf.

——. 2014. "Police-Reported Crime Statistics in Canada, 2013." *Juristat.* Accessed July 29, 2017. http://www.statcan.gc.ca/pub/85-002-x/2014001/ article/14040-eng.pdf.

Steinberg, Laurence, and Kathryn C. Monahan. 2007. "Age Differences in Resistance to Peer Influence." *Developmental Psychology* 43 (6): 1531–43.

Stevens, Alex, Daniele Berto, Ulrich Frick, Neil Hunt, Viktoria Kerschl, Tim McSweeney, Kerrie Oeuvray et al. 2006. "The Relationship Between Legal Status, Perceived Pressure and Motivation in Treatment for Drug Dependence: Results from a European Study of Quasi-Compulsory Treatment." *European Addiction Research* 12 (4): 197–209.

Stewart, Duncan. 2008. "The Problems and Needs of Newly Sentenced Prisoners: Results from a National Survey." Ministry of Justice Research Series no. 16/08. Accessed June 25, 2017. http://webarchive.nationalarchives. gov.uk/20100505212400/http:/www.justice.gov.uk/publications/docs/ research-problems-needs-prisoners.pdf.

Stone, Andrea L., Linda G. Becker, Alice M. Huber, and Richard F. Catalano. 2012. "Review of Risk and Protective Factors for Substance Use and Problem Use in Emerging Adulthood." *Addictive Behaviors* 37 (7): 747–75.

Strang, John, Thomas Babor, Jonathan Caulkins, Benedikt Fischer, David Foxcroft, and Keith Humphreys. 2012. "Drug Policy and the Public Good: Evidence for Effective Interventions." *The Lancet* 379 (9810): 71–83.

Strang, John, Michael Gossop, Joan Heuston, John Green, Christopher Whiteley, and Anthony Maden. 2006. "Persistence of Drug Use During Imprisonment: Relationship of Drug Type, Recency of Use and Severity of Dependence to Use of Heroin, Cocaine and Amphetamine in Prison." *Addiction* 101 (8): 1125–32.

Substance Abuse and Mental Health Services Administration. 2011. "Substance Abuse Treatment Admissions for Abuse of Benzodiazepines." *TEDS Report* 28. Accessed May 25, 2017. http://atforum.com/documents/ TEDS028BenzoAdmissions.pdf.

——. 2005. "Youth Violence and Illicit Drug Use." *National Survey on Drug Use and Health (NSDUH)* 5:1–4. Accessed May 29, 2017. http://files.eric. ed.gov/fulltext/ED495798.pdf.

Sullivan, Christopher J., Bonita M. Veysey, Zachary K. Hamilton, and Michelle Grillo. 2007. "Reducing Out-of-Community Placement and Recidivism: Diversion of Delinquent Youth with Mental Health and Substance Use Problems from the Justice System." *International Journal of Offender Therapy and Comparative Criminology* 51 (5): 555–77.

Sutherland, Rachel, Natasha Sindicich, Emma Barrett, Elizabeth Whittaker, Amy Peacock, Sophie Hickey, and Lucy Burns. 2015. "Motivations, Substance Use and Other Correlates Amongst Property and Violent Offenders Who Regularly Inject Drugs." *Addictive Behaviors* 45:207–13.

Szabo, Denis. 1992. "La criminologie dans l'Europe en cette fin de siècle: quelques enseignements de la criminologie comparée." Honorary doctorate acceptance speech. Montreal: Centre international de criminologie comparée.

Tavares, Ana, and Pedro Portugal. 2012. "The Impact of Drug Decriminalization in Portugal." NOVA School of Business and Economics.

Tellier, Claude, and Ralph C. Serin. 2000. "The Role of Staff in Effective Program Delivery." In *Compendium 2000 on Effective Correctional Programming*, edited by Laurence L. Motiuk and Ralph C. Serin, ch. 21. Ottawa: Correctional Service Canada. Accessed June 24, 2017. http://www.csc-scc.gc.ca/005/008/compendium/2000/chap_21-eng.shtml.

Temple, Jeff R., and Daniel H. Freeman. "Dating Violence and Substance Use Among Ethnically Diverse Adolescents." *Journal of Interpersonal Violence* 26 (4): 701–18.

Ternes, Marguerite, and Sara Johnson. 2011. "Linking Type of Substance Use and Type of Crime in Male Offenders." Correctional Service Canada, Addictions Research Centre, Research Branch no. RS-11-06. Accessed May 30, 2017. http://www.csc-scc.gc.ca/research/005008-rs11-06-eng.shtml.

Tétrault, Myriane, Serge Brochu, Louis-George Cournoyer, Jacques Bergeron, Natacha Brunelle, Michel Landry, and Joël Tremblay. 2007. "La persévérance en traitement des toxicomanes judiciarisés: une question de motivation." *Revue internationale de criminologie et de police technique et scientifique* 60: 41–54.

Thoumi, Francisco E. 2002. "Illegal Drugs in Colombia: From Illegal Economic Boom to Social Crisis." *Annals of the American Academy of Political and Social Science* 582: 102–16.

Titus, Janet C., Susan H. Godley, and Michelle K. White. 2006. "A Post-Treatment Examination of Adolescents' Reasons for Starting, Quitting, and Continuing the Use of Drugs and Alcohol." *Journal of Child & Adolescent Substance Abuse* 16 (2): 31–49.

Touzeau, Didier, and Pascal Courty. 2012. "Opiacés, réduction des risques et polyconsommation." *La Presse Médicale* 41 (2): 1192–200.

Tremblay, Joël, Natacha Brunelle, and Nadine Blanchette-Martin. 2007. "Portrait des activités délinquantes et de l'usage de substances psychoactives chez des jeunes consultant un centre de réadaptation pour personnes alcooliques et toxicomanes." *Criminologie* 41 (1): 79–104.

Tremblay, Joël, Natacha Brunelle, Nadine Blanchette-Martin, Michel Landry, Nadia L'Espérance, Myriam Laventure, Francine Ferland, Steve Jacob, Geneviève Demers-Lessard, and Annie-Claude Savard. 2014. *Évaluation des mécanismes d'accès jeunesse en toxicomanie (MAJT), Rapport final adressé aux Fonds de recherche du Québec - Société et culture (FRQSC)*, Université du Québec à Trois-Rivières. Accessed May 26, 2017. http://www.frqsc. gouv.qc.ca/documents/11326/448958/PC_TremblayJ_rapport+2014_ MAJT/932ee644-8ccd-42b0-92dc-2161741be083.

Tremblay, Joël, Pierre Rouillard, and Mario Sirois. 2004. *Assessment and Screening of Assistance Needs - Alcohol/Drugs (DÉBA-A/D)*. Québec: Service de recherche CRUV-CRAT-CA. https://oraprdnt.uqtr.uquebec. ca/pls/public/gscw031?owa_no_site=4242&owa_no_fiche=50&owa_ apercu=N&owa_imprimable=N&owa_bottin=.

Tripodi, Stephen J., David W. Springer, and Kevin Corcoran. "Determinants of Substance Abuse Among Incarcerated Adolescents: Implications for Brief Treatment and Crisis Intervention." *Brief Treatment and Crisis Intervention* 7 (1): 34–39.

United Nations Office on Drugs and Crime. 1959. *The Shanghai Opium Commission*. Accessed May 22, 2017. https://www.unodc.org/unodc/en/ data-and-analysis/bulletin/bulletin_1959-01-01_1_page006.html.

——. 2011. *World Drug Report 2011*. Vienna: Division for Policy Analysis and Public Affairs. Accessed May 27, 2017. https://www.unodc.org/ documents/data-and-analysis/WDR2011/World_Drug_Report_2011_ ebook.pdf.

——. 2013a. *The International Drug Control Conventions*. New York: United Nations. Accessed July 29, 2017. https://www.unodc.org/documents/ commissions/CND/Int_Drug_Control_Conventions/Ebook/The_ International_Drug_Control_Conventions_E.pdf.

——. 2013b. *World Drug Report 2013*. Vienna: Division for Policy Analysis and Public Affairs. Accessed May 27, 2017. https://www.unodc.org/ unodc/secured/wdr/wdr2013/World_Drug_Report_2013.pdf.

——. 2017. "Drug Trafficking." Accessed May 27, 2017. https://www.unodc. org/unodc/en/drug-trafficking/index.html.

UNODC. *See* United Nations Office on Drugs and Crime.

United States Department of Justice. 1998. "Drug Use Forecasting in 24 Cities in the United States, 1987–1997." Office of Justice Programs. National Institute of Justice. Ann Arbor, MI: Inter-university Consortium for Political and Social Research. Accessed May 29, 2017. http://www.icpsr. umich.edu/icpsrweb/NACJD/studies/9477/version/2.

U.S. Embassy, Mexico. 2015. "Fact Sheet: The Merida Initiative – An Overview." United States Diplomatic Mission to Mexico. Accessed

May 27, 2017. http://photos.state.gov/libraries/mexico/310329/july15/MeridaInitiativeOverview-Jul15.pdf.

Valleur, Marc, and Jean-Claude Matysiak. 2006. *Les pathologies de l'excès: Sexe, alcool, drogue, jeux...les dérives de nos passions.* Paris: JC Lattès.

van der Geest, Victor, Arjan Blokland, and Catrien Bijleveld. 2009. "Delinquent Development in a Sample of High-Risk Youth Shape, Content, and Predictors of Delinquent Trajectories from Age 12 to 32." *Journal of Research in Crime and Delinquency* 46 (2): 111–43.

Vandevelde, Stijn, Vicky Palmans, Eric Broekaert, Kathy Rousseau, and Kelly Vanderstraeten. 2006. "How Do Drug-Involved Incarcerated and Recently Released Offenders and Correctional Treatment Staff Perceive Treatment? A Qualitative Study on Treatment Needs and Motivation in Belgian Prisons." *Psychology, Crime & Law* 12 (3): 287–305.

Vandevelde, Stijn, Eric Broekaert, Rowdy Yates, and Martien Kooyman. 2004. "The Development of the Therapeutic Community in Correctional Establishments: A Comparative Retrospective Account of the 'Democratic' Maxwell Jones TC and the Hierarchical Concept-Based TC in Prison." *International Journal of Social Psychiatry* 50 (1): 66–79.

Van Ooyen-Houben, Marianne M. J. 2008. "Usage de substances illicites et politique néerlandaise en matière de drogues: vue d'ensemble et évaluation exploratoire." *Déviance et Société* 32 (3): 325–48.

Waldron, Holly Barrett, and Yifrah Kaminer. 2004. "On the Learning Curve: The Emerging Evidence Supporting Cognitive-Behavioral Therapies for Adolescent Substance Abuse." *Addiction* 99 (2): 99–105.

Wanberg, Kenneth W., and Harvey B. Milkman. 1998. *Criminal Conduct and Substance Abuse Treatment: Strategies for Self-Improvement and Change.* Newbury Park, CA: Sage Publications.

Wang, Min Qi, Resa F. Matthew, Nikki Bellamy, and Syretta James. 2005. "A Structural Model of the Substance Use Pathways Among Minority Youth." *American Journal of Health Behavior* 29 (6): 531–41.

Wanner, Brigitte, Frank Vitaro, René Carbonneau, and Richard E. Tremblay. 2009. "Cross-Lagged Links Among Gambling, Substance Use and Delinquency from Midadolescence to Young Adulthood: Additive and Moderating Effects of Common Risk Factors." *Psychology of Addictive Behaviors* 23 (1): 91–104.

Ward, Tony, and Shadd Maruna. 2007. *Rehabilitation: Beyond the Risk Paradigm.* New York: Routledge.

Webster, J. Matthew, Carl G. Leukefeld, Michele Staton Tindall, Allison Mateyoke-Scrivner, and Thomas F. Garrity. 2007. "Factors Related to Drug Abuse Treatment History Among Incarcerated Drug Abusers." *Journal of Correctional Health Care* 13 (1): 8–21.

Weekes, John, Andrea Moser, Marguerite Ternes, and Dan Kunic. "Substance Abuse Among Male Offenders." Research Snippet 09-2. Addiction

Research Centre, Correctional Service Canada. Accessed May 27, 2017. http://publications.gc.ca/collections/collection_2011/scc-csc/PS82-3-9-2-eng.pdf.

Werb, Daniel, Evan Wood, Julio Montaner, Thomas Kerr, Richard Elliott, and Benedikt Fischer. 2007. "Drug Treatment Courts in Canada: An Evidence-Based Review." *HIV/AIDS Policy & Law Review* 12 (2/3): 12–17.

Wikipedia. 2017. S.v. "History of opium in China." Accessed July 7, 2017. https://en.wikipedia.org/wiki/History_of_opium_in_China.

Wikipédia. 2017. "Première guerre de l'opium." Accessed November 20, 2017. https://fr.wikipedia.org/wiki/Première_guerre_de_l%27opium.

Wilkins, Chris, and Paul Sweetsur. "The Association Between Spending on Methamphetamine/Amphetamine and Cannabis for Personal Use and Earnings from Acquisitive Crime Among Police Detainees in New Zealand." *Addiction* 106 (4): 789–97.

Wilson, David B., Ojmarrh Mitchell, and Doris L. MacKenzie. 2006. "A Systematic Review of Drug Court Effects on Recidivism." *Journal of Experimental Criminology* 2 (4): 459–87.

Windle, Michael, and W. Alex Mason. 2004. "General and Specific Predictors of Behavioral and Emotional Problems Among Adolescents." *Journal of Emotional and Behavioral Disorders* 12 (1): 49–61.

Wisdom, Jennifer P., Jennifer I. Manuel, and Robert E. Drake. 2011. "Substance Use Disorder Among People with First-Episode Psychosis: A Systematic Review of Course and Treatment." *Psychiatric Services* 62 (9): 1007–12.

Wisdom, Jennifer P., Mary Cavaleri, Leah Gogel, and Michele Nacht. 2011. "Barriers and Facilitators to Adolescent Drug Treatment: Youth, Family, and Staff Reports." *Addiction Research & Theory* 19 (2): 179–88.

World Health Organization. 2017. *Lexicon of Alcohol and Drug Terms*. Geneva: World Health Organization. Accessed May 24, 2017. http://www.who.int/substance_abuse/terminology/who_lexicon/en/#.

Wright, Sam, and Hilary Klee. 2001. "Violent Crime, Aggression and Amphetamine: What Are the Implications for Drug Treatment Services?" *Drugs: Education, Prevention and Policy* 8 (1): 73–90. http://www.tandfonline.com/doi/abs/10.1080/09687630124890.

Xue, Yange, Marc A. Zimmerman, and Rebecca Cunningham. 2009. "Relationship Between Alcohol Use and Violent Behavior Among Urban African American Youths from Adolescence to Emerging Adulthood: A Longitudinal Study." *American Journal of Public Health* 99 (11): 2041–48.

Young, Amy M., Carol Boyd, and Amy Hubbell. "Prostitution, Drug Use, and Coping with Psychological Distress." *Journal of Drug Issues* 30 (4): 789–800.

Zaitch, Damián. 2005. "The Ambiguity of Violence, Secrecy, and Trust among Colombian Drug Entrepreneurs." *Journal of Drug Issues* 35 (1): 201–28.

Zakaria, Dianne, Jennie Mae Thompson, Ashley Jarvis, and Frederic Borgatta. 2010. *Summary of Emerging Findings from the 2007 National Inmate Infectious Disease and Risk-Behaviours Survey.* Ottawa: Correctional Service of Canada, Research Branch. Accessed May 27, 2017. http://www.csc-scc.gc.ca/research/005008-0211-01-eng.shtml.

Zarkin, Gary A., Laura J. Dunlap, Jeremy W. Bray, and Wendee M. Wechsberg. 2002. "The Effect of Treatment Completion and Length of Stay on Employment and Crime in Outpatient Drug-Free Treatment." *Journal of Substance Abuse Treatment* 23 (4): 261–71.

Zhang, Zhiwei. 2003. *Drug and Alcohol Use and Related Matters Among Arrestees.* Arrestee Drug Abuse Monitoring Program, National Institute of Justice, Office of Justice Programs, U.S. Department of Justice. Accessed July 4, 2017. https://www.ncjrs.gov/nij/adam/adam2003.pdf.

Zinberg, Norman E. 1981. "Alcohol Addiction: Toward a More Comprehensive Definition." In *Dynamic Approaches to the Understanding and Treatment of Alcoholism,* edited by Margaret H. Bean and Norman E. Zinberg, 97–127. New York: The Free Press.

——. 1984. *Drug, Set, and Setting: The Basis for Controlled Intoxicant Use.* New Haven, CT: Yale University Press.

Authors and Translator

Serge Brochu, PhD, was a professor at the Université de Montréal's School of Criminology for thirty years before becoming the scientific director of the Institut universitaire sur les dépendances (IUD), in Montreal. He is a founding member of the Groupe de recherche et intervention sur les substances psychoactives – Québec (RISQ), where he is a regular researcher.

Natacha Brunelle, PhD, is a professor in the Department of Psychoeducation at the Université du Québec à Trois-Rivières (UQTR) and the Canada Research Chair in Drug Use Patterns and Related Problems. She is a regular researcher at RISQ, the International Centre for Comparative Criminology (ICCC), and the IUD.

Chantal Plourde, PhD, is a professor in the Department of Psychoeducation at the UQTR and a regular researcher at RISQ and the ICCC. She also heads the UQTR wing of the ICCC.

Julie da Silva is an Ottawa-based translator.

Health and Society

Series editor: Sanni Yaya

The *Health and Society* series provides a space for dialogue where different fields of expertise (sociology, psychology, political science, biology, nutrition, medicine, nursing, human kinetics, and rehabilitation sciences) generate new insights into health matters from the individual as well as the global perspectives on population health.

Previous titles in this collection

Marie Drolet, Pier Bouchard and Jacinthe Savard (editors), with the collaboration of Josée Benoît and Solange van Kemenade, *Accessibility and Active Offer: Health Care and Social Services in Linguistic Minority Communities*, 2017

Martin Rovers, Judith Malette and Manal Guirguis-Younger (editors), *Therapeutic Touch: Research, Practice and Ethics*, 2017

Manal Guirguis-Younger, Ryan McNeil and Stephen W. Hwang (editors), *Homelessness & Health in Canada*, 2014

www.press.uottawa.ca

MIX
Paper from
responsible sources
FSC
www.fsc.org   FSC® C100212

Printed in February 2018
at Gauvin, Gatineau, Quebec, Canada.